PORTRAITS of VIOLENCE

An Illustrated History of Radical Thinking

Foreword by **Henry A Giroux**

Written by **Brad Evans** and **Sean Michael Wilson**

Illustrated by
**Inko • Carl Thompson • Robert Brown
Chris Mackenzie • Michiru Morikawa • Yen Quach**

New Internationalist

Portraits of Violence
An Illustrated History of Radical Thinking
First published in 2016 by
New Internationalist Publications Ltd
The Old Music Hall
106-108 Cowley Road
Oxford OX4 1JE, UK
newint.org

Artwork by Robert Brown, Inko, Chris Mackenzie, Michiru Morikawa, Yen Quach and
Carl Thompson.

Printed by PBtisk s.t.o., Czech Republic, who hold environmental accreditation
ISO 14001.

British Library Cataloguing-in-Publication Data
A catalogue record for this book is available from the British Library.

Library of Congress Cataloging-in-Publication Data.
A catalog record for this book is available from the Library of Congress.

ISBN 978-1-78026-318-2
(ebook ISBN 978-1-78026-319-9)

PORTRAITS of VIOLENCE

Contents

How do we educate about violence?

Henry A Giroux

There has never been a more urgent time to develop the necessary pedagogical tools to critique forms of violence in the contemporary period. Unfortunately, we live at a moment in which ignorance appears to be one of the defining features of political and cultural life. Ignorance has become a form of weaponized refusal to acknowledge the violence of the past, and revels in a culture of media spectacles in which public concerns are translated into private obsessions, consumerism and fatuous entertainment. As James Baldwin rightly warned, 'Ignorance, allied with power, is the most ferocious enemy justice can have.'

What I have called in my work the violence of organized forgetting signals how contemporary politics are those in which emotion triumphs over reason, and spectacle over truth, thereby erasing history by producing an endless flow of fragmented and disingenuous knowledge. The lessons here are clear. Without a critical formative culture, and the public spheres that nourish it, a type of symbolic violence, engineered by the active disavowal of thought, emerges in which it becomes difficult for people to think critically and act with responsibility and informed judgment.

What I have stressed is that the culture of ignorance functions to depoliticize people by immersing them in a culture of immediacy, thrill and pleasure, a withdrawal into private obsessions, conspicuous consumption and the spectacle of keeping up with popular celebrities.

We live at a time when memory and its capacity to inform critical thought is either under attack or undervalued by a number of forces in our societies. Historical memory has become dangerous, because it offers reflection on lost acts of resistance, collective struggles, and a legacy of what might be called troubling knowledge. The violence of organized forgetting signals how mainstream politics and the new communication cultures largely function to erase history by producing a notion of time wedded to speed, instant information and an endless flow of fragmented knowledge. This is a culture of immediacy that devalues reason, dissent and critique and those institutions, such as public education and higher education, that support critical thinking, informed agency and collective struggles necessary for a democracy itself.

At a time when the shadow of authoritarianism once again looms large, the social and political attacks upon memory, history and thought itself must be seen as an attack not only on basic civil rights and human decency, but also on the very possibility of social agency. That is why developing the necessary education tools that address multiple audiences is central to this fight. We need to remember the importance of analyzing the crucial questions regarding what education should accomplish in a democracy and what work educators, artists and other cultural workers might do to create the economic, political and ethical conditions necessary to endow young people with the capacities to think, question, imagine the unimaginable, be autonomous, learn skills necessary for meaningful work, and defend the civic purpose of education.

Education is fundamental to democracy and no democratic society can survive without a formative culture shaped by pedagogical practices capable of creating the conditions for producing citizens who are critical, self-reflective, knowledgeable, and willing to make moral judgments and act in a socially responsible way. Understood this way, education as a moral and political practice does more than emphasize the importance of critical analysis and moral judgments. It also provides tools to theorize matters of self and social agency and the ever-changing demands and promise of a democratic polity. Education, in short, is inextricably linked to the arc of hope, one that both imagines and struggles for expanding democratic institutions. Moreover, a critical education takes as one of its central projects an attempt to be discerning and attentive to those places and practices in which social agency has been denied, and sometimes subject to a form of intellectual violence.

Education then does more than create critical and autonomous citizens and a culture of critique; it also calls for self-reflection and the ability to call power into question. It enables young people and others to connect individual troubles to wider systemic concerns and, as a critical mode of translation, empowers people to address important issues not as isolated individuals but as part of a wider social movement. This notion of education is especially important at a time in which issues of racialized violence, violence against women, and the ongoing assaults on the future of younger generations cannot be solved on an individual basis.

This notion of critical education is particularly important at a time when our societies are not only saturated in violence, but reproduced in all spheres of life, from popular culture to the real violence waged against minorities in the streets and school environments. A critical education draws attention to the fact that violence is not only structural but also symbolic and, as Pierre Bourdieu has argued, 'lies on the side of belief and persuasion'. Such a recognition makes education central to politics and the struggle against all forms of violence in that it makes clear that at the heart of any viable notion of agency and struggle is the need to change the way people view themselves, their relationship with others, and the larger world. A critical education can pose serious challenges to diverse forms of institutional violence because it offers individuals the tools to press the claims for economic and social justice, transform self-destructive behavior into productive collective action, make power visible, and enable the development of a discourse of both critique and possibility.

Violence maims not only the body but also the mind and spirit. Recognizing the latter enables the development of a critical education in which questions can be raised about what it means to gain the knowledge and skill that enhance one's agency, but also what it means to unlearn those ideologies, values, ideas and falsehoods that lead people to believe that they are individually responsible for the violence they experience and that nothing can be done to challenge the ideological and institutional conditions that produce it.

Authoritarian systems have always used public pedagogy as a form of ideology to persuade many in the masses that the only solution to addressing social issues is to blame vulnerable groups for their plight. This is no less apparent in the contemporary moment, as the white underclasses are being mobilized against people of a different religion and color across the world. When politics becomes an extension of hate and economic distress, it offers no guarantee to enlighten people politically. We now live at a time in which people are diverted into a politics that celebrates saviors, denigrates relations of power and policy, and provides a mode of escape in which heartfelt trauma and pain are used not to mobilize people into democratic movements but to blame others who are equally oppressed.

Atomization on a global scale thus points to a new form of invisible violence because it shackles people to become prisoners of their own experiences, cut off from the larger systemic forces that both shape them and for which they bear little responsibility and over which they have no control. Anger, indignation and misery need to take a detour through those ethical, political and social models of analysis that connect individual issues to larger social problems in ways that fight, rather than justify, that transformation of grievances into a contemporary version of political fascism.

While there are no guarantees that a critical education will prompt individuals to contest various forms of oppression and violence, it is clear that in the absence of a critical formative democratic culture the forces of authoritarianism and state violence will only become stronger. One can easily extend this insight by arguing that as long as oppression and violence are normalized and the larger public depoliticized through educational practices that legitimate various forms of domination, any vestige of a strong democracy will wither and violence will reign unchecked.

Such a task does, however, come with its challenges. Troubling knowledge cannot be condemned on the basis of making students uncomfortable, especially if the desire for safety serves merely to limit access to difficult knowledge and the resources needed to analyze it. Critical education should be viewed as the art of the possible rather than a space organized around timidity, caution and fear. Confronting the intolerable should be challenging and upsetting. Who could read the works of the authors and deal with the examples featured here and not feel intellectually and emotionally exhausted? It is the conditions that produce violence that should upset us ethically and prompt us to act responsibly.

Under the present circumstances, it is time to remind ourselves that critical ideas are a matter of critical importance. Those public spheres in which critical thought is nurtured provide the minimal conditions for people to become worldly, take hold of important social issues and alleviate human suffering as the means of making more equitable and just societies. Ideas are not empty gestures and they do more than express a free-floating idealism. Ideas provide a crucial foundation for assessing the limits and strengths of our senses of individual and collective agency and what it might mean to exercise civic courage in order to not merely live in the world, but to shape it in light of democratic ideals that would make it a better place for everyone. Critical ideas and the technologies, institutions and public spheres that enable them matter because they offer us the opportunity to think and act otherwise, challenge common sense, cross over into new lines of inquiry and take positions without standing still – in short, to become border crossers who refuse the silos that isolate and determine the future of thought.

Some intellectuals refute the values of criticality. They don't engage in debates; they simply offer already rehearsed positions in which unsubstantiated opinion and sustained argument collapse into each other. It is time then for critical thinkers with a public interest to make pedagogy central to any viable notion of politics. It is time to initiate a cultural campaign in which the positive virtues of radical criticality can be reclaimed, courage to tell the truth defended, and where learning is connected to social change. Our task in short is to demand a return of the political as a matter of critical urgency.

Creating alternative futures requires serious and sustained investment in arresting the cycle of violence, imagining better futures and styles for living amongst the world of peoples. It is to destroy the image of a violently fated world we have created for ourselves by taking pedagogy and education seriously, harnessing the power of imagination and equipping young people with the confidence that the world can be transformed for the better. This illustrated book is an excellent step in that direction.

Brad Evans

Thinking
Against Violence

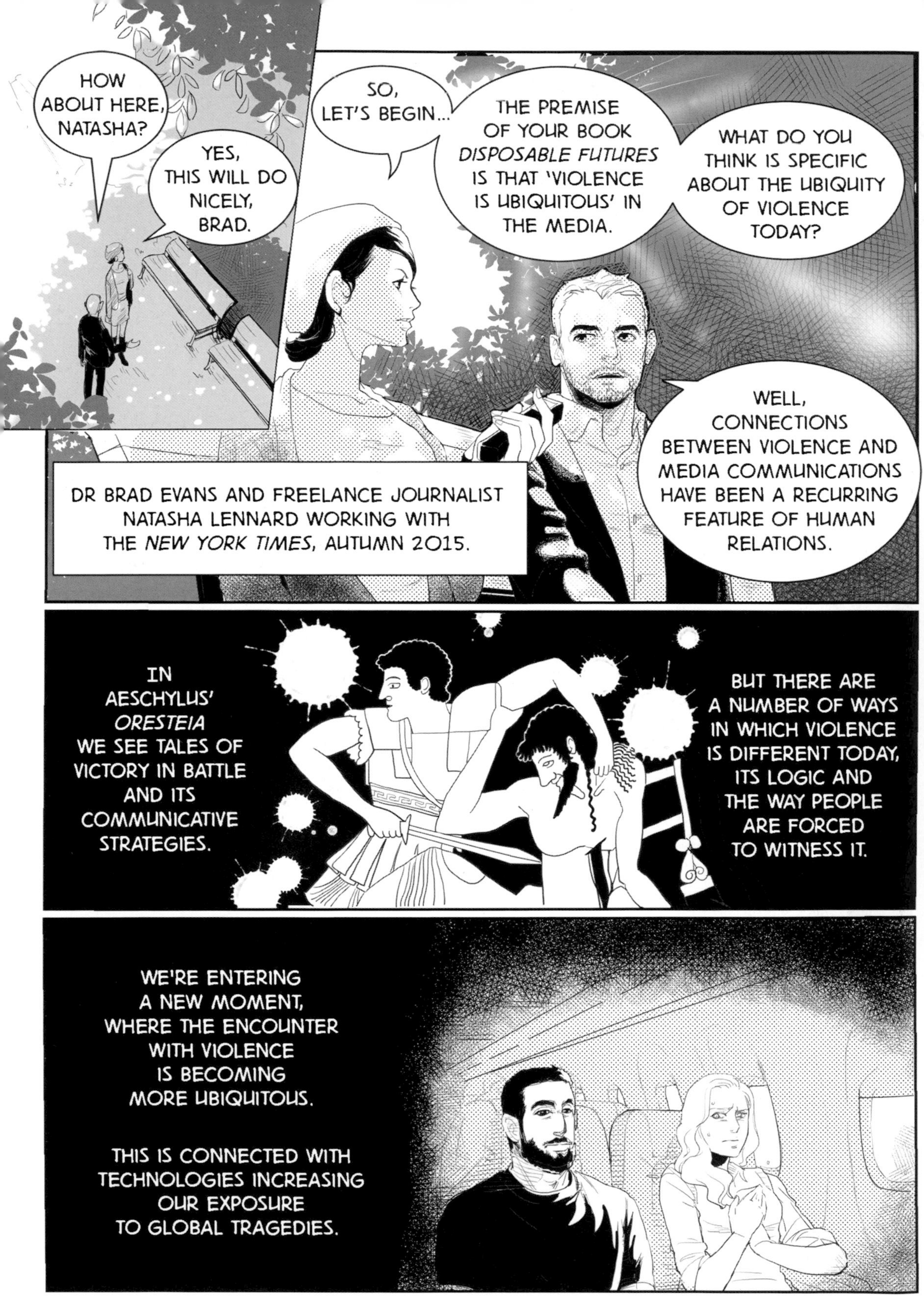
HOW ABOUT HERE, NATASHA?
YES, THIS WILL DO NICELY, BRAD.
SO, LET'S BEGIN...
THE PREMISE OF YOUR BOOK *DISPOSABLE FUTURES* IS THAT 'VIOLENCE IS UBIQUITOUS' IN THE MEDIA.
WHAT DO YOU THINK IS SPECIFIC ABOUT THE UBIQUITY OF VIOLENCE TODAY?
DR BRAD EVANS AND FREELANCE JOURNALIST NATASHA LENNARD WORKING WITH THE *NEW YORK TIMES*, AUTUMN 2015.
WELL, CONNECTIONS BETWEEN VIOLENCE AND MEDIA COMMUNICATIONS HAVE BEEN A RECURRING FEATURE OF HUMAN RELATIONS.
IN AESCHYLUS' *ORESTEIA* WE SEE TALES OF VICTORY IN BATTLE AND ITS COMMUNICATIVE STRATEGIES.
BUT THERE ARE A NUMBER OF WAYS IN WHICH VIOLENCE IS DIFFERENT TODAY, ITS LOGIC AND THE WAY PEOPLE ARE FORCED TO WITNESS IT.
WE'RE ENTERING A NEW MOMENT, WHERE THE ENCOUNTER WITH VIOLENCE IS BECOMING MORE UBIQUITOUS.
THIS IS CONNECTED WITH TECHNOLOGIES INCREASING OUR EXPOSURE TO GLOBAL TRAGEDIES.

VIOLENCE HAS BECOME THE DEFINING ORGANIZATIONAL PRINCIPLE FOR CONTEMPORARY SOCIETIES. IT MATTERS LESS IF WE ARE ACTUAL VICTIMS OF VIOLENCE.

IT IS THE POSSIBILITY THAT WE COULD FACE SOME FORM OF VIOLENT ENCOUNTER WHICH SHAPES THE LOGICS OF POWER IN LIBERAL SOCIETIES.

OUR POLITICAL IMAGINATION HAS BECOME DOMINATED BY POTENTIAL CATASTROPHES, SUCH AS THE CLOSING OF THE LOS ANGELES CITY SCHOOL SYSTEM AFTER A REPORTED TERRORIST THREAT.

WE SEE THIS PLAYED OUT ON MANY LEVELS, AS THE BLURRING BETWEEN OLDER NOTIONS OF HOMELAND/BATTLEFIELDS, FRIENDS/ENEMIES, PEACE/WAR HAS LED TO THE WIDESPREAD MILITARIZATION OF EVERYDAY BEHAVIORS.

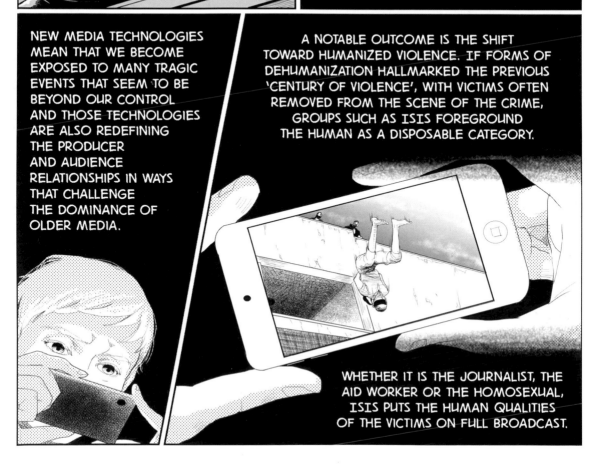

NEW MEDIA TECHNOLOGIES MEAN THAT WE BECOME EXPOSED TO MANY TRAGIC EVENTS THAT SEEM TO BE BEYOND OUR CONTROL AND THOSE TECHNOLOGIES ARE ALSO REDEFINING THE PRODUCER AND AUDIENCE RELATIONSHIPS IN WAYS THAT CHALLENGE THE DOMINANCE OF OLDER MEDIA.

A NOTABLE OUTCOME IS THE SHIFT TOWARD HUMANIZED VIOLENCE. IF FORMS OF DEHUMANIZATION HALLMARKED THE PREVIOUS 'CENTURY OF VIOLENCE', WITH VICTIMS OFTEN REMOVED FROM THE SCENE OF THE CRIME, GROUPS SUCH AS ISIS FOREGROUND THE HUMAN AS A DISPOSABLE CATEGORY.

WHETHER IT IS THE JOURNALIST, THE AID WORKER OR THE HOMOSEXUAL, ISIS PUTS THE HUMAN QUALITIES OF THE VICTIMS ON FULL BROADCAST.

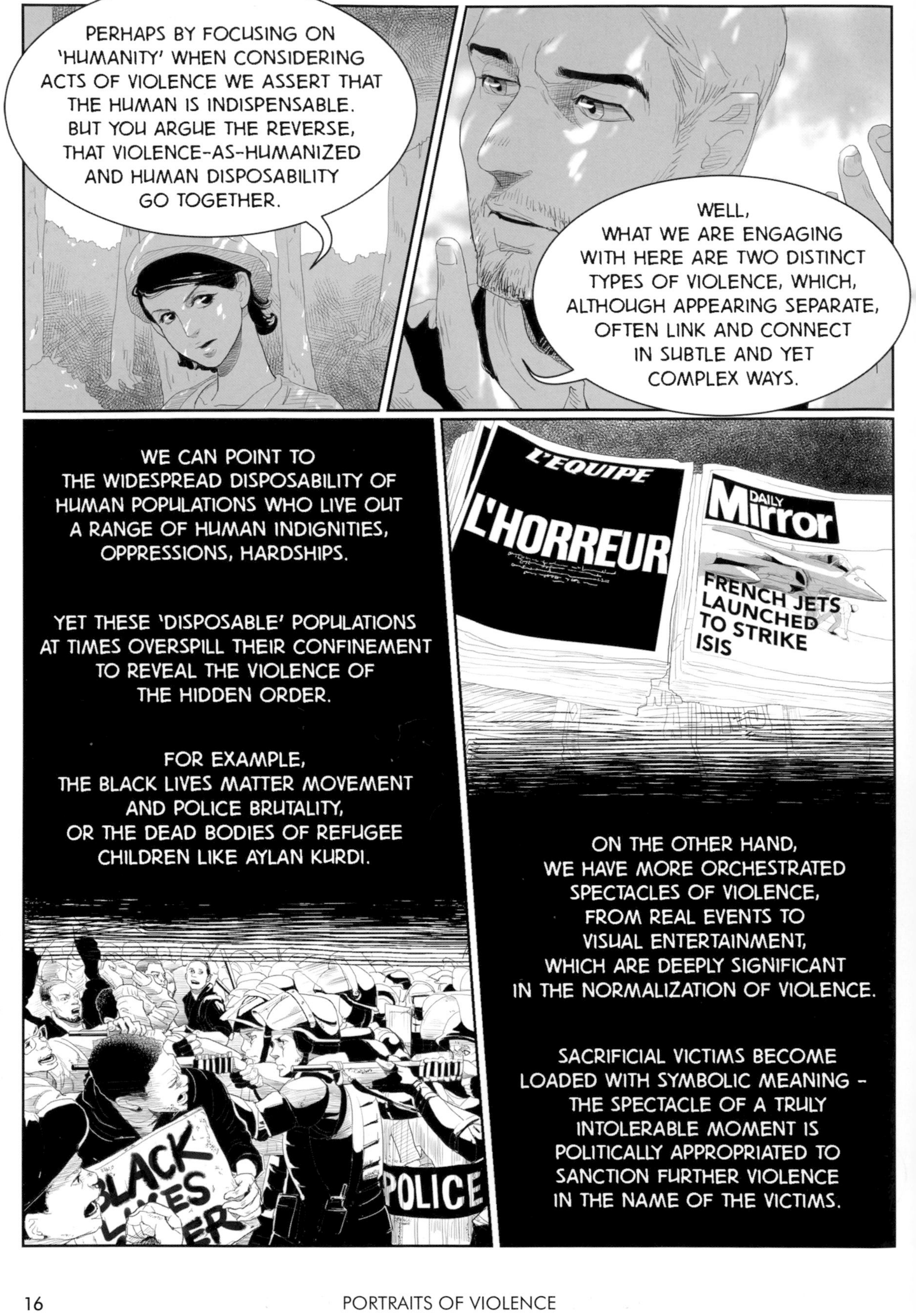
PERHAPS BY FOCUSING ON 'HUMANITY' WHEN CONSIDERING ACTS OF VIOLENCE WE ASSERT THAT THE HUMAN IS INDISPENSABLE. BUT YOU ARGUE THE REVERSE, THAT VIOLENCE-AS-HUMANIZED AND HUMAN DISPOSABILITY GO TOGETHER.
WELL, WHAT WE ARE ENGAGING WITH HERE ARE TWO DISTINCT TYPES OF VIOLENCE, WHICH, ALTHOUGH APPEARING SEPARATE, OFTEN LINK AND CONNECT IN SUBTLE AND YET COMPLEX WAYS.
WE CAN POINT TO THE WIDESPREAD DISPOSABILITY OF HUMAN POPULATIONS WHO LIVE OUT A RANGE OF HUMAN INDIGNITIES, OPPRESSIONS, HARDSHIPS.
YET THESE 'DISPOSABLE' POPULATIONS AT TIMES OVERSPILL THEIR CONFINEMENT TO REVEAL THE VIOLENCE OF THE HIDDEN ORDER.
FOR EXAMPLE, THE BLACK LIVES MATTER MOVEMENT AND POLICE BRUTALITY, OR THE DEAD BODIES OF REFUGEE CHILDREN LIKE AYLAN KURDI.
BLACK
POLICE
L'EQUIPE
L'HORREUR
DAILY Mirror
FRENCH JETS LAUNCHED TO STRIKE ISIS
ON THE OTHER HAND, WE HAVE MORE ORCHESTRATED SPECTACLES OF VIOLENCE, FROM REAL EVENTS TO VISUAL ENTERTAINMENT, WHICH ARE DEEPLY SIGNIFICANT IN THE NORMALIZATION OF VIOLENCE.
SACRIFICIAL VICTIMS BECOME LOADED WITH SYMBOLIC MEANING – THE SPECTACLE OF A TRULY INTOLERABLE MOMENT IS POLITICALLY APPROPRIATED TO SANCTION FURTHER VIOLENCE IN THE NAME OF THE VICTIMS.

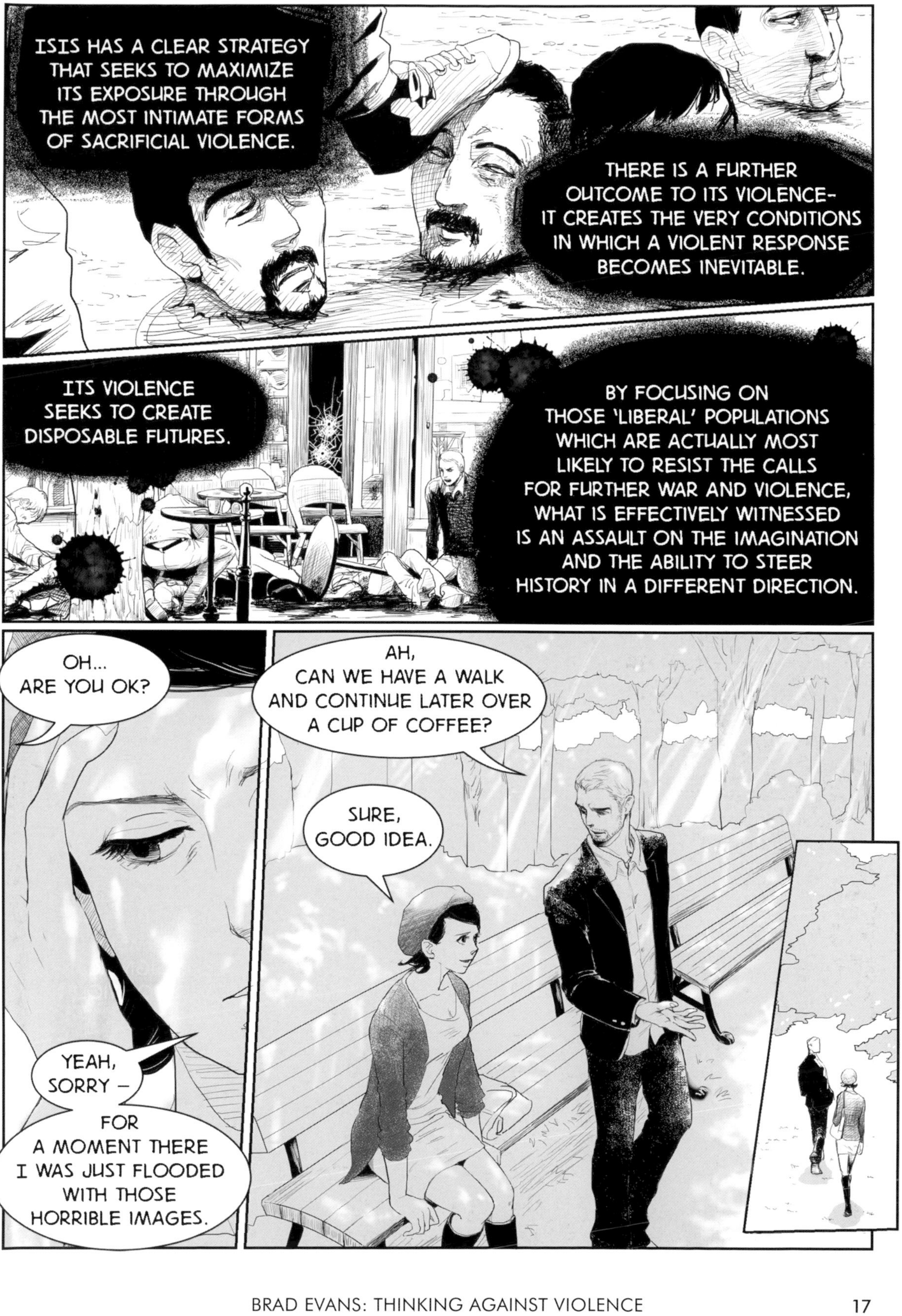
ISIS HAS A CLEAR STRATEGY THAT SEEKS TO MAXIMIZE ITS EXPOSURE THROUGH THE MOST INTIMATE FORMS OF SACRIFICIAL VIOLENCE.
THERE IS A FURTHER OUTCOME TO ITS VIOLENCE- IT CREATES THE VERY CONDITIONS IN WHICH A VIOLENT RESPONSE BECOMES INEVITABLE.
ITS VIOLENCE SEEKS TO CREATE DISPOSABLE FUTURES.
BY FOCUSING ON THOSE 'LIBERAL' POPULATIONS WHICH ARE ACTUALLY MOST LIKELY TO RESIST THE CALLS FOR FURTHER WAR AND VIOLENCE, WHAT IS EFFECTIVELY WITNESSED IS AN ASSAULT ON THE IMAGINATION AND THE ABILITY TO STEER HISTORY IN A DIFFERENT DIRECTION.
OH... ARE YOU OK?
YEAH, SORRY –
FOR A MOMENT THERE I WAS JUST FLOODED WITH THOSE HORRIBLE IMAGES.
AH, CAN WE HAVE A WALK AND CONTINUE LATER OVER A CUP OF COFFEE?
SURE, GOOD IDEA.

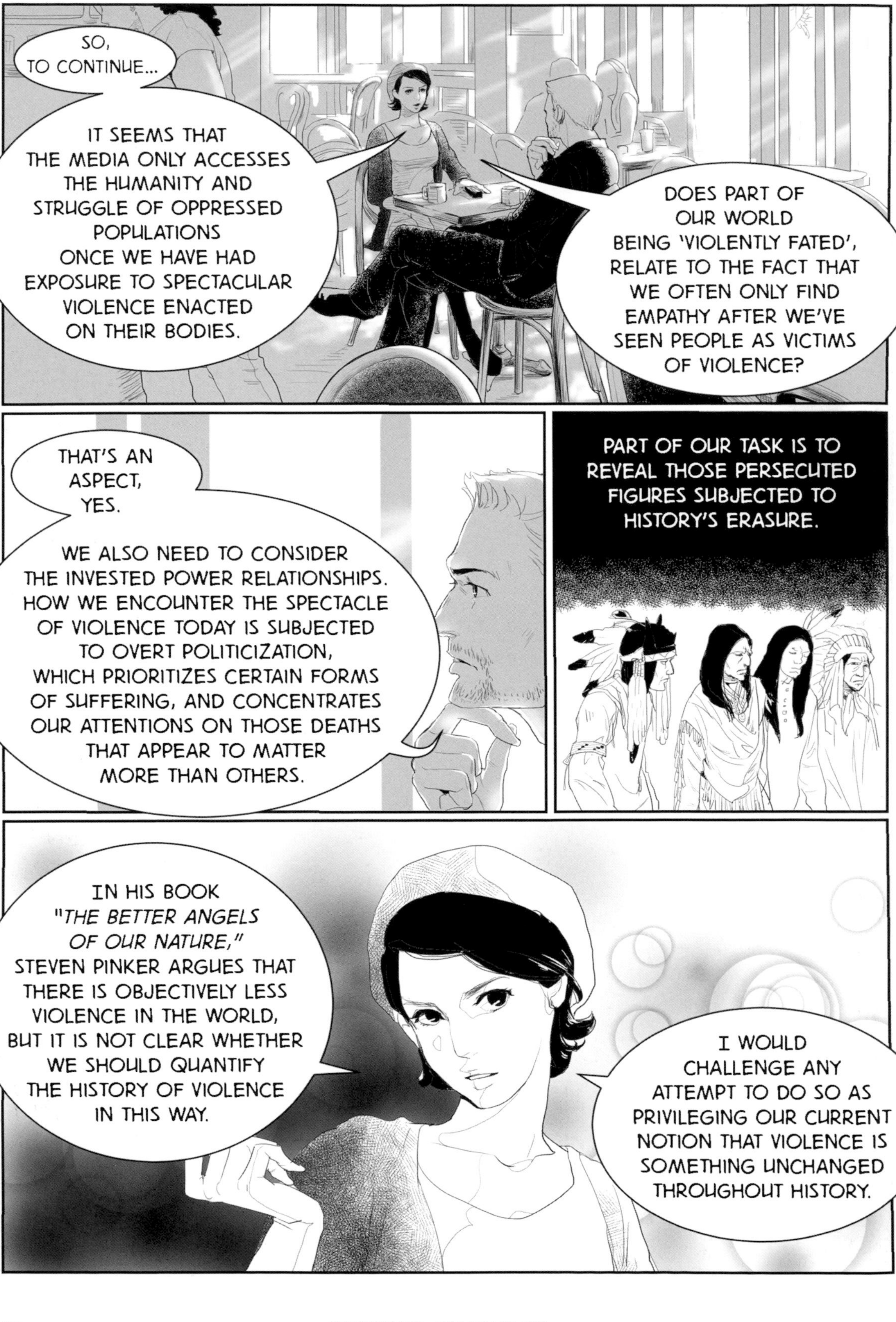
SO, TO CONTINUE...
IT SEEMS THAT THE MEDIA ONLY ACCESSES THE HUMANITY AND STRUGGLE OF OPPRESSED POPULATIONS ONCE WE HAVE HAD EXPOSURE TO SPECTACULAR VIOLENCE ENACTED ON THEIR BODIES.
DOES PART OF OUR WORLD BEING 'VIOLENTLY FATED', RELATE TO THE FACT THAT WE OFTEN ONLY FIND EMPATHY AFTER WE'VE SEEN PEOPLE AS VICTIMS OF VIOLENCE?
THAT'S AN ASPECT, YES.
WE ALSO NEED TO CONSIDER THE INVESTED POWER RELATIONSHIPS. HOW WE ENCOUNTER THE SPECTACLE OF VIOLENCE TODAY IS SUBJECTED TO OVERT POLITICIZATION, WHICH PRIORITIZES CERTAIN FORMS OF SUFFERING, AND CONCENTRATES OUR ATTENTIONS ON THOSE DEATHS THAT APPEAR TO MATTER MORE THAN OTHERS.
PART OF OUR TASK IS TO REVEAL THOSE PERSECUTED FIGURES SUBJECTED TO HISTORY'S ERASURE.
IN HIS BOOK "*THE BETTER ANGELS OF OUR NATURE,*" STEVEN PINKER ARGUES THAT THERE IS OBJECTIVELY LESS VIOLENCE IN THE WORLD, BUT IT IS NOT CLEAR WHETHER WE SHOULD QUANTIFY THE HISTORY OF VIOLENCE IN THIS WAY.
I WOULD CHALLENGE ANY ATTEMPT TO DO SO AS PRIVILEGING OUR CURRENT NOTION THAT VIOLENCE IS SOMETHING UNCHANGED THROUGHOUT HISTORY.

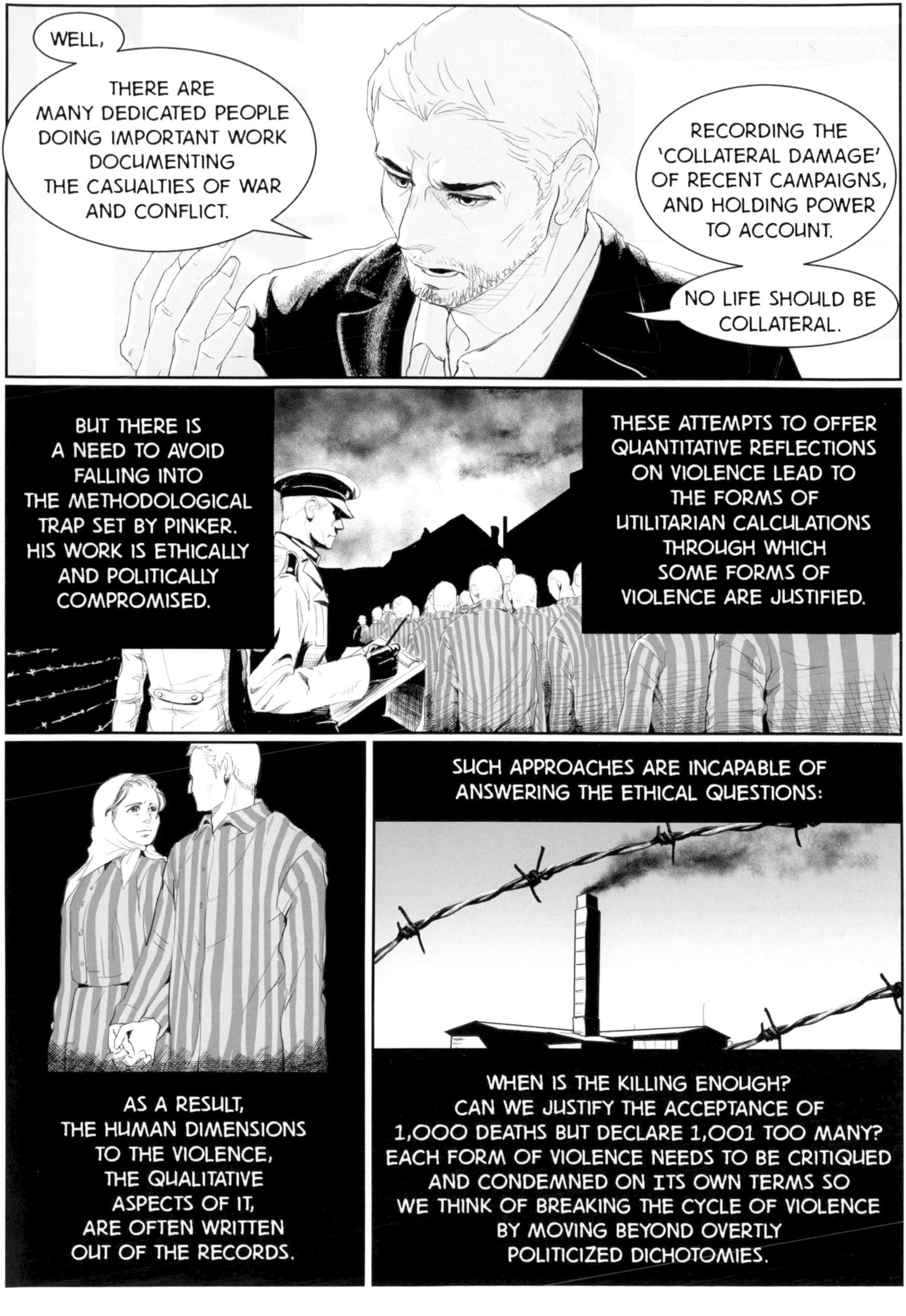
WELL,
THERE ARE MANY DEDICATED PEOPLE DOING IMPORTANT WORK DOCUMENTING THE CASUALTIES OF WAR AND CONFLICT.
RECORDING THE 'COLLATERAL DAMAGE' OF RECENT CAMPAIGNS, AND HOLDING POWER TO ACCOUNT.
NO LIFE SHOULD BE COLLATERAL.
BUT THERE IS A NEED TO AVOID FALLING INTO THE METHODOLOGICAL TRAP SET BY PINKER. HIS WORK IS ETHICALLY AND POLITICALLY COMPROMISED.
THESE ATTEMPTS TO OFFER QUANTITATIVE REFLECTIONS ON VIOLENCE LEAD TO THE FORMS OF UTILITARIAN CALCULATIONS THROUGH WHICH SOME FORMS OF VIOLENCE ARE JUSTIFIED.
AS A RESULT, THE HUMAN DIMENSIONS TO THE VIOLENCE, THE QUALITATIVE ASPECTS OF IT, ARE OFTEN WRITTEN OUT OF THE RECORDS.
SUCH APPROACHES ARE INCAPABLE OF ANSWERING THE ETHICAL QUESTIONS:
WHEN IS THE KILLING ENOUGH? CAN WE JUSTIFY THE ACCEPTANCE OF 1,000 DEATHS BUT DECLARE 1,001 TOO MANY? EACH FORM OF VIOLENCE NEEDS TO BE CRITIQUED AND CONDEMNED ON ITS OWN TERMS SO WE THINK OF BREAKING THE CYCLE OF VIOLENCE BY MOVING BEYOND OVERTLY POLITICIZED DICHOTOMIES.

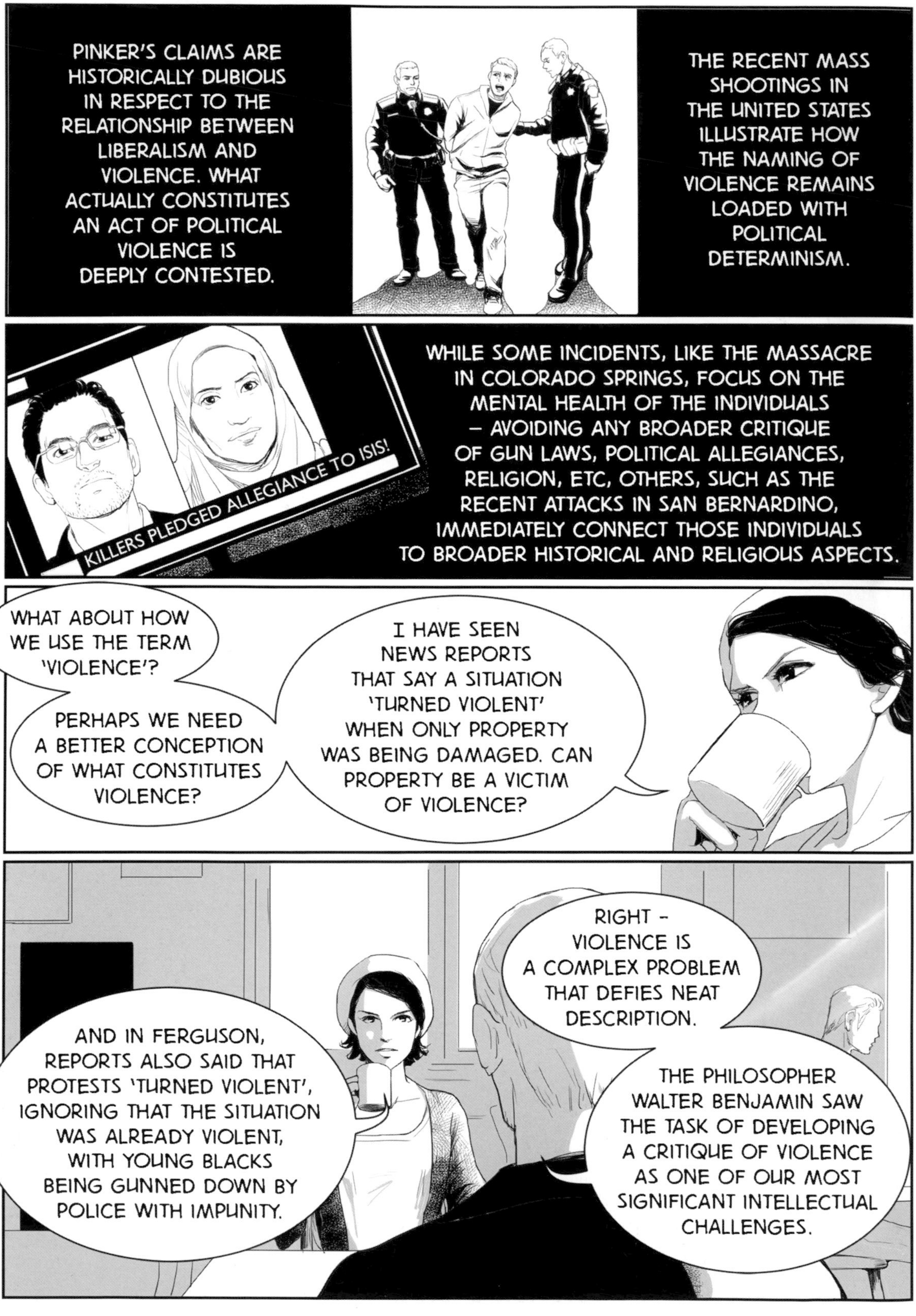
PINKER'S CLAIMS ARE HISTORICALLY DUBIOUS IN RESPECT TO THE RELATIONSHIP BETWEEN LIBERALISM AND VIOLENCE. WHAT ACTUALLY CONSTITUTES AN ACT OF POLITICAL VIOLENCE IS DEEPLY CONTESTED.
THE RECENT MASS SHOOTINGS IN THE UNITED STATES ILLUSTRATE HOW THE NAMING OF VIOLENCE REMAINS LOADED WITH POLITICAL DETERMINISM.
KILLERS PLEDGED ALLEGIANCE TO ISIS!
WHILE SOME INCIDENTS, LIKE THE MASSACRE IN COLORADO SPRINGS, FOCUS ON THE MENTAL HEALTH OF THE INDIVIDUALS – AVOIDING ANY BROADER CRITIQUE OF GUN LAWS, POLITICAL ALLEGIANCES, RELIGION, ETC, OTHERS, SUCH AS THE RECENT ATTACKS IN SAN BERNARDINO, IMMEDIATELY CONNECT THOSE INDIVIDUALS TO BROADER HISTORICAL AND RELIGIOUS ASPECTS.
WHAT ABOUT HOW WE USE THE TERM 'VIOLENCE'?
PERHAPS WE NEED A BETTER CONCEPTION OF WHAT CONSTITUTES VIOLENCE?
I HAVE SEEN NEWS REPORTS THAT SAY A SITUATION 'TURNED VIOLENT' WHEN ONLY PROPERTY WAS BEING DAMAGED. CAN PROPERTY BE A VICTIM OF VIOLENCE?
AND IN FERGUSON, REPORTS ALSO SAID THAT PROTESTS 'TURNED VIOLENT', IGNORING THAT THE SITUATION WAS ALREADY VIOLENT, WITH YOUNG BLACKS BEING GUNNED DOWN BY POLICE WITH IMPUNITY.
RIGHT – VIOLENCE IS A COMPLEX PROBLEM THAT DEFIES NEAT DESCRIPTION.
THE PHILOSOPHER WALTER BENJAMIN SAW THE TASK OF DEVELOPING A CRITIQUE OF VIOLENCE AS ONE OF OUR MOST SIGNIFICANT INTELLECTUAL CHALLENGES.

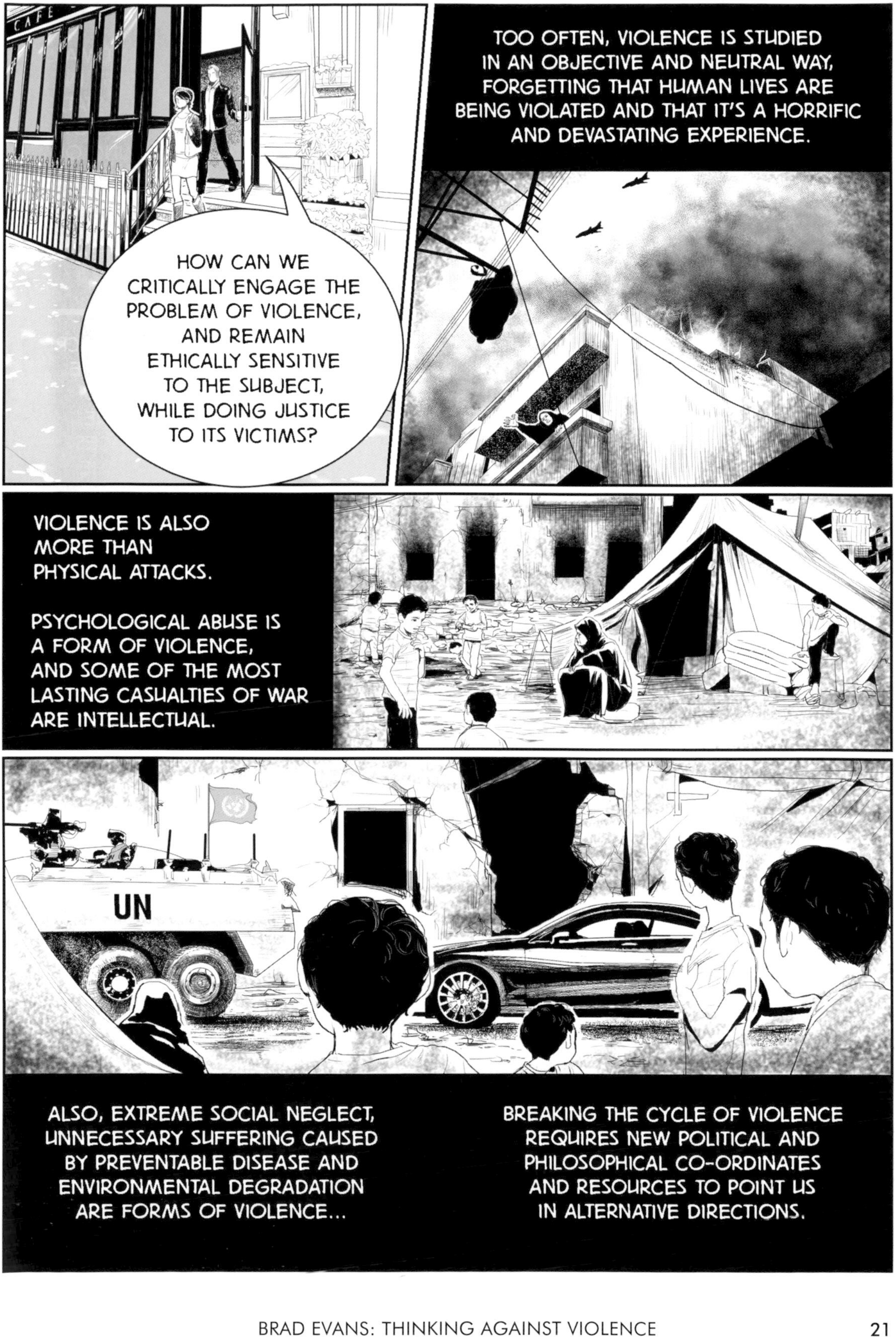
CAFE
HOW CAN WE CRITICALLY ENGAGE THE PROBLEM OF VIOLENCE, AND REMAIN ETHICALLY SENSITIVE TO THE SUBJECT, WHILE DOING JUSTICE TO ITS VICTIMS?
TOO OFTEN, VIOLENCE IS STUDIED IN AN OBJECTIVE AND NEUTRAL WAY, FORGETTING THAT HUMAN LIVES ARE BEING VIOLATED AND THAT IT'S A HORRIFIC AND DEVASTATING EXPERIENCE.
VIOLENCE IS ALSO MORE THAN PHYSICAL ATTACKS.
PSYCHOLOGICAL ABUSE IS A FORM OF VIOLENCE, AND SOME OF THE MOST LASTING CASUALTIES OF WAR ARE INTELLECTUAL.
UN
ALSO, EXTREME SOCIAL NEGLECT, UNNECESSARY SUFFERING CAUSED BY PREVENTABLE DISEASE AND ENVIRONMENTAL DEGRADATION ARE FORMS OF VIOLENCE...
BREAKING THE CYCLE OF VIOLENCE REQUIRES NEW POLITICAL AND PHILOSOPHICAL CO-ORDINATES AND RESOURCES TO POINT US IN ALTERNATIVE DIRECTIONS.

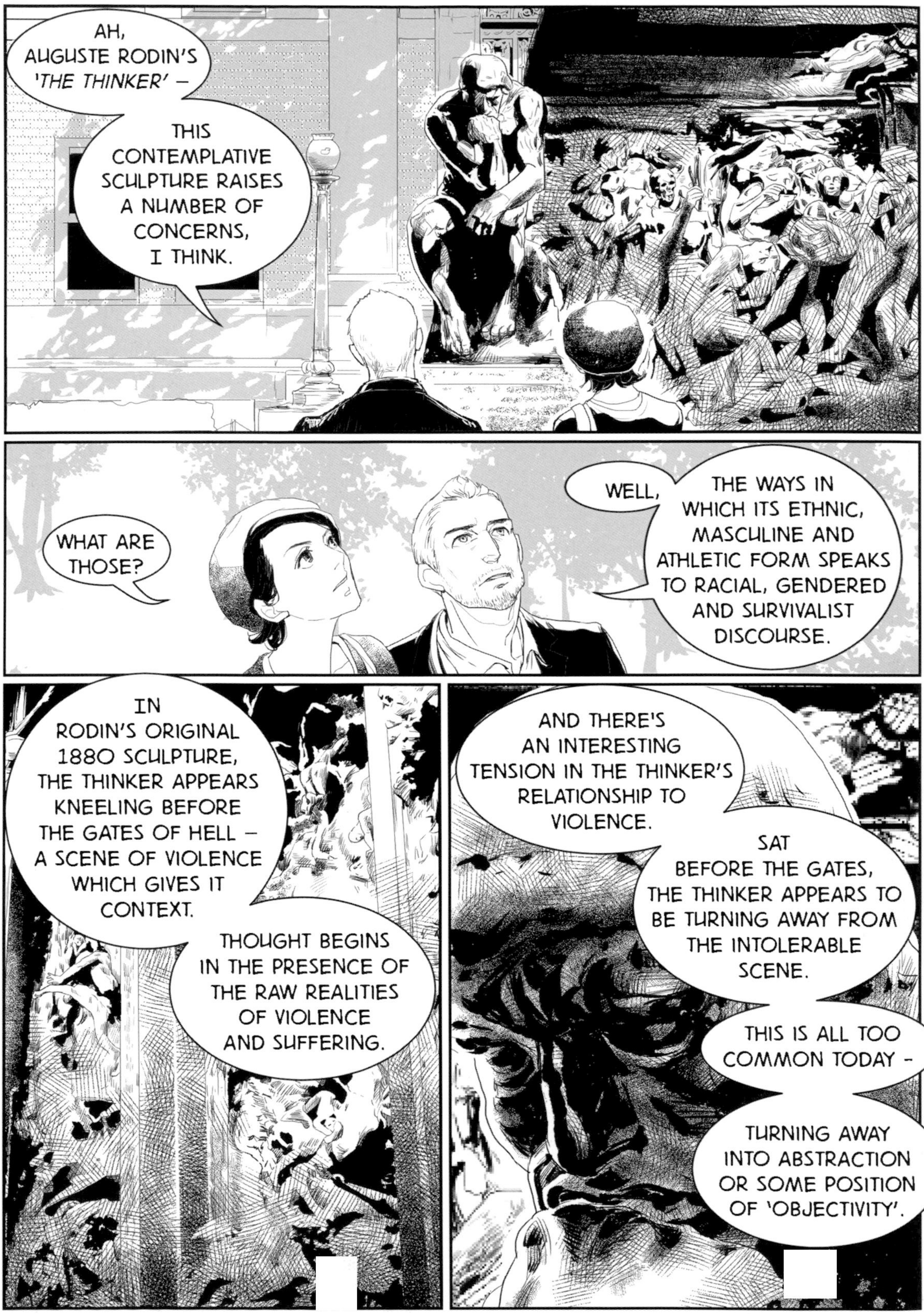
AH, AUGUSTE RODIN'S *'THE THINKER'* –
THIS CONTEMPLATIVE SCULPTURE RAISES A NUMBER OF CONCERNS, I THINK.
WHAT ARE THOSE?
WELL,
THE WAYS IN WHICH ITS ETHNIC, MASCULINE AND ATHLETIC FORM SPEAKS TO RACIAL, GENDERED AND SURVIVALIST DISCOURSE.
IN RODIN'S ORIGINAL 1880 SCULPTURE, THE THINKER APPEARS KNEELING BEFORE THE GATES OF HELL – A SCENE OF VIOLENCE WHICH GIVES IT CONTEXT.
THOUGHT BEGINS IN THE PRESENCE OF THE RAW REALITIES OF VIOLENCE AND SUFFERING.
AND THERE'S AN INTERESTING TENSION IN THE THINKER'S RELATIONSHIP TO VIOLENCE.
SAT BEFORE THE GATES, THE THINKER APPEARS TO BE TURNING AWAY FROM THE INTOLERABLE SCENE.
THIS IS ALL TOO COMMON TODAY -
TURNING AWAY INTO ABSTRACTION OR SOME POSITION OF 'OBJECTIVITY'.

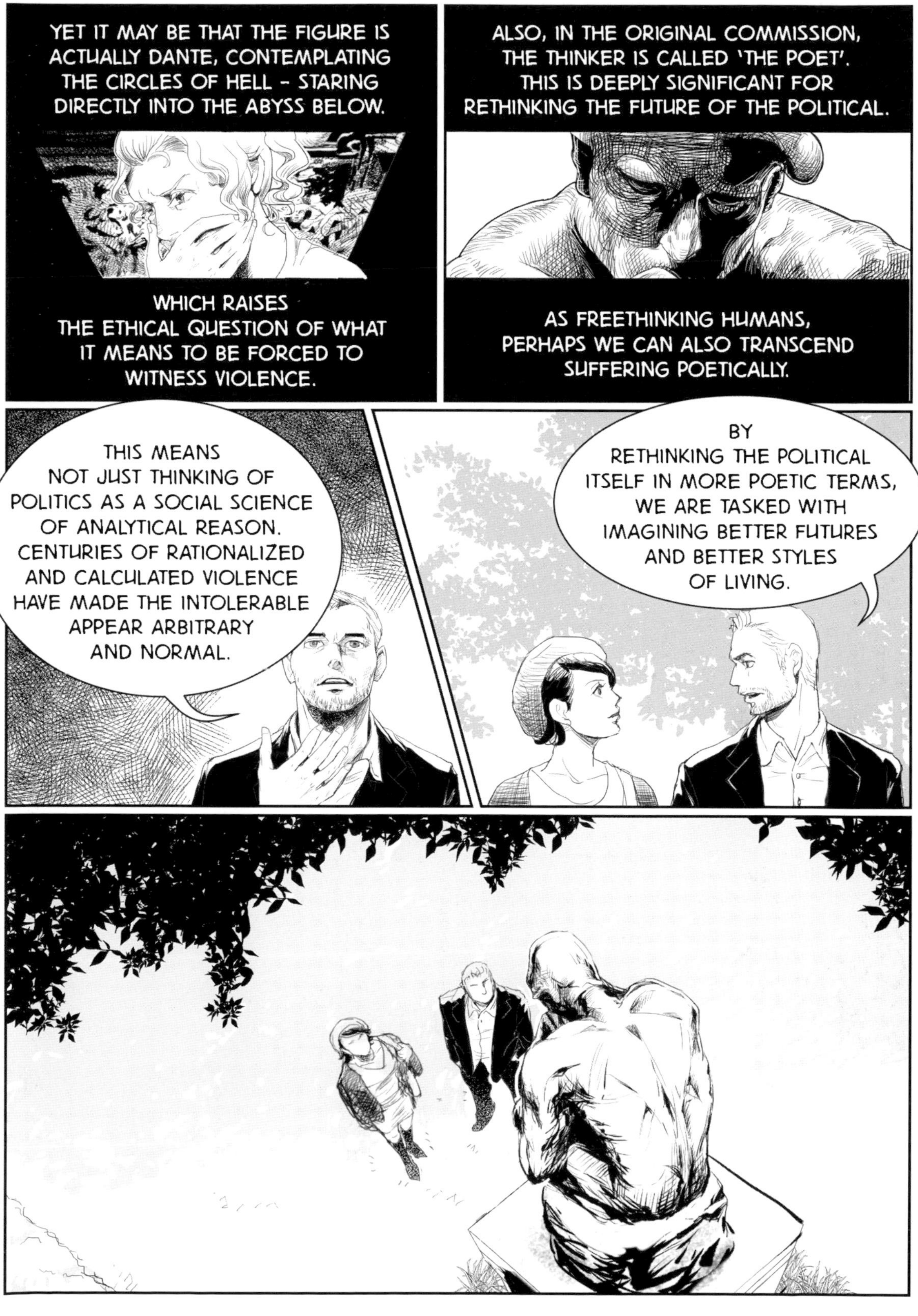
YET IT MAY BE THAT THE FIGURE IS ACTUALLY DANTE, CONTEMPLATING THE CIRCLES OF HELL – STARING DIRECTLY INTO THE ABYSS BELOW.
WHICH RAISES THE ETHICAL QUESTION OF WHAT IT MEANS TO BE FORCED TO WITNESS VIOLENCE.
ALSO, IN THE ORIGINAL COMMISSION, THE THINKER IS CALLED 'THE POET'. THIS IS DEEPLY SIGNIFICANT FOR RETHINKING THE FUTURE OF THE POLITICAL.
AS FREETHINKING HUMANS, PERHAPS WE CAN ALSO TRANSCEND SUFFERING POETICALLY.
THIS MEANS NOT JUST THINKING OF POLITICS AS A SOCIAL SCIENCE OF ANALYTICAL REASON. CENTURIES OF RATIONALIZED AND CALCULATED VIOLENCE HAVE MADE THE INTOLERABLE APPEAR ARBITRARY AND NORMAL.
BY RETHINKING THE POLITICAL ITSELF IN MORE POETIC TERMS, WE ARE TASKED WITH IMAGINING BETTER FUTURES AND BETTER STYLES OF LIVING.

Hannah Arendt

The Banality of Evil

Robert Brown

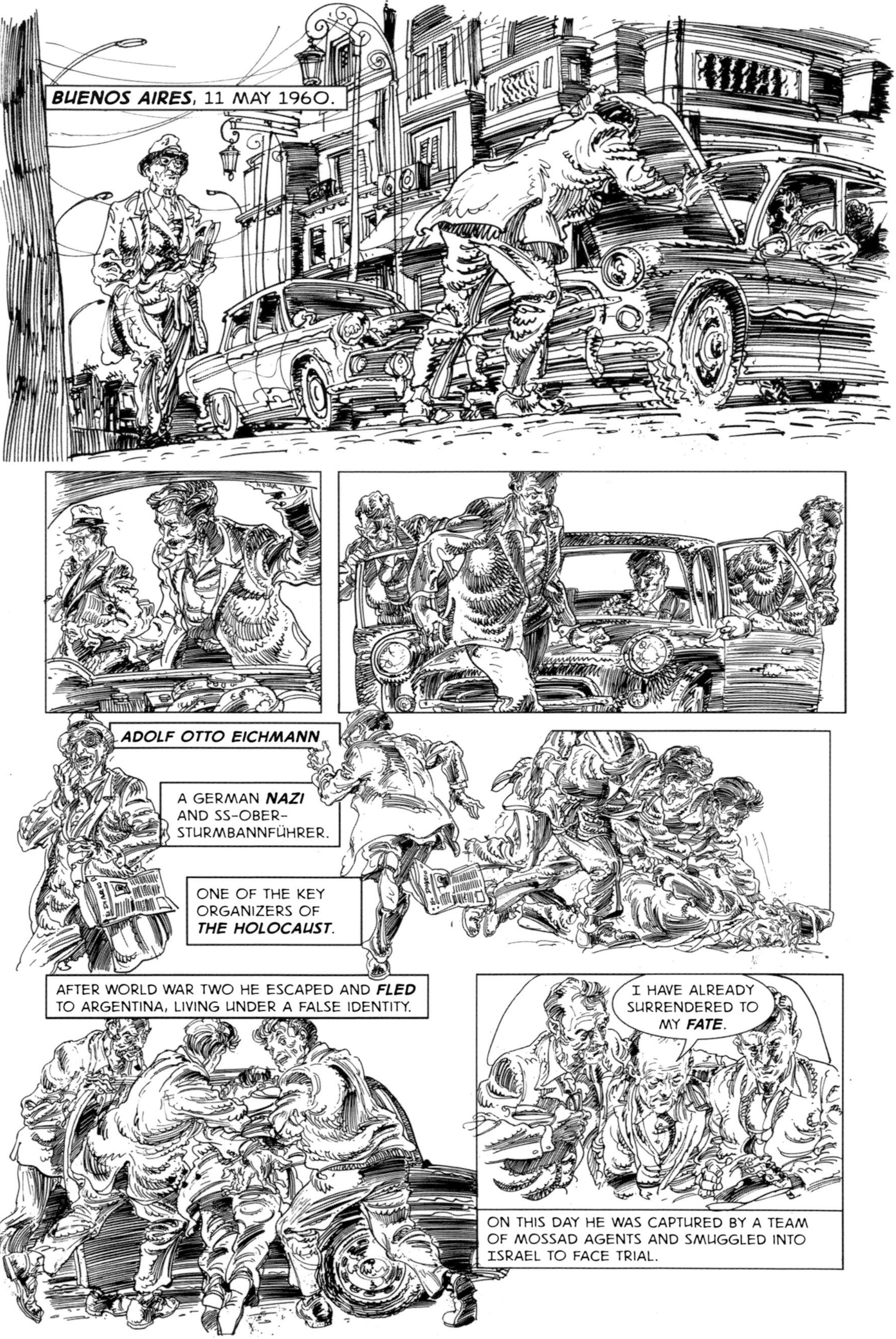

BUENOS AIRES, 11 MAY 1960.
ADOLF OTTO EICHMANN
A GERMAN NAZI AND SS-OBER-STURMBANNFÜHRER.
ONE OF THE KEY ORGANIZERS OF THE HOLOCAUST.
AFTER WORLD WAR TWO HE ESCAPED AND FLED TO ARGENTINA, LIVING UNDER A FALSE IDENTITY.
I HAVE ALREADY SURRENDERED TO MY FATE.
ON THIS DAY HE WAS CAPTURED BY A TEAM OF MOSSAD AGENTS AND SMUGGLED INTO ISRAEL TO FACE TRIAL.

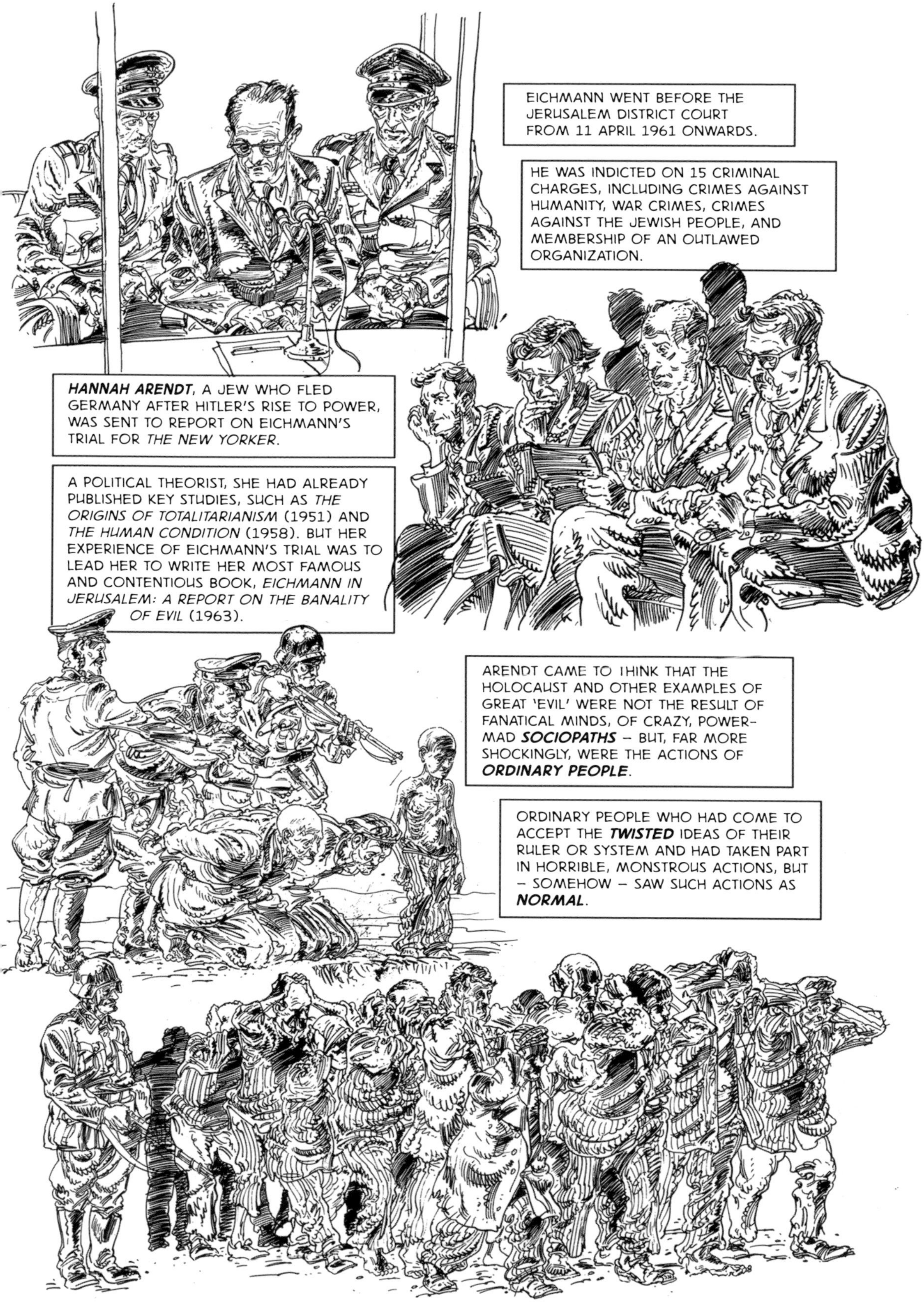
EICHMANN WENT BEFORE THE JERUSALEM DISTRICT COURT FROM 11 APRIL 1961 ONWARDS.
HE WAS INDICTED ON 15 CRIMINAL CHARGES, INCLUDING CRIMES AGAINST HUMANITY, WAR CRIMES, CRIMES AGAINST THE JEWISH PEOPLE, AND MEMBERSHIP OF AN OUTLAWED ORGANIZATION.
HANNAH ARENDT, A JEW WHO FLED GERMANY AFTER HITLER'S RISE TO POWER, WAS SENT TO REPORT ON EICHMANN'S TRIAL FOR *THE NEW YORKER*.
A POLITICAL THEORIST, SHE HAD ALREADY PUBLISHED KEY STUDIES, SUCH AS *THE ORIGINS OF TOTALITARIANISM* (1951) AND *THE HUMAN CONDITION* (1958). BUT HER EXPERIENCE OF EICHMANN'S TRIAL WAS TO LEAD HER TO WRITE HER MOST FAMOUS AND CONTENTIOUS BOOK, *EICHMANN IN JERUSALEM: A REPORT ON THE BANALITY OF EVIL* (1963).
ARENDT CAME TO THINK THAT THE HOLOCAUST AND OTHER EXAMPLES OF GREAT 'EVIL' WERE NOT THE RESULT OF FANATICAL MINDS, OF CRAZY, POWER-MAD ***SOCIOPATHS*** – BUT, FAR MORE SHOCKINGLY, WERE THE ACTIONS OF ***ORDINARY PEOPLE***.
ORDINARY PEOPLE WHO HAD COME TO ACCEPT THE ***TWISTED*** IDEAS OF THEIR RULER OR SYSTEM AND HAD TAKEN PART IN HORRIBLE, MONSTROUS ACTIONS, BUT – SOMEHOW – SAW SUCH ACTIONS AS ***NORMAL***.

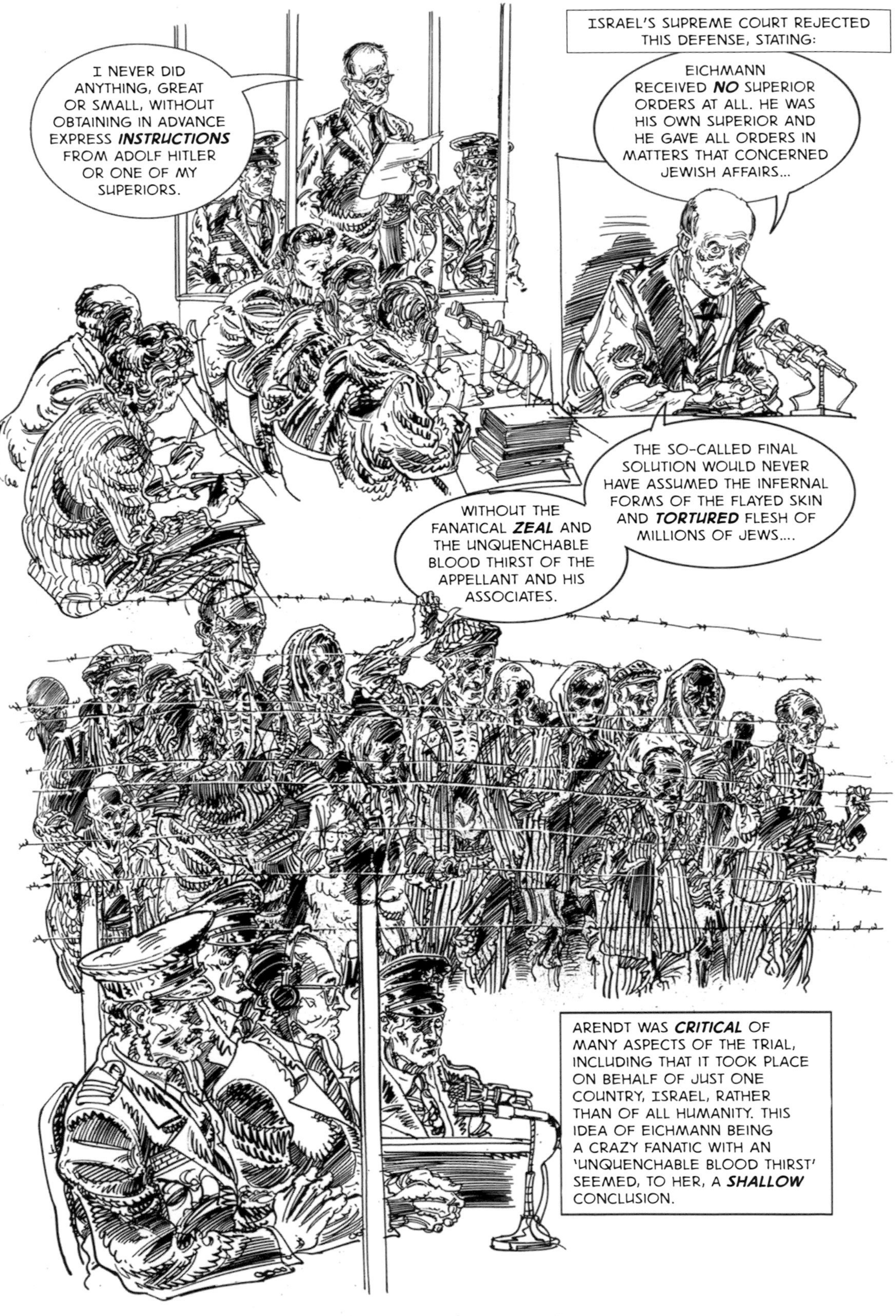

I NEVER DID ANYTHING, GREAT OR SMALL, WITHOUT OBTAINING IN ADVANCE EXPRESS ***INSTRUCTIONS*** FROM ADOLF HITLER OR ONE OF MY SUPERIORS.
ISRAEL'S SUPREME COURT REJECTED THIS DEFENSE, STATING:
EICHMANN RECEIVED ***NO*** SUPERIOR ORDERS AT ALL. HE WAS HIS OWN SUPERIOR AND HE GAVE ALL ORDERS IN MATTERS THAT CONCERNED JEWISH AFFAIRS...
THE SO-CALLED FINAL SOLUTION WOULD NEVER HAVE ASSUMED THE INFERNAL FORMS OF THE FLAYED SKIN AND ***TORTURED*** FLESH OF MILLIONS OF JEWS....
WITHOUT THE FANATICAL ***ZEAL*** AND THE UNQUENCHABLE BLOOD THIRST OF THE APPELLANT AND HIS ASSOCIATES.
ARENDT WAS ***CRITICAL*** OF MANY ASPECTS OF THE TRIAL, INCLUDING THAT IT TOOK PLACE ON BEHALF OF JUST ONE COUNTRY, ISRAEL, RATHER THAN OF ALL HUMANITY. THIS IDEA OF EICHMANN BEING A CRAZY FANATIC WITH AN 'UNQUENCHABLE BLOOD THIRST' SEEMED, TO HER, A ***SHALLOW*** CONCLUSION.

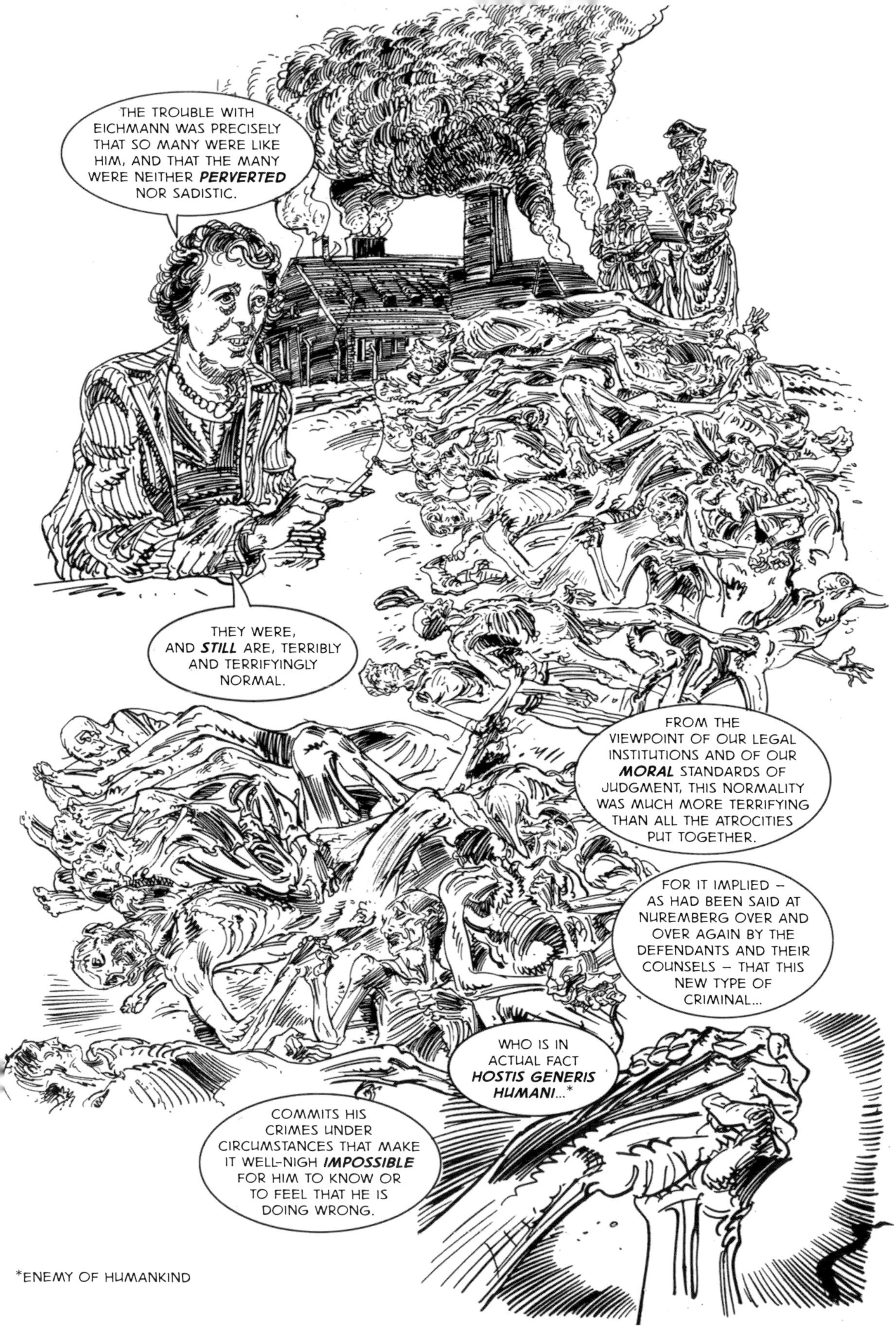
THE TROUBLE WITH EICHMANN WAS PRECISELY THAT SO MANY WERE LIKE HIM, AND THAT THE MANY WERE NEITHER **PERVERTED** NOR SADISTIC.
THEY WERE, AND **STILL** ARE, TERRIBLY AND TERRIFYINGLY NORMAL.
FROM THE VIEWPOINT OF OUR LEGAL INSTITUTIONS AND OF OUR **MORAL** STANDARDS OF JUDGMENT, THIS NORMALITY WAS MUCH MORE TERRIFYING THAN ALL THE ATROCITIES PUT TOGETHER.
FOR IT IMPLIED – AS HAD BEEN SAID AT NUREMBERG OVER AND OVER AGAIN BY THE DEFENDANTS AND THEIR COUNSELS – THAT THIS NEW TYPE OF CRIMINAL...
WHO IS IN ACTUAL FACT ***HOSTIS GENERIS HUMANI***...*
COMMITS HIS CRIMES UNDER CIRCUMSTANCES THAT MAKE IT WELL-NIGH ***IMPOSSIBLE*** FOR HIM TO KNOW OR TO FEEL THAT HE IS DOING WRONG.

*ENEMY OF HUMANKIND

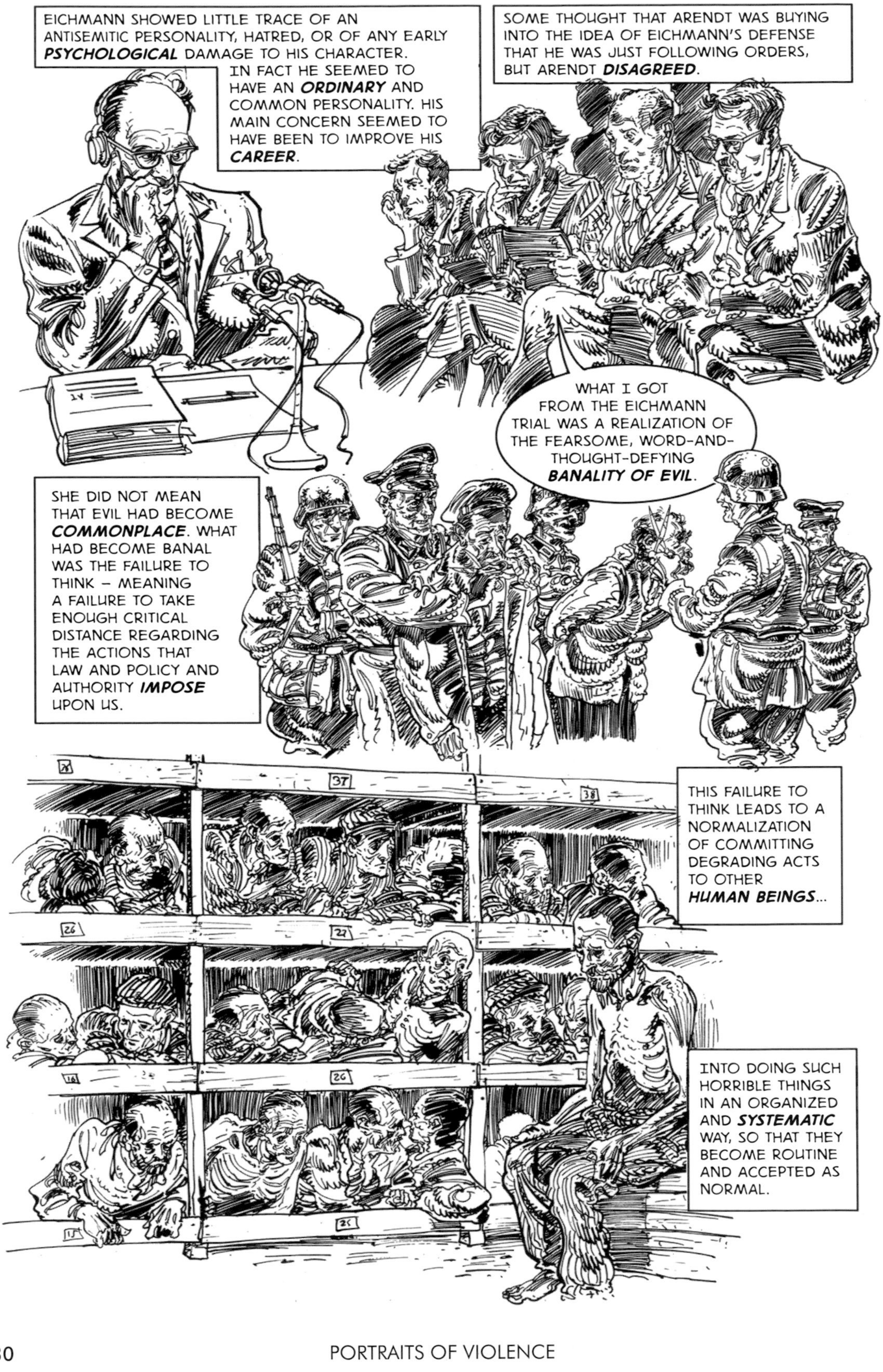
EICHMANN SHOWED LITTLE TRACE OF AN ANTISEMITIC PERSONALITY, HATRED, OR OF ANY EARLY **PSYCHOLOGICAL** DAMAGE TO HIS CHARACTER.
IN FACT HE SEEMED TO HAVE AN **ORDINARY** AND COMMON PERSONALITY. HIS MAIN CONCERN SEEMED TO HAVE BEEN TO IMPROVE HIS **CAREER**.
SOME THOUGHT THAT ARENDT WAS BUYING INTO THE IDEA OF EICHMANN'S DEFENSE THAT HE WAS JUST FOLLOWING ORDERS, BUT ARENDT **DISAGREED**.
WHAT I GOT FROM THE EICHMANN TRIAL WAS A REALIZATION OF THE FEARSOME, WORD-AND-THOUGHT-DEFYING **BANALITY OF EVIL**.
SHE DID NOT MEAN THAT EVIL HAD BECOME **COMMONPLACE**. WHAT HAD BECOME BANAL WAS THE FAILURE TO THINK – MEANING A FAILURE TO TAKE ENOUGH CRITICAL DISTANCE REGARDING THE ACTIONS THAT LAW AND POLICY AND AUTHORITY **IMPOSE** UPON US.
THIS FAILURE TO THINK LEADS TO A NORMALIZATION OF COMMITTING DEGRADING ACTS TO OTHER **HUMAN BEINGS**...
INTO DOING SUCH HORRIBLE THINGS IN AN ORGANIZED AND **SYSTEMATIC** WAY, SO THAT THEY BECOME ROUTINE AND ACCEPTED AS NORMAL.

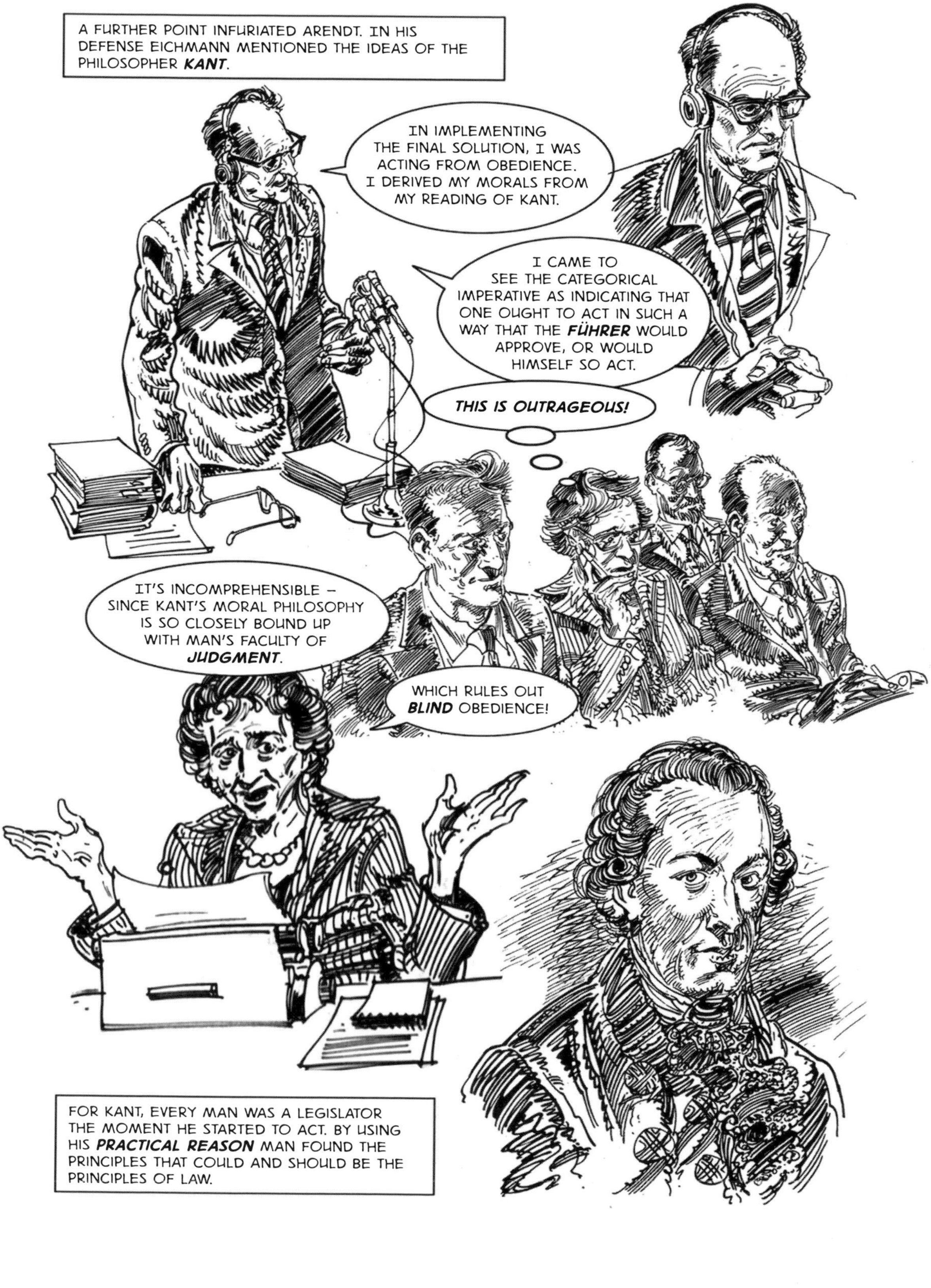
A FURTHER POINT INFURIATED ARENDT. IN HIS DEFENSE EICHMANN MENTIONED THE IDEAS OF THE PHILOSOPHER **KANT**.
IN IMPLEMENTING THE FINAL SOLUTION, I WAS ACTING FROM OBEDIENCE. I DERIVED MY MORALS FROM MY READING OF KANT.
I CAME TO SEE THE CATEGORICAL IMPERATIVE AS INDICATING THAT ONE OUGHT TO ACT IN SUCH A WAY THAT THE **FÜHRER** WOULD APPROVE, OR WOULD HIMSELF SO ACT.
THIS IS OUTRAGEOUS!
IT'S INCOMPREHENSIBLE – SINCE KANT'S MORAL PHILOSOPHY IS SO CLOSELY BOUND UP WITH MAN'S FACULTY OF **JUDGMENT**.
WHICH RULES OUT **BLIND** OBEDIENCE!
FOR KANT, EVERY MAN WAS A LEGISLATOR THE MOMENT HE STARTED TO ACT. BY USING HIS **PRACTICAL REASON** MAN FOUND THE PRINCIPLES THAT COULD AND SHOULD BE THE PRINCIPLES OF LAW.

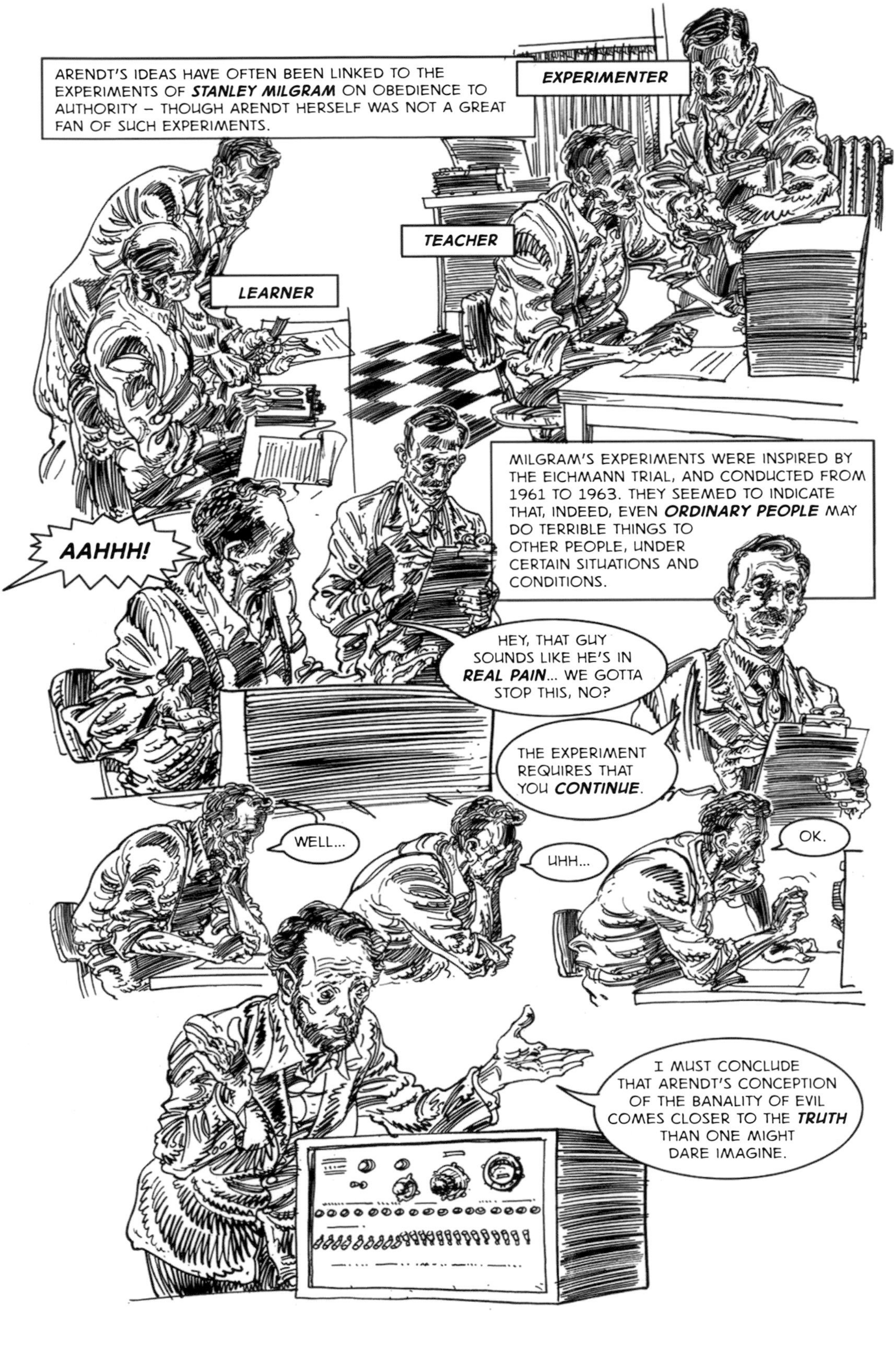
ARENDT'S IDEAS HAVE OFTEN BEEN LINKED TO THE EXPERIMENTS OF **STANLEY MILGRAM** ON OBEDIENCE TO AUTHORITY – THOUGH ARENDT HERSELF WAS NOT A GREAT FAN OF SUCH EXPERIMENTS.
EXPERIMENTER
TEACHER
LEARNER
MILGRAM'S EXPERIMENTS WERE INSPIRED BY THE EICHMANN TRIAL, AND CONDUCTED FROM 1961 TO 1963. THEY SEEMED TO INDICATE THAT, INDEED, EVEN **ORDINARY PEOPLE** MAY DO TERRIBLE THINGS TO OTHER PEOPLE, UNDER CERTAIN SITUATIONS AND CONDITIONS.
AAHHH!
HEY, THAT GUY SOUNDS LIKE HE'S IN **REAL PAIN**... WE GOTTA STOP THIS, NO?
THE EXPERIMENT REQUIRES THAT YOU **CONTINUE**.
WELL...
UHH...
OK.
I MUST CONCLUDE THAT ARENDT'S CONCEPTION OF THE BANALITY OF EVIL COMES CLOSER TO THE **TRUTH** THAN ONE MIGHT DARE IMAGINE.

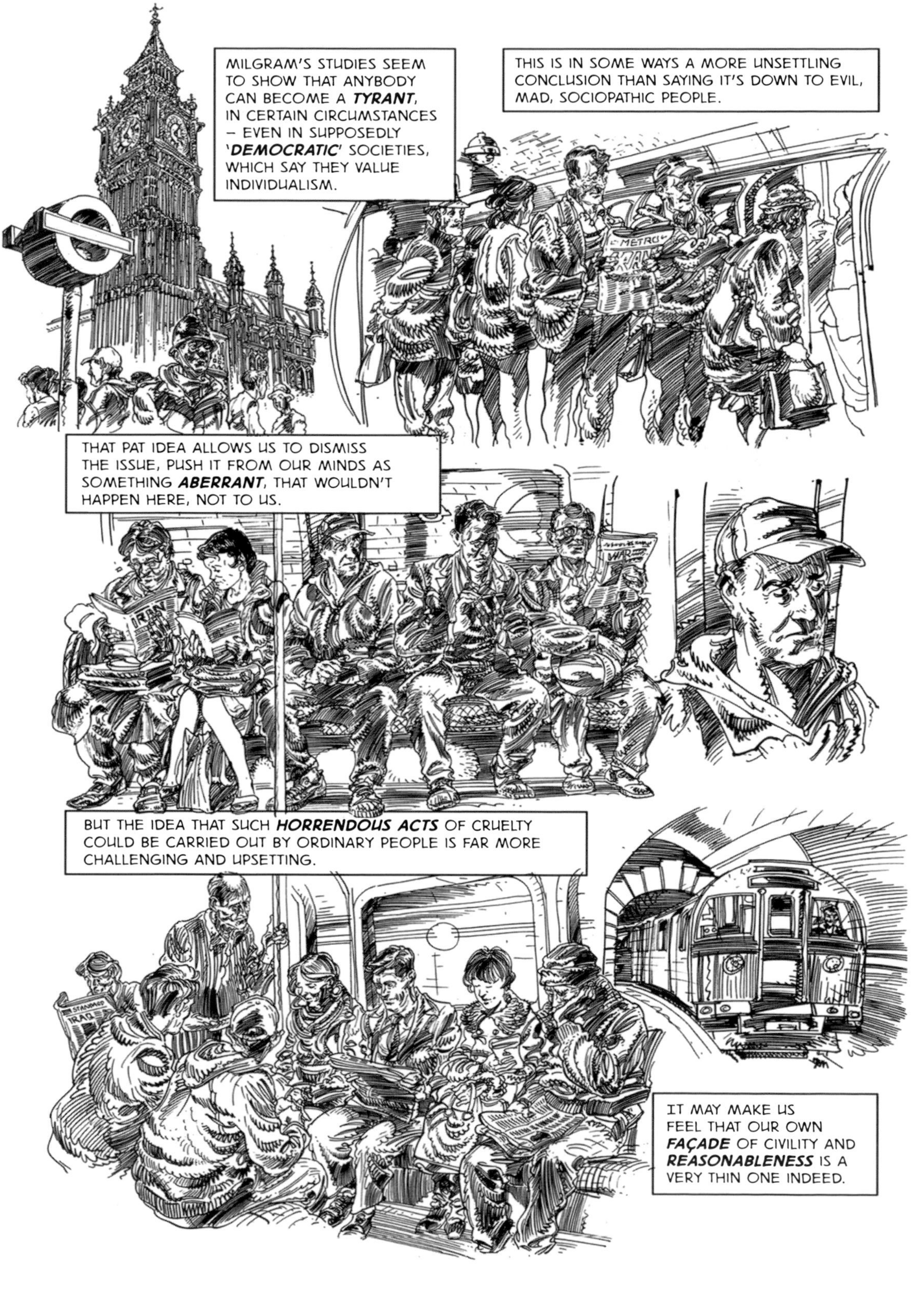
MILGRAM'S STUDIES SEEM TO SHOW THAT ANYBODY CAN BECOME A ***TYRANT***, IN CERTAIN CIRCUMSTANCES – EVEN IN SUPPOSEDLY '***DEMOCRATIC***' SOCIETIES, WHICH SAY THEY VALUE INDIVIDUALISM.
THIS IS IN SOME WAYS A MORE UNSETTLING CONCLUSION THAN SAYING IT'S DOWN TO EVIL, MAD, SOCIOPATHIC PEOPLE.
THAT PAT IDEA ALLOWS US TO DISMISS THE ISSUE, PUSH IT FROM OUR MINDS AS SOMETHING ***ABERRANT***, THAT WOULDN'T HAPPEN HERE, NOT TO US.
BUT THE IDEA THAT SUCH ***HORRENDOUS ACTS*** OF CRUELTY COULD BE CARRIED OUT BY ORDINARY PEOPLE IS FAR MORE CHALLENGING AND UPSETTING.
IT MAY MAKE US FEEL THAT OUR OWN ***FAÇADE*** OF CIVILITY AND ***REASONABLENESS*** IS A VERY THIN ONE INDEED.

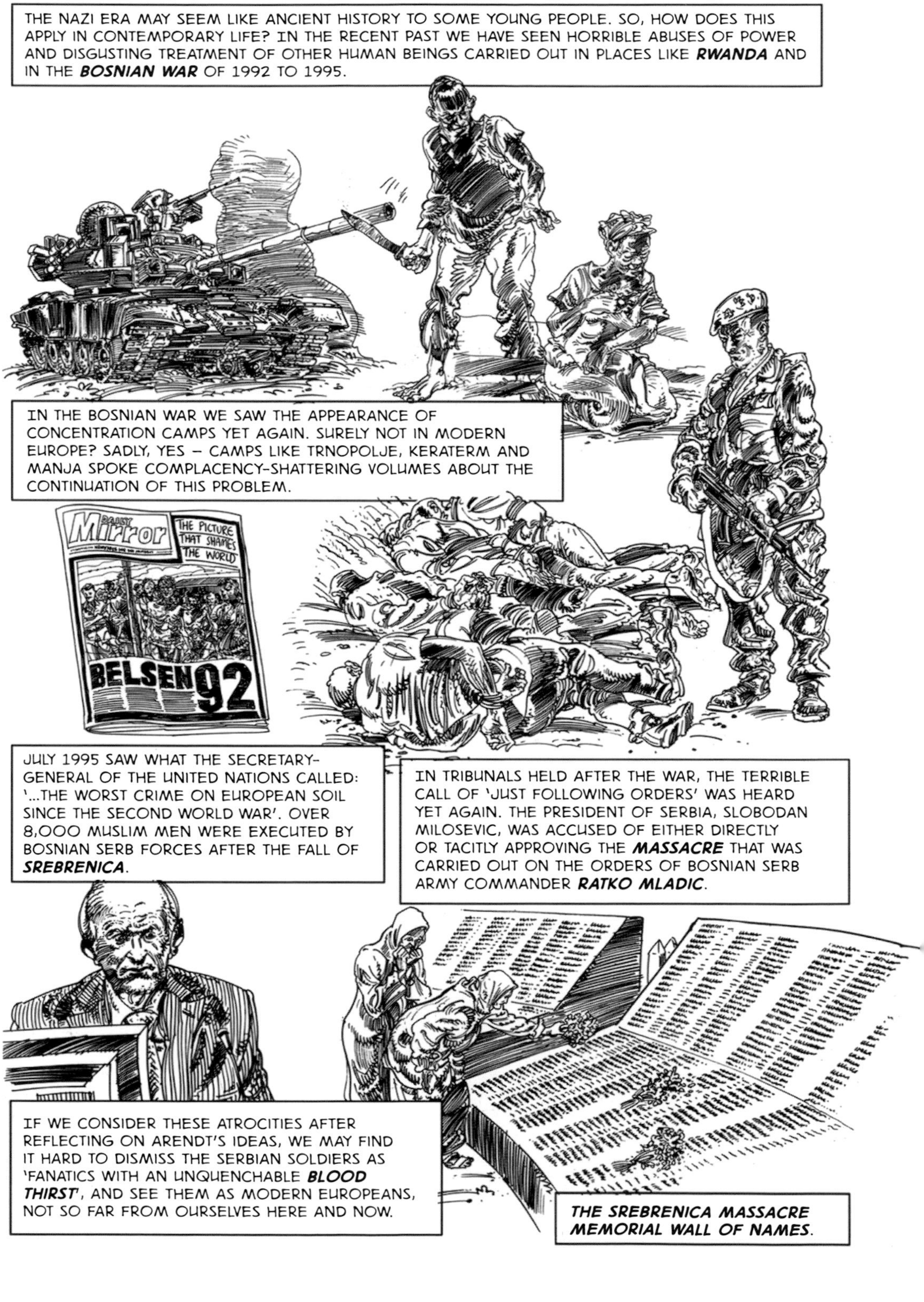
THE NAZI ERA MAY SEEM LIKE ANCIENT HISTORY TO SOME YOUNG PEOPLE. SO, HOW DOES THIS APPLY IN CONTEMPORARY LIFE? IN THE RECENT PAST WE HAVE SEEN HORRIBLE ABUSES OF POWER AND DISGUSTING TREATMENT OF OTHER HUMAN BEINGS CARRIED OUT IN PLACES LIKE **RWANDA** AND IN THE **BOSNIAN WAR** OF 1992 TO 1995.
IN THE BOSNIAN WAR WE SAW THE APPEARANCE OF CONCENTRATION CAMPS YET AGAIN. SURELY NOT IN MODERN EUROPE? SADLY, YES – CAMPS LIKE TRNOPOLJE, KERATERM AND MANJA SPOKE COMPLACENCY-SHATTERING VOLUMES ABOUT THE CONTINUATION OF THIS PROBLEM.
Mirror
THE PICTURE THAT SHAMES THE WORLD
BELSEN 92
JULY 1995 SAW WHAT THE SECRETARY-GENERAL OF THE UNITED NATIONS CALLED: '...THE WORST CRIME ON EUROPEAN SOIL SINCE THE SECOND WORLD WAR'. OVER 8,000 MUSLIM MEN WERE EXECUTED BY BOSNIAN SERB FORCES AFTER THE FALL OF ***SREBRENICA***.
IN TRIBUNALS HELD AFTER THE WAR, THE TERRIBLE CALL OF 'JUST FOLLOWING ORDERS' WAS HEARD YET AGAIN. THE PRESIDENT OF SERBIA, SLOBODAN MILOSEVIC, WAS ACCUSED OF EITHER DIRECTLY OR TACITLY APPROVING THE ***MASSACRE*** THAT WAS CARRIED OUT ON THE ORDERS OF BOSNIAN SERB ARMY COMMANDER ***RATKO MLADIC***.
IF WE CONSIDER THESE ATROCITIES AFTER REFLECTING ON ARENDT'S IDEAS, WE MAY FIND IT HARD TO DISMISS THE SERBIAN SOLDIERS AS 'FANATICS WITH AN UNQUENCHABLE ***BLOOD THIRST***', AND SEE THEM AS MODERN EUROPEANS, NOT SO FAR FROM OURSELVES HERE AND NOW.
THE SREBRENICA MASSACRE MEMORIAL WALL OF NAMES.

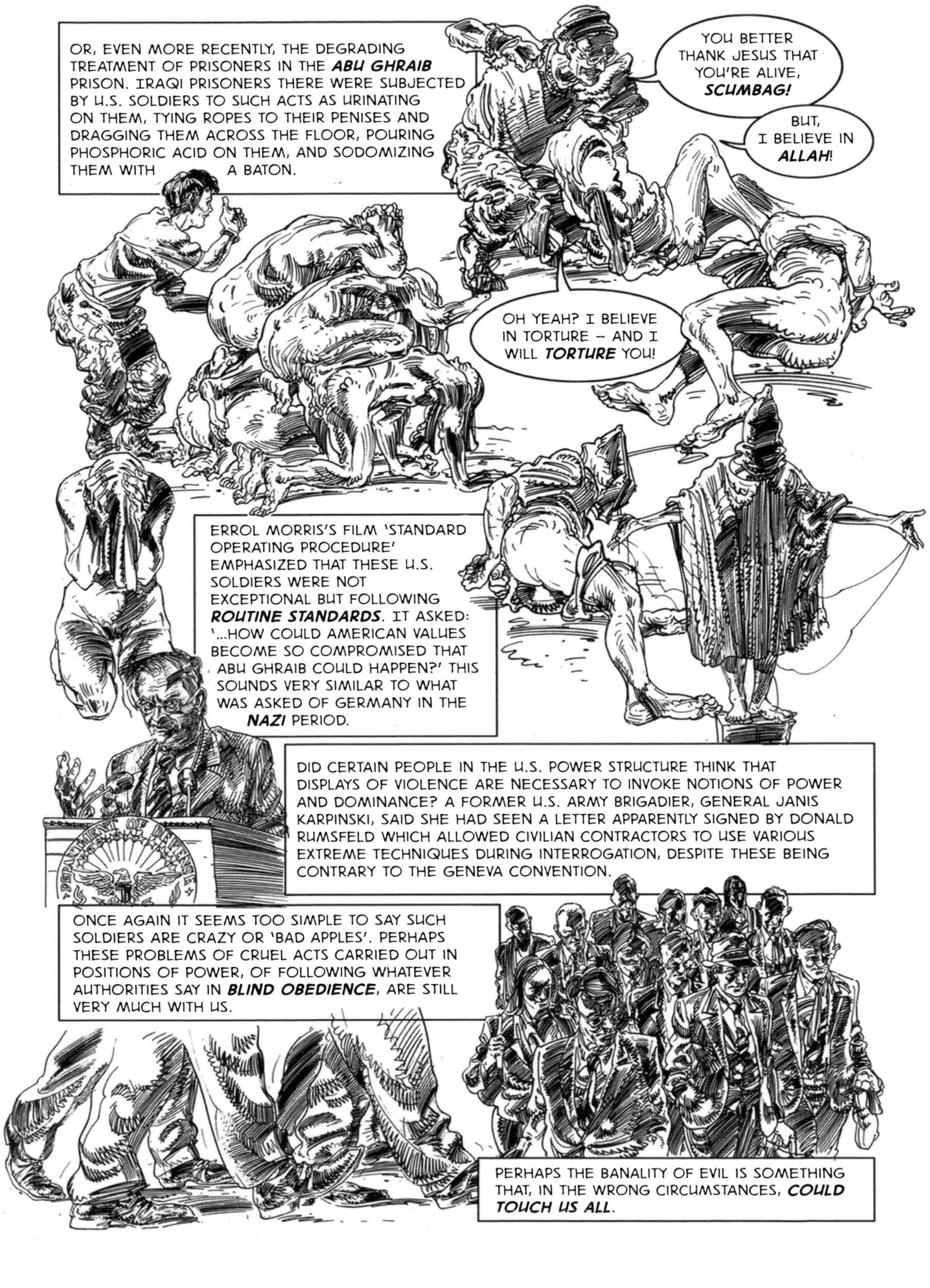
OR, EVEN MORE RECENTLY, THE DEGRADING TREATMENT OF PRISONERS IN THE ABU GHRAIB PRISON. IRAQI PRISONERS THERE WERE SUBJECTED BY U.S. SOLDIERS TO SUCH ACTS AS URINATING ON THEM, TYING ROPES TO THEIR PENISES AND DRAGGING THEM ACROSS THE FLOOR, POURING PHOSPHORIC ACID ON THEM, AND SODOMIZING THEM WITH A BATON.
YOU BETTER THANK JESUS THAT YOU'RE ALIVE, SCUMBAG!
BUT, I BELIEVE IN ALLAH!
OH YEAH? I BELIEVE IN TORTURE – AND I WILL TORTURE YOU!
ERROL MORRIS'S FILM 'STANDARD OPERATING PROCEDURE' EMPHASIZED THAT THESE U.S. SOLDIERS WERE NOT EXCEPTIONAL BUT FOLLOWING ROUTINE STANDARDS. IT ASKED: '...HOW COULD AMERICAN VALUES BECOME SO COMPROMISED THAT ABU GHRAIB COULD HAPPEN?' THIS SOUNDS VERY SIMILAR TO WHAT WAS ASKED OF GERMANY IN THE NAZI PERIOD.
DID CERTAIN PEOPLE IN THE U.S. POWER STRUCTURE THINK THAT DISPLAYS OF VIOLENCE ARE NECESSARY TO INVOKE NOTIONS OF POWER AND DOMINANCE? A FORMER U.S. ARMY BRIGADIER, GENERAL JANIS KARPINSKI, SAID SHE HAD SEEN A LETTER APPARENTLY SIGNED BY DONALD RUMSFELD WHICH ALLOWED CIVILIAN CONTRACTORS TO USE VARIOUS EXTREME TECHNIQUES DURING INTERROGATION, DESPITE THESE BEING CONTRARY TO THE GENEVA CONVENTION.
DEPARTMENT OF DEFENSE
ONCE AGAIN IT SEEMS TOO SIMPLE TO SAY SUCH SOLDIERS ARE CRAZY OR 'BAD APPLES'. PERHAPS THESE PROBLEMS OF CRUEL ACTS CARRIED OUT IN POSITIONS OF POWER, OF FOLLOWING WHATEVER AUTHORITIES SAY IN BLIND OBEDIENCE, ARE STILL VERY MUCH WITH US.
PERHAPS THE BANALITY OF EVIL IS SOMETHING THAT, IN THE WRONG CIRCUMSTANCES, COULD TOUCH US ALL.

Frantz Fanon

The Wretched
of the Earth

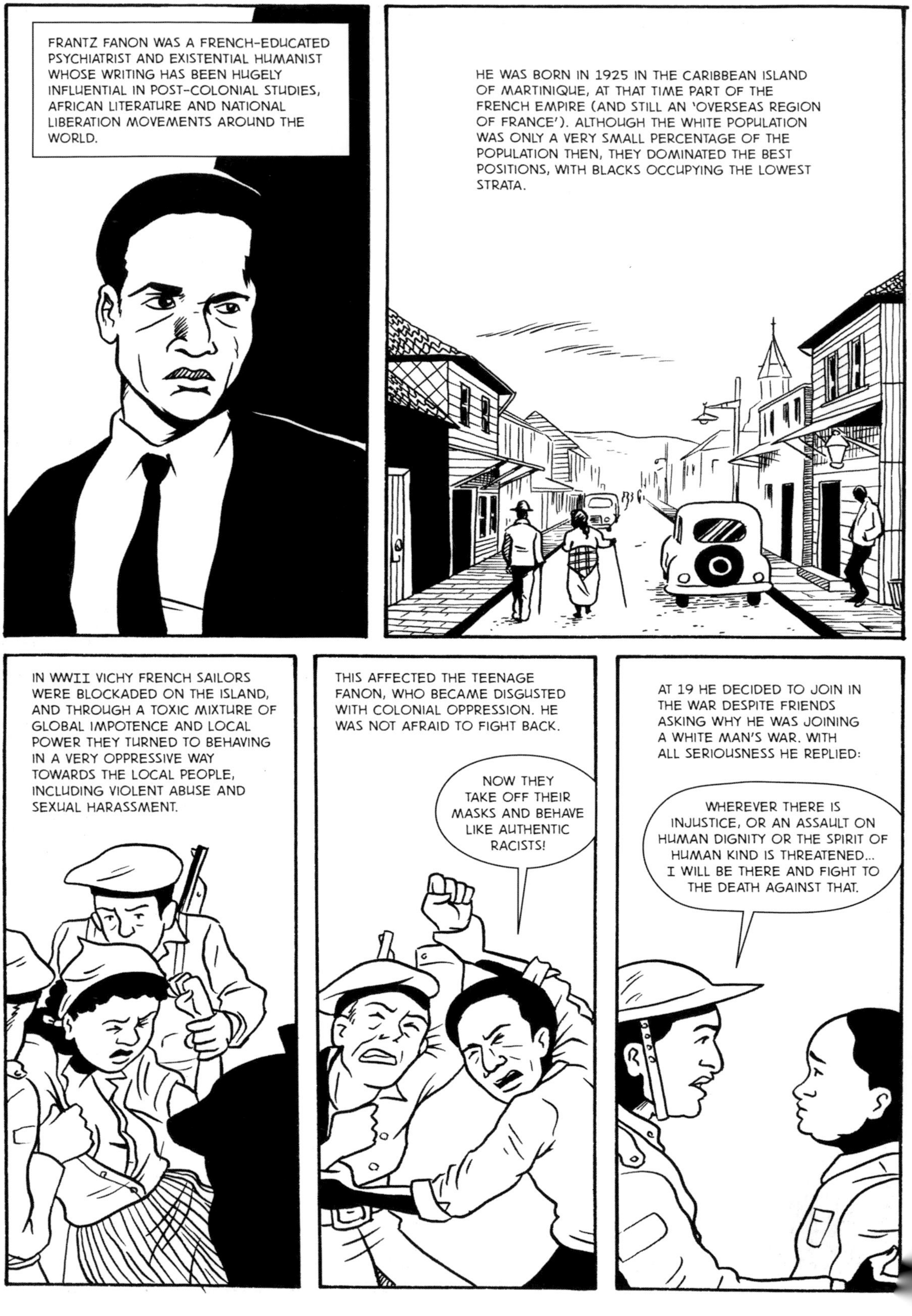
FRANTZ FANON WAS A FRENCH-EDUCATED PSYCHIATRIST AND EXISTENTIAL HUMANIST WHOSE WRITING HAS BEEN HUGELY INFLUENTIAL IN POST-COLONIAL STUDIES, AFRICAN LITERATURE AND NATIONAL LIBERATION MOVEMENTS AROUND THE WORLD.
HE WAS BORN IN 1925 IN THE CARIBBEAN ISLAND OF MARTINIQUE, AT THAT TIME PART OF THE FRENCH EMPIRE (AND STILL AN 'OVERSEAS REGION OF FRANCE'). ALTHOUGH THE WHITE POPULATION WAS ONLY A VERY SMALL PERCENTAGE OF THE POPULATION THEN, THEY DOMINATED THE BEST POSITIONS, WITH BLACKS OCCUPYING THE LOWEST STRATA.
IN WWII VICHY FRENCH SAILORS WERE BLOCKADED ON THE ISLAND, AND THROUGH A TOXIC MIXTURE OF GLOBAL IMPOTENCE AND LOCAL POWER THEY TURNED TO BEHAVING IN A VERY OPPRESSIVE WAY TOWARDS THE LOCAL PEOPLE, INCLUDING VIOLENT ABUSE AND SEXUAL HARASSMENT.
THIS AFFECTED THE TEENAGE FANON, WHO BECAME DISGUSTED WITH COLONIAL OPPRESSION. HE WAS NOT AFRAID TO FIGHT BACK.
NOW THEY TAKE OFF THEIR MASKS AND BEHAVE LIKE AUTHENTIC RACISTS!
AT 19 HE DECIDED TO JOIN IN THE WAR DESPITE FRIENDS ASKING WHY HE WAS JOINING A WHITE MAN'S WAR. WITH ALL SERIOUSNESS HE REPLIED:
WHEREVER THERE IS INJUSTICE, OR AN ASSAULT ON HUMAN DIGNITY OR THE SPIRIT OF HUMAN KIND IS THREATENED... I WILL BE THERE AND FIGHT TO THE DEATH AGAINST THAT.

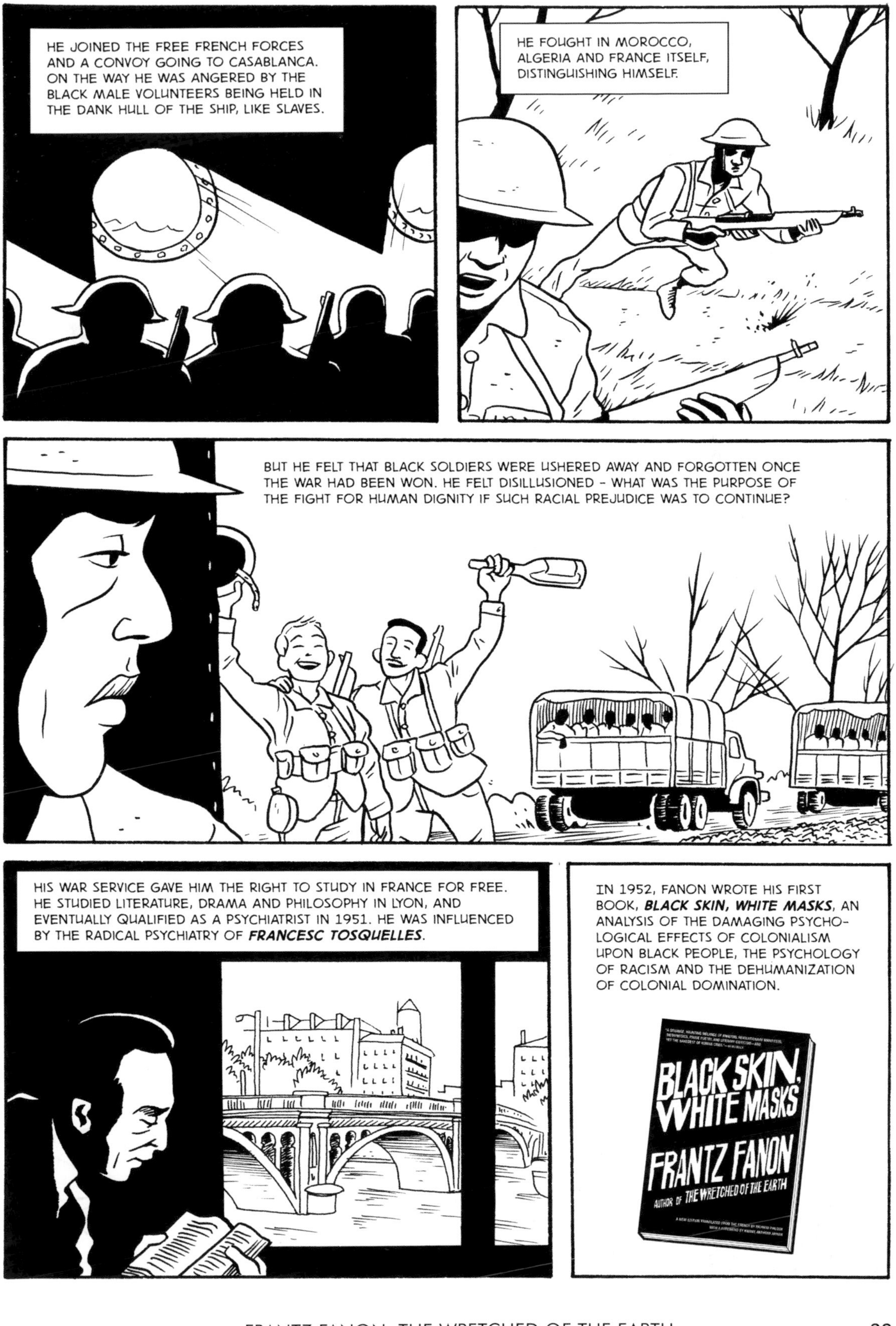
HE JOINED THE FREE FRENCH FORCES AND A CONVOY GOING TO CASABLANCA. ON THE WAY HE WAS ANGERED BY THE BLACK MALE VOLUNTEERS BEING HELD IN THE DANK HULL OF THE SHIP, LIKE SLAVES.
HE FOUGHT IN MOROCCO, ALGERIA AND FRANCE ITSELF, DISTINGUISHING HIMSELF.
BUT HE FELT THAT BLACK SOLDIERS WERE USHERED AWAY AND FORGOTTEN ONCE THE WAR HAD BEEN WON. HE FELT DISILLUSIONED - WHAT WAS THE PURPOSE OF THE FIGHT FOR HUMAN DIGNITY IF SUCH RACIAL PREJUDICE WAS TO CONTINUE?
HIS WAR SERVICE GAVE HIM THE RIGHT TO STUDY IN FRANCE FOR FREE. HE STUDIED LITERATURE, DRAMA AND PHILOSOPHY IN LYON, AND EVENTUALLY QUALIFIED AS A PSYCHIATRIST IN 1951. HE WAS INFLUENCED BY THE RADICAL PSYCHIATRY OF ***FRANCESC TOSQUELLES***.
IN 1952, FANON WROTE HIS FIRST BOOK, ***BLACK SKIN, WHITE MASKS***, AN ANALYSIS OF THE DAMAGING PSYCHOLOGICAL EFFECTS OF COLONIALISM UPON BLACK PEOPLE, THE PSYCHOLOGY OF RACISM AND THE DEHUMANIZATION OF COLONIAL DOMINATION.
BLACK SKIN, WHITE MASKS
FRANTZ FANON
AUTHOR OF THE WRETCHED OF THE EARTH

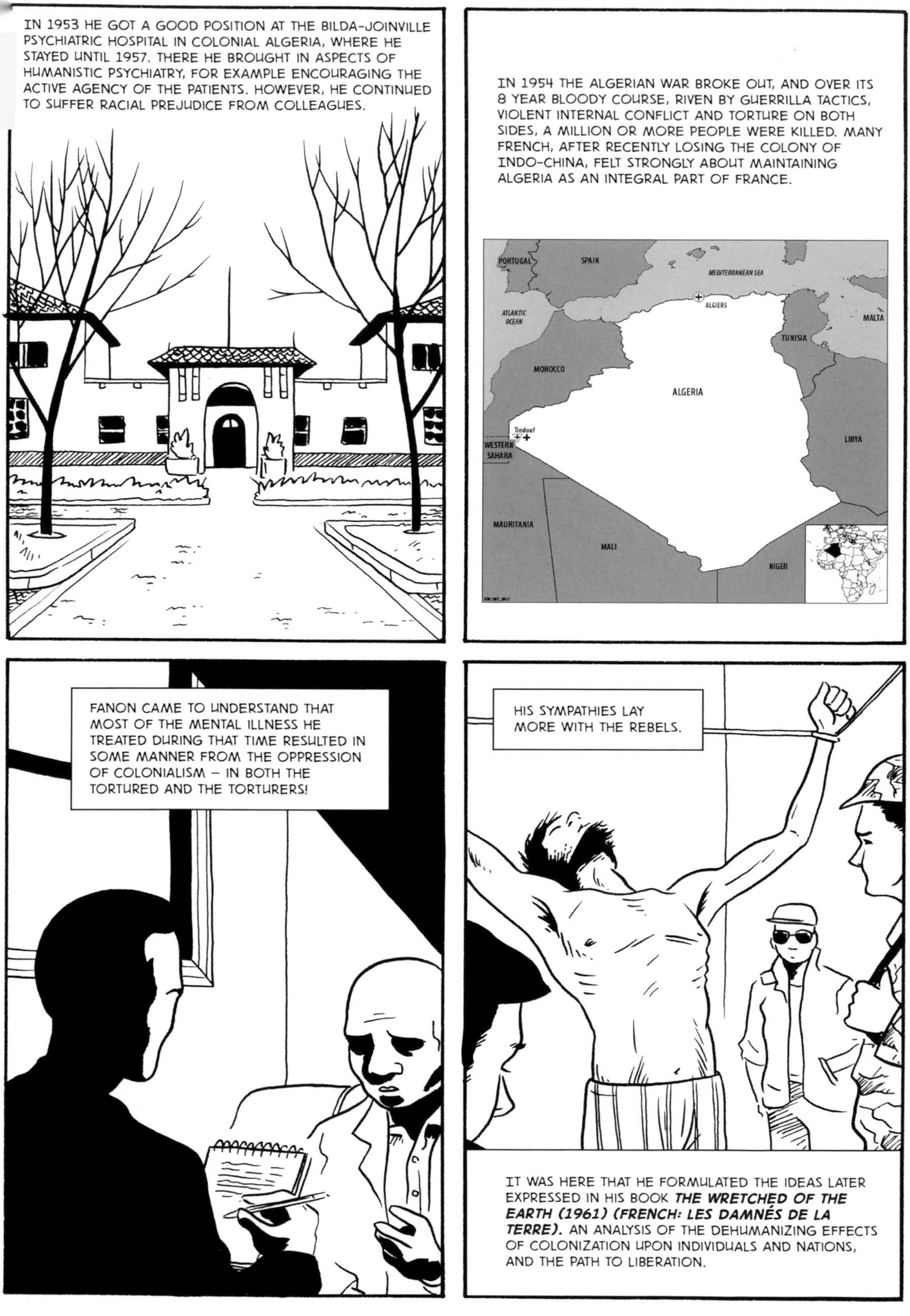
IN 1953 HE GOT A GOOD POSITION AT THE BILDA-JOINVILLE PSYCHIATRIC HOSPITAL IN COLONIAL ALGERIA, WHERE HE STAYED UNTIL 1957. THERE HE BROUGHT IN ASPECTS OF HUMANISTIC PSYCHIATRY, FOR EXAMPLE ENCOURAGING THE ACTIVE AGENCY OF THE PATIENTS. HOWEVER, HE CONTINUED TO SUFFER RACIAL PREJUDICE FROM COLLEAGUES.
IN 1954 THE ALGERIAN WAR BROKE OUT, AND OVER ITS 8 YEAR BLOODY COURSE, RIVEN BY GUERRILLA TACTICS, VIOLENT INTERNAL CONFLICT AND TORTURE ON BOTH SIDES, A MILLION OR MORE PEOPLE WERE KILLED. MANY FRENCH, AFTER RECENTLY LOSING THE COLONY OF INDO-CHINA, FELT STRONGLY ABOUT MAINTAINING ALGERIA AS AN INTEGRAL PART OF FRANCE.
PORTUGAL
SPAIN
MEDITERRANEAN SEA
ALGIERS
ATLANTIC OCEAN
MALTA
TUNISIA
MOROCCO
ALGERIA
Tindouf
WESTERN SAHARA
LIBYA
MAURITANIA
MALI
NIGER
FANON CAME TO UNDERSTAND THAT MOST OF THE MENTAL ILLNESS HE TREATED DURING THAT TIME RESULTED IN SOME MANNER FROM THE OPPRESSION OF COLONIALISM – IN BOTH THE TORTURED AND THE TORTURERS!
HIS SYMPATHIES LAY MORE WITH THE REBELS.
IT WAS HERE THAT HE FORMULATED THE IDEAS LATER EXPRESSED IN HIS BOOK ***THE WRETCHED OF THE EARTH (1961) (FRENCH: LES DAMNÉS DE LA TERRE).*** AN ANALYSIS OF THE DEHUMANIZING EFFECTS OF COLONIZATION UPON INDIVIDUALS AND NATIONS, AND THE PATH TO LIBERATION.

THE COMMON IDEAL OF COLONIES WAS OF SUPERIOR WESTERNERS CIVILIZING MORE BACKWARD AREAS, OF DOING SO TOUGHLY, BUT BASICALLY WITH GOOD INTENTIONS; OF THE NATIVE PEOPLE BEING 'NOBLE SAVAGES' — INFERIOR, BUT NOT BEYOND REDEMPTION.

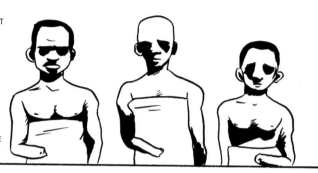

FANON WAS A KEY FIGURE WHO CHANGED THAT IMAGE INTO SOMETHING MORE REALISTIC, AND BRUTAL. HE FOCUSED ON THE VIOLENCE INHERENT IN THE COLONIAL SYSTEM.

*CONGO LABORERS WHO FAILED TO MEET RUBBER COLLECTION QUOTAS WERE SOMETIMES PUNISHED BY HAVING A HAND CUT OFF BY THEIR BELGIAN OVERLORDS.

FANON, VIA HIS EXPERIENCES AND HIS INTELLECTUAL INFLUENCES, DEVELOPED THE IDEA THAT COLONIALISM WAS A SYSTEM OF VIOLENCE BASED ON DIALECTICAL RACIAL ENMITY. THAT IS, ON THE DYNAMIC OF HOSTILITY BETWEEN TWO OPPOSING RACIAL GROUPS.

COLONIALISM CREATED A SYSTEM OF LOGIC THAT WAS BASED ON VIOLENCE.

ANY COLONY TENDS TO BECOME ONE VAST FARMYARD, ONE VAST CONCENTRATION CAMP WHERE THE ONLY LAW IS THAT OF THE KNIFE.

FRANTZ FANON: THE WRETCHED OF THE EARTH

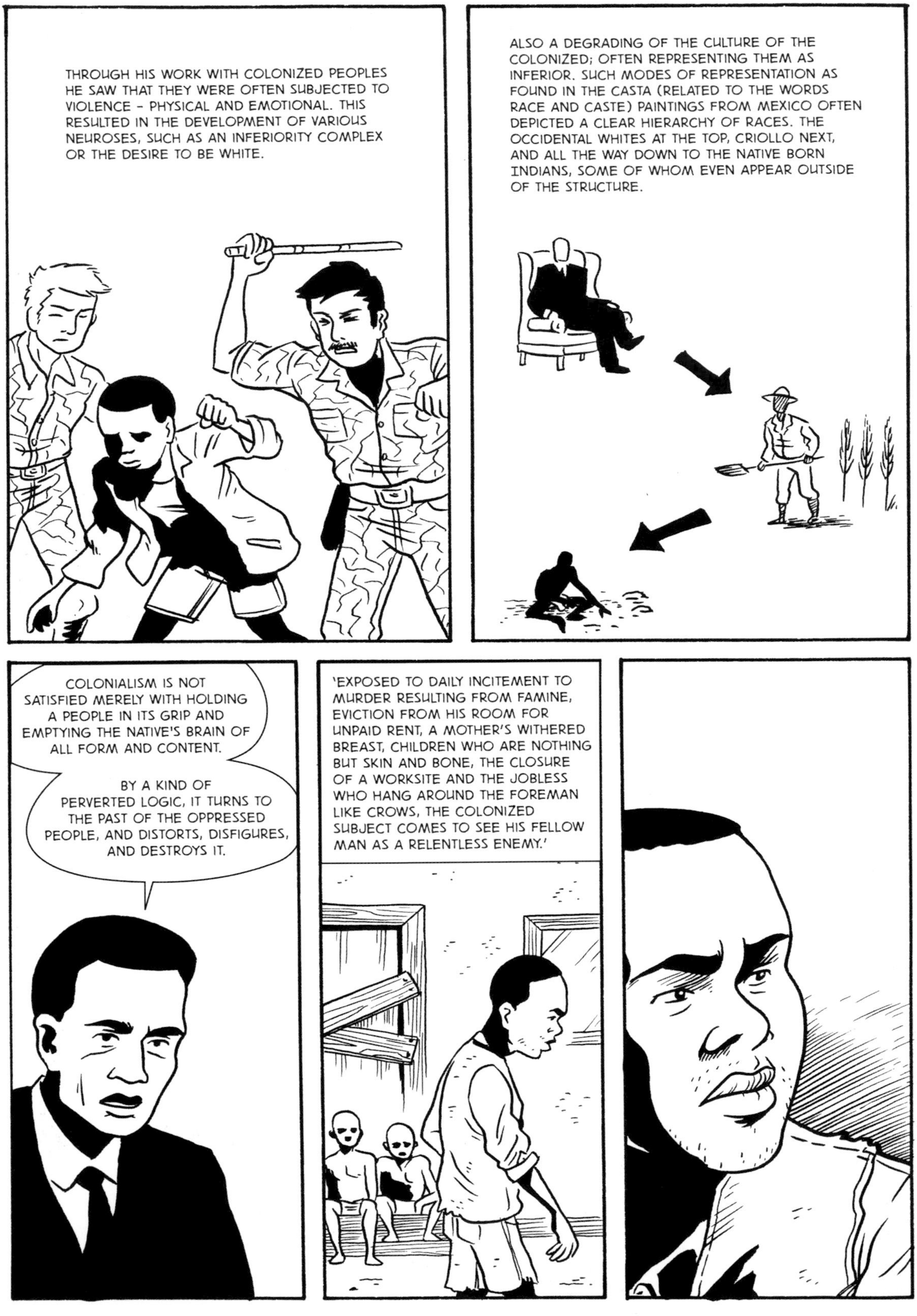
THROUGH HIS WORK WITH COLONIZED PEOPLES HE SAW THAT THEY WERE OFTEN SUBJECTED TO VIOLENCE - PHYSICAL AND EMOTIONAL. THIS RESULTED IN THE DEVELOPMENT OF VARIOUS NEUROSES, SUCH AS AN INFERIORITY COMPLEX OR THE DESIRE TO BE WHITE.
ALSO A DEGRADING OF THE CULTURE OF THE COLONIZED; OFTEN REPRESENTING THEM AS INFERIOR. SUCH MODES OF REPRESENTATION AS FOUND IN THE CASTA (RELATED TO THE WORDS RACE AND CASTE) PAINTINGS FROM MEXICO OFTEN DEPICTED A CLEAR HIERARCHY OF RACES. THE OCCIDENTAL WHITES AT THE TOP, CRIOLLO NEXT, AND ALL THE WAY DOWN TO THE NATIVE BORN INDIANS, SOME OF WHOM EVEN APPEAR OUTSIDE OF THE STRUCTURE.
COLONIALISM IS NOT SATISFIED MERELY WITH HOLDING A PEOPLE IN ITS GRIP AND EMPTYING THE NATIVE'S BRAIN OF ALL FORM AND CONTENT.
BY A KIND OF PERVERTED LOGIC, IT TURNS TO THE PAST OF THE OPPRESSED PEOPLE, AND DISTORTS, DISFIGURES, AND DESTROYS IT.
'EXPOSED TO DAILY INCITEMENT TO MURDER RESULTING FROM FAMINE, EVICTION FROM HIS ROOM FOR UNPAID RENT, A MOTHER'S WITHERED BREAST, CHILDREN WHO ARE NOTHING BUT SKIN AND BONE, THE CLOSURE OF A WORKSITE AND THE JOBLESS WHO HANG AROUND THE FOREMAN LIKE CROWS, THE COLONIZED SUBJECT COMES TO SEE HIS FELLOW MAN AS A RELENTLESS ENEMY.'

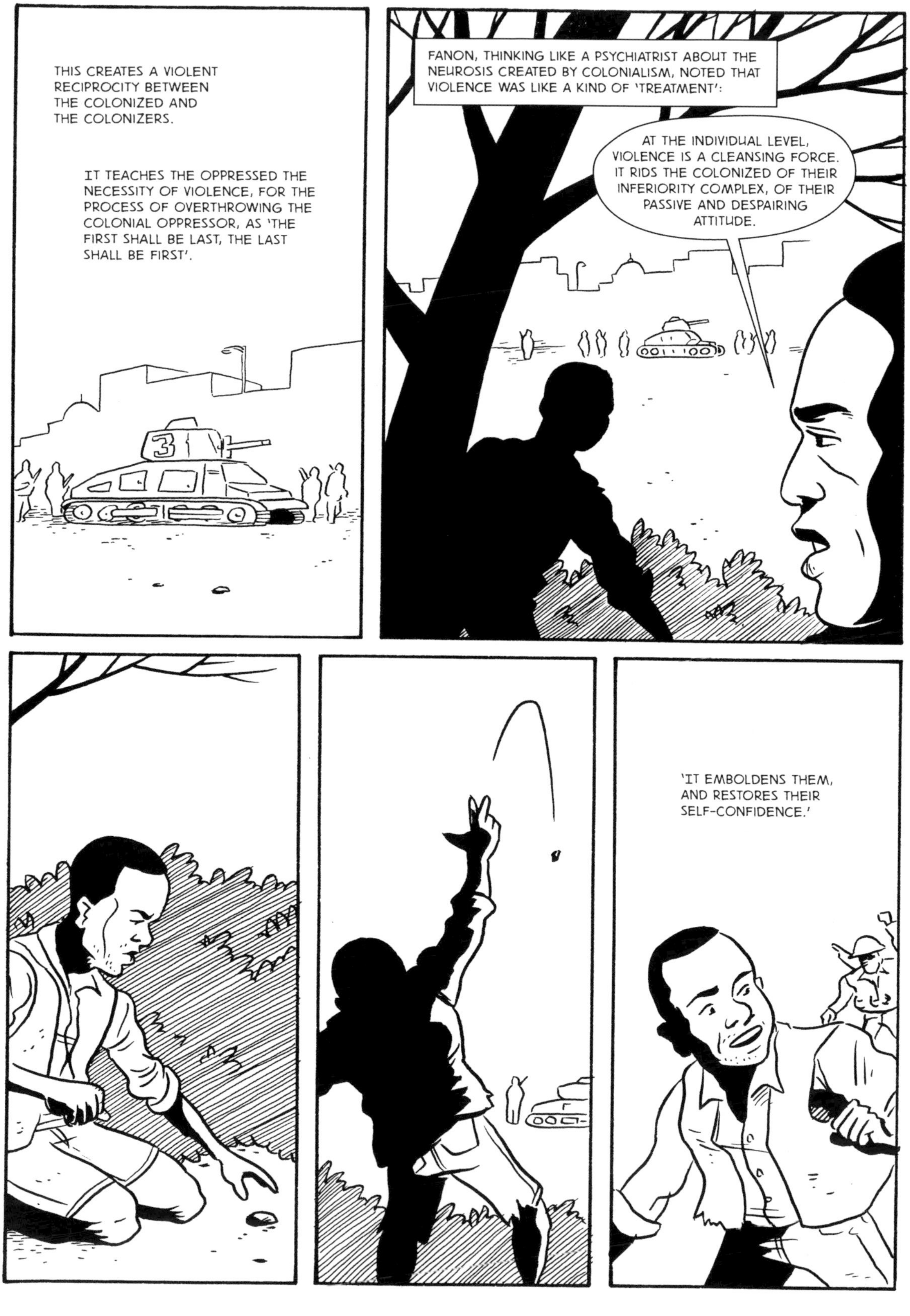
THIS CREATES A VIOLENT RECIPROCITY BETWEEN THE COLONIZED AND THE COLONIZERS.
IT TEACHES THE OPPRESSED THE NECESSITY OF VIOLENCE, FOR THE PROCESS OF OVERTHROWING THE COLONIAL OPPRESSOR, AS 'THE FIRST SHALL BE LAST, THE LAST SHALL BE FIRST'.
3
FANON, THINKING LIKE A PSYCHIATRIST ABOUT THE NEUROSIS CREATED BY COLONIALISM, NOTED THAT VIOLENCE WAS LIKE A KIND OF 'TREATMENT':
AT THE INDIVIDUAL LEVEL, VIOLENCE IS A CLEANSING FORCE. IT RIDS THE COLONIZED OF THEIR INFERIORITY COMPLEX, OF THEIR PASSIVE AND DESPAIRING ATTITUDE.
'IT EMBOLDENS THEM, AND RESTORES THEIR SELF-CONFIDENCE.'

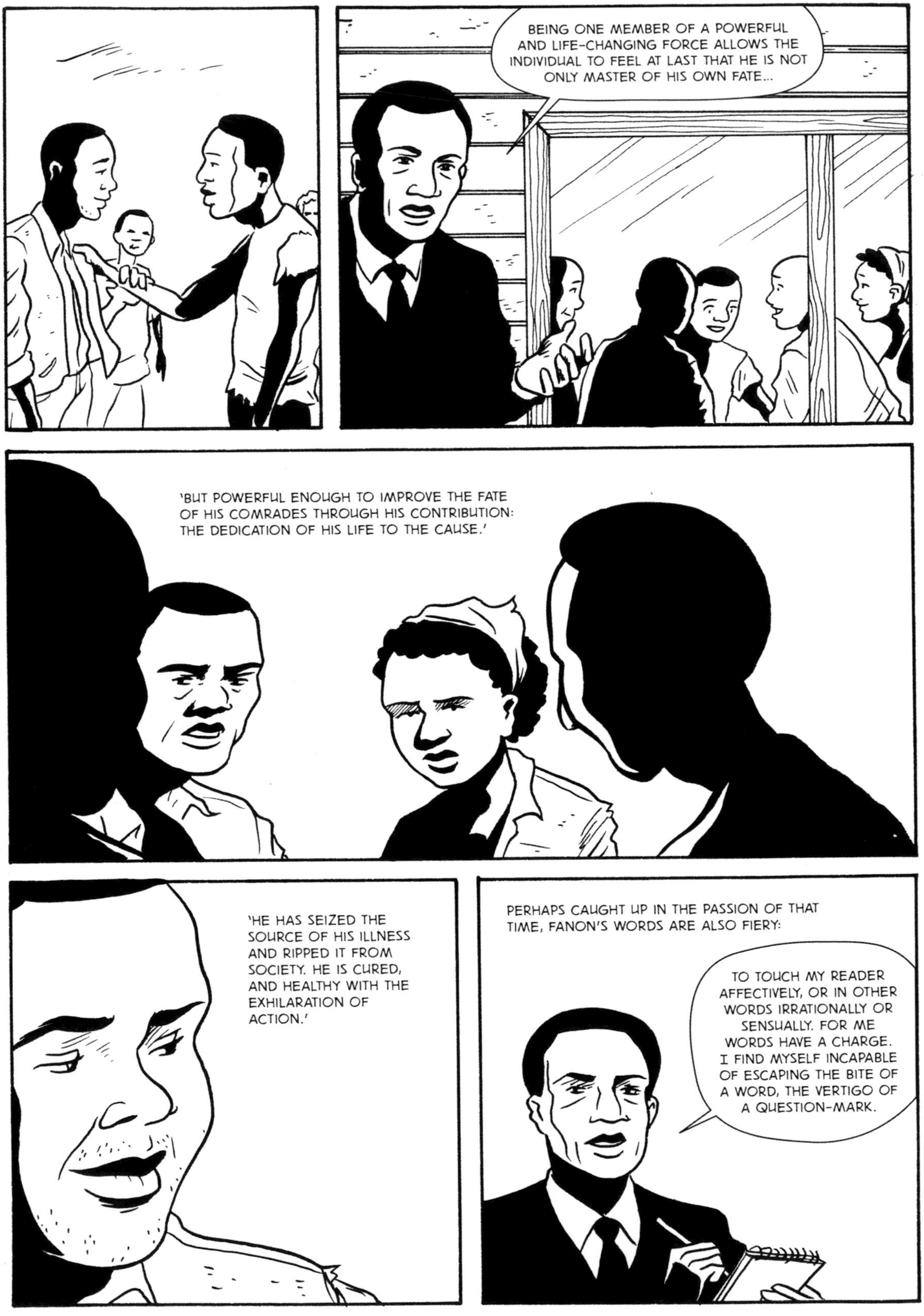
BEING ONE MEMBER OF A POWERFUL AND LIFE-CHANGING FORCE ALLOWS THE INDIVIDUAL TO FEEL AT LAST THAT HE IS NOT ONLY MASTER OF HIS OWN FATE...
'BUT POWERFUL ENOUGH TO IMPROVE THE FATE OF HIS COMRADES THROUGH HIS CONTRIBUTION: THE DEDICATION OF HIS LIFE TO THE CAUSE.'
'HE HAS SEIZED THE SOURCE OF HIS ILLNESS AND RIPPED IT FROM SOCIETY. HE IS CURED, AND HEALTHY WITH THE EXHILARATION OF ACTION.'
PERHAPS CAUGHT UP IN THE PASSION OF THAT TIME, FANON'S WORDS ARE ALSO FIERY:
TO TOUCH MY READER AFFECTIVELY, OR IN OTHER WORDS IRRATIONALLY OR SENSUALLY. FOR ME WORDS HAVE A CHARGE. I FIND MYSELF INCAPABLE OF ESCAPING THE BITE OF A WORD, THE VERTIGO OF A QUESTION-MARK.

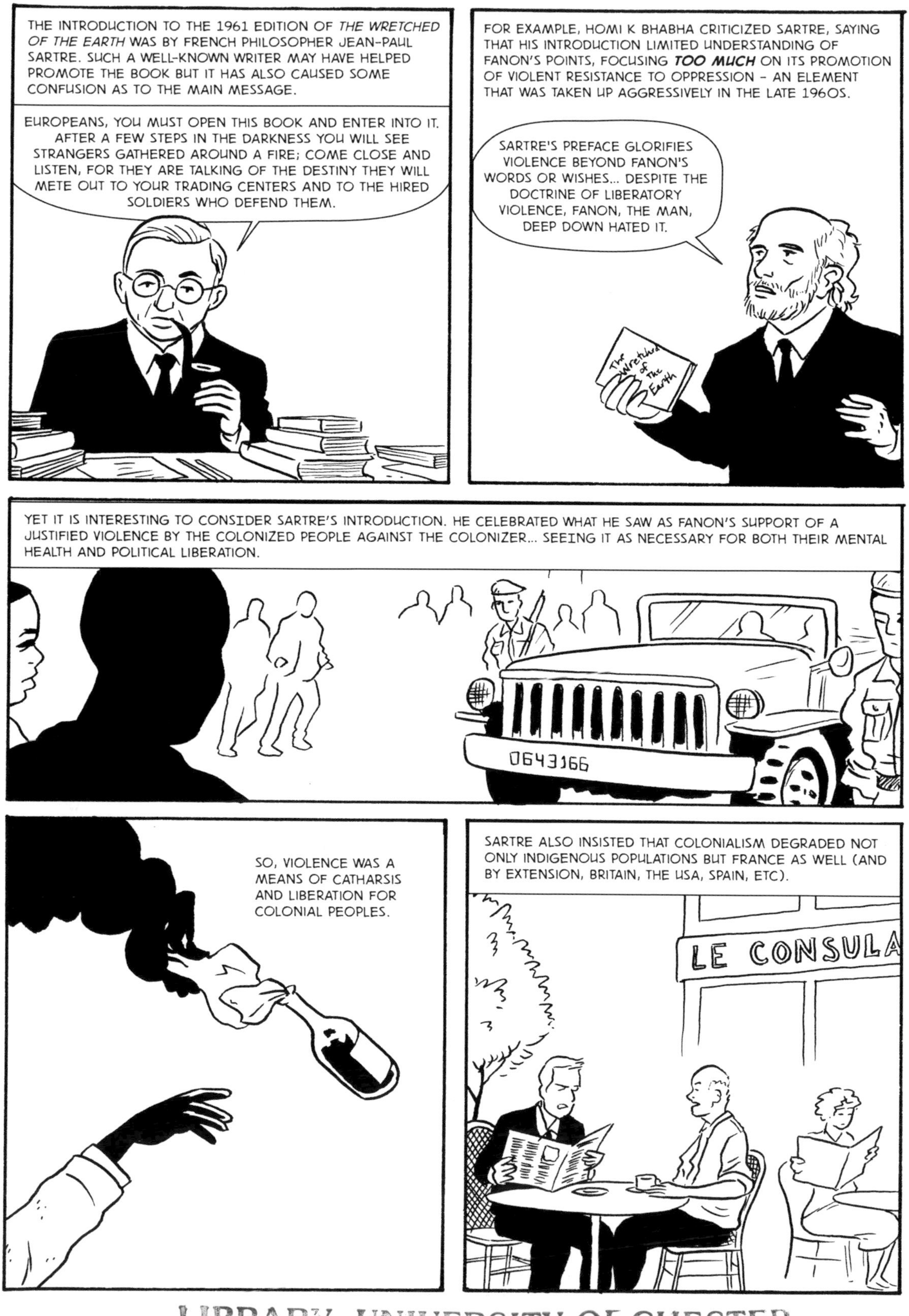
THE INTRODUCTION TO THE 1961 EDITION OF *THE WRETCHED OF THE EARTH* WAS BY FRENCH PHILOSOPHER JEAN-PAUL SARTRE. SUCH A WELL-KNOWN WRITER MAY HAVE HELPED PROMOTE THE BOOK BUT IT HAS ALSO CAUSED SOME CONFUSION AS TO THE MAIN MESSAGE.
EUROPEANS, YOU MUST OPEN THIS BOOK AND ENTER INTO IT. AFTER A FEW STEPS IN THE DARKNESS YOU WILL SEE STRANGERS GATHERED AROUND A FIRE; COME CLOSE AND LISTEN, FOR THEY ARE TALKING OF THE DESTINY THEY WILL METE OUT TO YOUR TRADING CENTERS AND TO THE HIRED SOLDIERS WHO DEFEND THEM.
FOR EXAMPLE, HOMI K BHABHA CRITICIZED SARTRE, SAYING THAT HIS INTRODUCTION LIMITED UNDERSTANDING OF FANON'S POINTS, FOCUSING **TOO MUCH** ON ITS PROMOTION OF VIOLENT RESISTANCE TO OPPRESSION – AN ELEMENT THAT WAS TAKEN UP AGGRESSIVELY IN THE LATE 1960S.
SARTRE'S PREFACE GLORIFIES VIOLENCE BEYOND FANON'S WORDS OR WISHES... DESPITE THE DOCTRINE OF LIBERATORY VIOLENCE, FANON, THE MAN, DEEP DOWN HATED IT.
The Wretched of The Earth
YET IT IS INTERESTING TO CONSIDER SARTRE'S INTRODUCTION. HE CELEBRATED WHAT HE SAW AS FANON'S SUPPORT OF A JUSTIFIED VIOLENCE BY THE COLONIZED PEOPLE AGAINST THE COLONIZER... SEEING IT AS NECESSARY FOR BOTH THEIR MENTAL HEALTH AND POLITICAL LIBERATION.
0643166
SO, VIOLENCE WAS A MEANS OF CATHARSIS AND LIBERATION FOR COLONIAL PEOPLES.
SARTRE ALSO INSISTED THAT COLONIALISM DEGRADED NOT ONLY INDIGENOUS POPULATIONS BUT FRANCE AS WELL (AND BY EXTENSION, BRITAIN, THE USA, SPAIN, ETC).
LE CONSULA

CRITICISM OF SARTRE'S INTRODUCTION SHOWS THAT FANON'S VIEWS ON VIOLENCE WERE NOT AS SIMPLE AS A LITERAL READING MIGHT SUGGEST. THE 'VIOLENCE AS PURIFICATION' ELEMENT CAN BE SEEN AS A WARNING, NOT A PROMISE. A WARNING OF ABUSES LIKE THE VIOLENT DESTRUCTION OF PERCEIVED ENEMY CULTURES.

THE PROCESS OF WINNING INDEPENDENCE VIA VIOLENCE CAN BE POLLUTING, IT CAN END UP REPRODUCING THAT WHICH YOU ARE FIGHTING TO ESCAPE. CREATING A POST-COLONIAL MESS IN WHICH USING VIOLENCE TO ASSERT AUTHORITY BECOMES NORMALIZED, WITH TRAGIC CONSEQUENCES.

THERE IS ANOTHER READING OF FANON THAT LENDS ITSELF TO WHAT MIGHT SEEM TO BE JUST THE OPPOSITE: TO **NON-VIOLENCE**. INDEED, WE CAN SEE EXAMPLES IN HISTORY WHERE PEOPLE AND GROUPS HAVE CHOSEN NOT TO CONFRONT A REGIME OF VIOLENCE WITH **MORE** VIOLENCE, BUT INSTEAD HAVE SOUGHT MORE DIGNIFIED SOLUTIONS.

LIKE ROSA PARKS POLITELY, BUT FIRMLY, REFUSING TO CHANGE SEATS ON A SEGREGATED BUS IN THE 1950S.

OR THE LONE PROTESTER IN THE TIANANMEN SQUARE PROTESTS OF 1989.

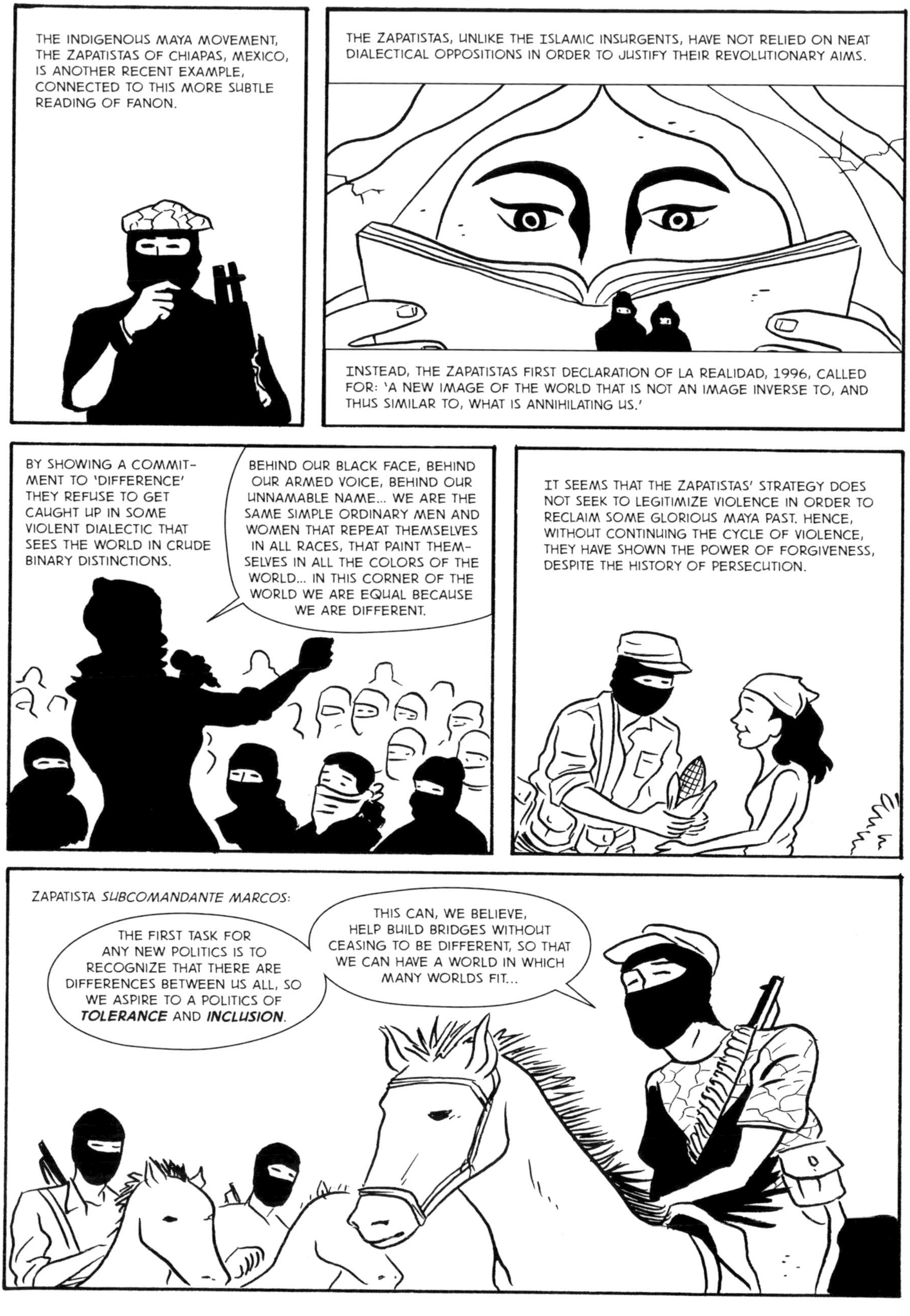
THE INDIGENOUS MAYA MOVEMENT, THE ZAPATISTAS OF CHIAPAS, MEXICO, IS ANOTHER RECENT EXAMPLE, CONNECTED TO THIS MORE SUBTLE READING OF FANON.
THE ZAPATISTAS, UNLIKE THE ISLAMIC INSURGENTS, HAVE NOT RELIED ON NEAT DIALECTICAL OPPOSITIONS IN ORDER TO JUSTIFY THEIR REVOLUTIONARY AIMS.
INSTEAD, THE ZAPATISTAS FIRST DECLARATION OF LA REALIDAD, 1996, CALLED FOR: 'A NEW IMAGE OF THE WORLD THAT IS NOT AN IMAGE INVERSE TO, AND THUS SIMILAR TO, WHAT IS ANNIHILATING US.'
BY SHOWING A COMMITMENT TO 'DIFFERENCE' THEY REFUSE TO GET CAUGHT UP IN SOME VIOLENT DIALECTIC THAT SEES THE WORLD IN CRUDE BINARY DISTINCTIONS.
BEHIND OUR BLACK FACE, BEHIND OUR ARMED VOICE, BEHIND OUR UNNAMABLE NAME... WE ARE THE SAME SIMPLE ORDINARY MEN AND WOMEN THAT REPEAT THEMSELVES IN ALL RACES, THAT PAINT THEMSELVES IN ALL THE COLORS OF THE WORLD... IN THIS CORNER OF THE WORLD WE ARE EQUAL BECAUSE WE ARE DIFFERENT.
IT SEEMS THAT THE ZAPATISTAS' STRATEGY DOES NOT SEEK TO LEGITIMIZE VIOLENCE IN ORDER TO RECLAIM SOME GLORIOUS MAYA PAST. HENCE, WITHOUT CONTINUING THE CYCLE OF VIOLENCE, THEY HAVE SHOWN THE POWER OF FORGIVENESS, DESPITE THE HISTORY OF PERSECUTION.
ZAPATISTA *SUBCOMANDANTE MARCOS*:
THE FIRST TASK FOR ANY NEW POLITICS IS TO RECOGNIZE THAT THERE ARE DIFFERENCES BETWEEN US ALL, SO WE ASPIRE TO A POLITICS OF ***TOLERANCE*** AND ***INCLUSION***.
THIS CAN, WE BELIEVE, HELP BUILD BRIDGES WITHOUT CEASING TO BE DIFFERENT, SO THAT WE CAN HAVE A WORLD IN WHICH MANY WORLDS FIT...

Paulo Freire

Pedagogy
of the Oppressed

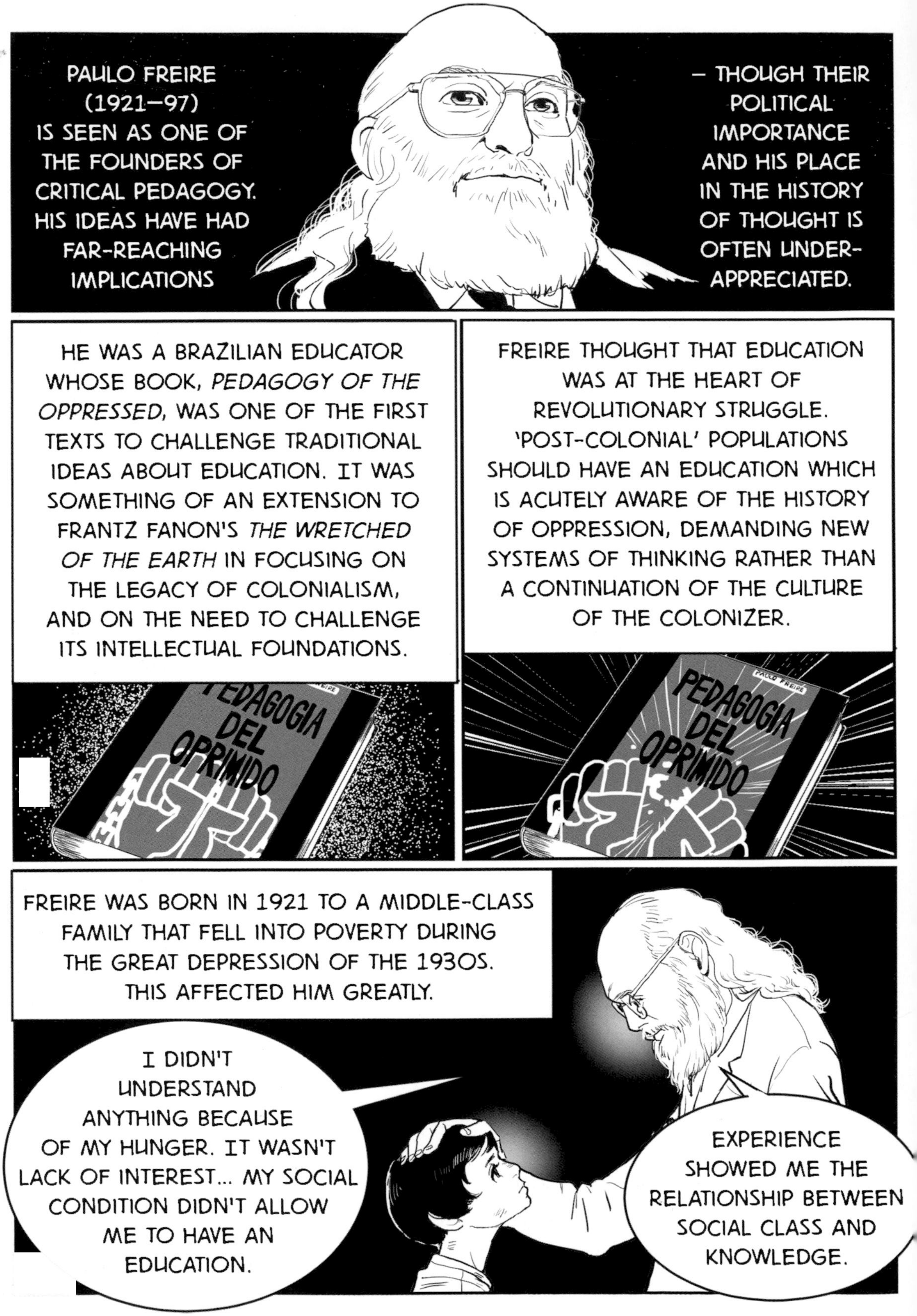

PAULO FREIRE (1921–97) IS SEEN AS ONE OF THE FOUNDERS OF CRITICAL PEDAGOGY. HIS IDEAS HAVE HAD FAR-REACHING IMPLICATIONS
– THOUGH THEIR POLITICAL IMPORTANCE AND HIS PLACE IN THE HISTORY OF THOUGHT IS OFTEN UNDER-APPRECIATED.
HE WAS A BRAZILIAN EDUCATOR WHOSE BOOK, *PEDAGOGY OF THE OPPRESSED*, WAS ONE OF THE FIRST TEXTS TO CHALLENGE TRADITIONAL IDEAS ABOUT EDUCATION. IT WAS SOMETHING OF AN EXTENSION TO FRANTZ FANON'S *THE WRETCHED OF THE EARTH* IN FOCUSING ON THE LEGACY OF COLONIALISM, AND ON THE NEED TO CHALLENGE ITS INTELLECTUAL FOUNDATIONS.
PEDAGOGIA DEL OPRIMIDO
FREIRE THOUGHT THAT EDUCATION WAS AT THE HEART OF REVOLUTIONARY STRUGGLE. 'POST-COLONIAL' POPULATIONS SHOULD HAVE AN EDUCATION WHICH IS ACUTELY AWARE OF THE HISTORY OF OPPRESSION, DEMANDING NEW SYSTEMS OF THINKING RATHER THAN A CONTINUATION OF THE CULTURE OF THE COLONIZER.
PAULO FREIRE
PEDAGOGIA DEL OPRIMIDO
FREIRE WAS BORN IN 1921 TO A MIDDLE-CLASS FAMILY THAT FELL INTO POVERTY DURING THE GREAT DEPRESSION OF THE 1930S. THIS AFFECTED HIM GREATLY.
I DIDN'T UNDERSTAND ANYTHING BECAUSE OF MY HUNGER. IT WASN'T LACK OF INTEREST... MY SOCIAL CONDITION DIDN'T ALLOW ME TO HAVE AN EDUCATION.
EXPERIENCE SHOWED ME THE RELATIONSHIP BETWEEN SOCIAL CLASS AND KNOWLEDGE.

FREIRE STUDIED LAW AND PHILOSOPHY AT THE UNIVERSITY OF RECIFE FROM 1943. HE CHOSE NOT TO PRACTICE LAW, BUT TO TEACH IN SECONDARY SCHOOLS. LATER HE WORKED WITH THE ILLITERATE POOR, INCORPORATING MARXIST IDEAS WITH ANTI-COLONIAL NARRATIVES, AND BLENDED THEM WITH THE LIBERATION TEACHINGS BEING PROMOTED BY THE CHURCH IN LATIN AMERICA.

IN 1961, HE BECAME DIRECTOR OF THE DEPARTMENT OF CULTURAL EXTENSION OF RECIFE UNIVERSITY AND APPLIED HIS UNUSUAL TECHNIQUES OF EDUCATION, TEACHING 300 SUGAR-CANE WORKERS TO READ AND WRITE IN JUST 45 DAYS.

HE ALSO HELPED TO SET UP MANY 'CULTURAL CIRCLES' WITH BRAZILIAN GOVERNMENT APPROVAL.

BUT THE 1964 MILITARY COUP IN BRAZIL ENDED THESE EXPERIMENTS AND FREIRE WAS EVEN IMPRISONED.

AFTER HIS RELEASE HE WORKED IN CHILE FOR THE CHRISTIAN DEMOCRATIC AGRARIAN REFORM MOVEMENT AND PUBLISHED HIS FIRST BOOK IN 1967 – *EDUCATION AS THE PRACTICE OF FREEDOM*.

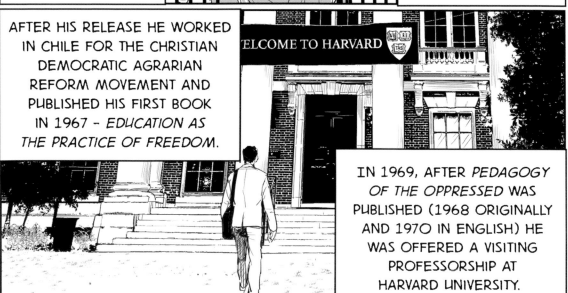

IN 1969, AFTER *PEDAGOGY OF THE OPPRESSED* WAS PUBLISHED (1968 ORIGINALLY AND 1970 IN ENGLISH) HE WAS OFFERED A VISITING PROFESSORSHIP AT HARVARD UNIVERSITY.

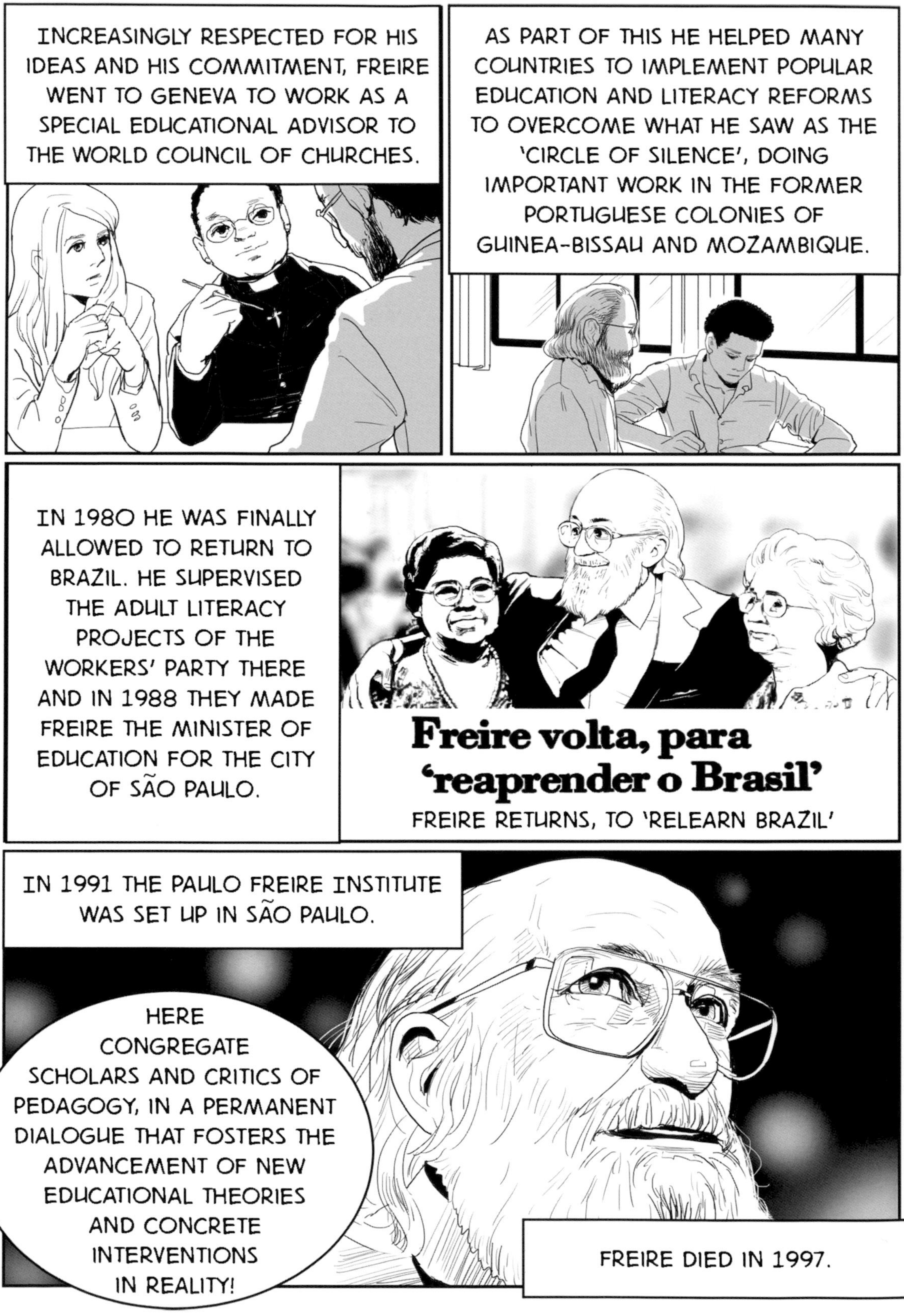
INCREASINGLY RESPECTED FOR HIS IDEAS AND HIS COMMITMENT, FREIRE WENT TO GENEVA TO WORK AS A SPECIAL EDUCATIONAL ADVISOR TO THE WORLD COUNCIL OF CHURCHES.
AS PART OF THIS HE HELPED MANY COUNTRIES TO IMPLEMENT POPULAR EDUCATION AND LITERACY REFORMS TO OVERCOME WHAT HE SAW AS THE 'CIRCLE OF SILENCE', DOING IMPORTANT WORK IN THE FORMER PORTUGUESE COLONIES OF GUINEA-BISSAU AND MOZAMBIQUE.
IN 1980 HE WAS FINALLY ALLOWED TO RETURN TO BRAZIL. HE SUPERVISED THE ADULT LITERACY PROJECTS OF THE WORKERS' PARTY THERE AND IN 1988 THEY MADE FREIRE THE MINISTER OF EDUCATION FOR THE CITY OF SÃO PAULO.
Freire volta, para 'reaprender o Brasil'
FREIRE RETURNS, TO 'RELEARN BRAZIL'
IN 1991 THE PAULO FREIRE INSTITUTE WAS SET UP IN SÃO PAULO.
HERE CONGREGATE SCHOLARS AND CRITICS OF PEDAGOGY, IN A PERMANENT DIALOGUE THAT FOSTERS THE ADVANCEMENT OF NEW EDUCATIONAL THEORIES AND CONCRETE INTERVENTIONS IN REALITY!
FREIRE DIED IN 1997.

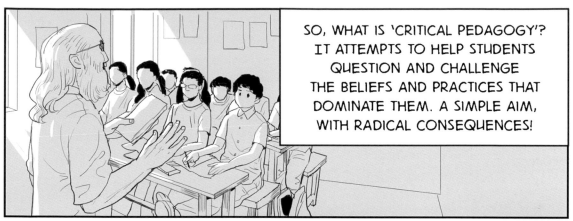

SO, WHAT IS 'CRITICAL PEDAGOGY'? IT ATTEMPTS TO HELP STUDENTS QUESTION AND CHALLENGE THE BELIEFS AND PRACTICES THAT DOMINATE THEM. A SIMPLE AIM, WITH RADICAL CONSEQUENCES!

EDUCATION EITHER FUNCTIONS AS AN INSTRUMENT WHICH IS USED TO FACILITATE INTEGRATION OF THE YOUNGER GENERATION INTO THE LOGIC OF THE PRESENT SYSTEM AND BRING ABOUT CONFORMITY...

OR...

IT BECOMES THE PRACTICE OF FREEDOM, THE MEANS BY WHICH WE DEAL CRITICALLY AND CREATIVELY WITH REALITY AND DISCOVER HOW TO PARTICIPATE IN THE TRANSFORMATION OF OUR WORLD.

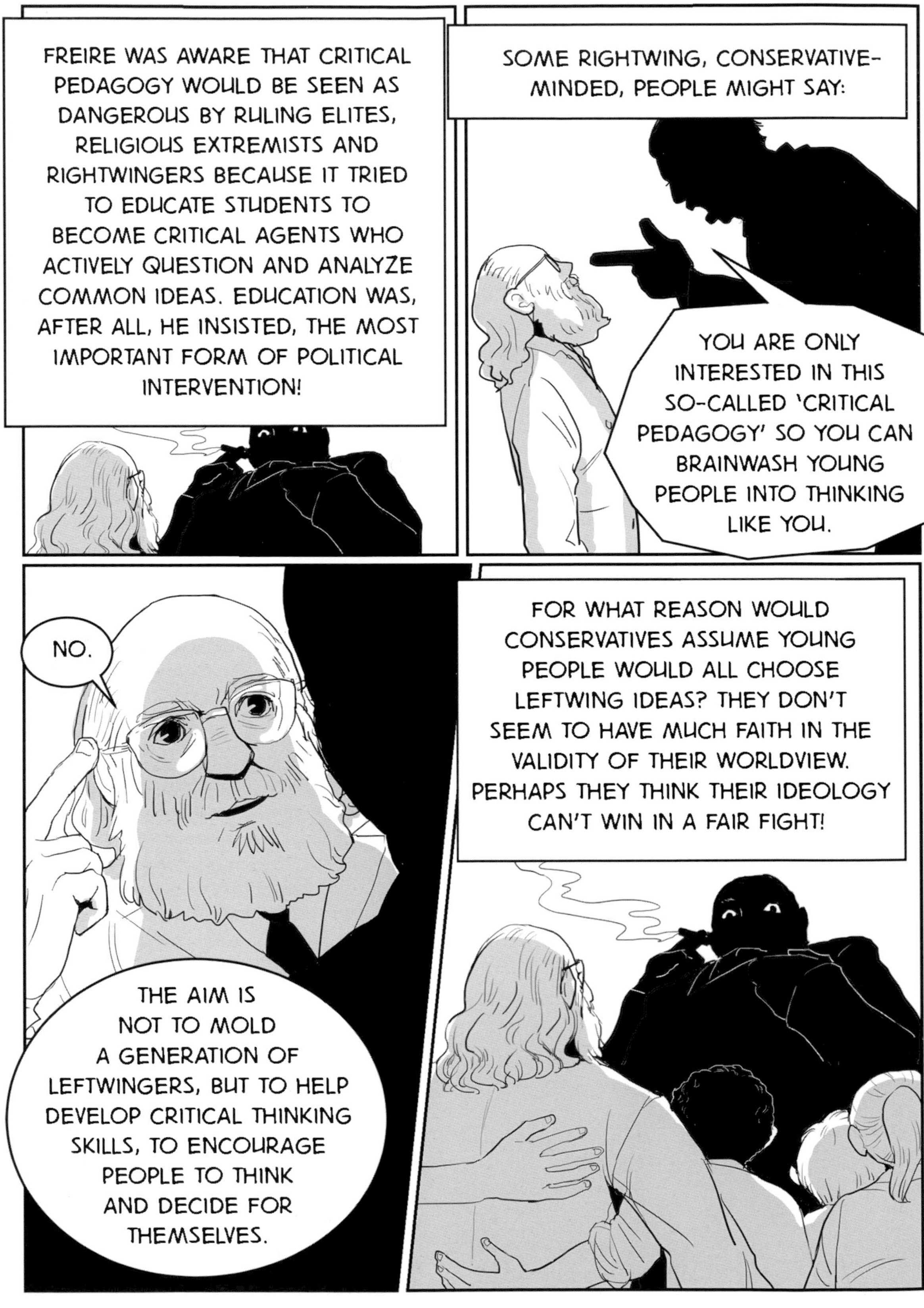
FREIRE WAS AWARE THAT CRITICAL PEDAGOGY WOULD BE SEEN AS DANGEROUS BY RULING ELITES, RELIGIOUS EXTREMISTS AND RIGHTWINGERS BECAUSE IT TRIED TO EDUCATE STUDENTS TO BECOME CRITICAL AGENTS WHO ACTIVELY QUESTION AND ANALYZE COMMON IDEAS. EDUCATION WAS, AFTER ALL, HE INSISTED, THE MOST IMPORTANT FORM OF POLITICAL INTERVENTION!
SOME RIGHTWING, CONSERVATIVE-MINDED, PEOPLE MIGHT SAY:
YOU ARE ONLY INTERESTED IN THIS SO-CALLED 'CRITICAL PEDAGOGY' SO YOU CAN BRAINWASH YOUNG PEOPLE INTO THINKING LIKE YOU.
NO.
THE AIM IS NOT TO MOLD A GENERATION OF LEFTWINGERS, BUT TO HELP DEVELOP CRITICAL THINKING SKILLS, TO ENCOURAGE PEOPLE TO THINK AND DECIDE FOR THEMSELVES.
FOR WHAT REASON WOULD CONSERVATIVES ASSUME YOUNG PEOPLE WOULD ALL CHOOSE LEFTWING IDEAS? THEY DON'T SEEM TO HAVE MUCH FAITH IN THE VALIDITY OF THEIR WORLDVIEW. PERHAPS THEY THINK THEIR IDEOLOGY CAN'T WIN IN A FAIR FIGHT!

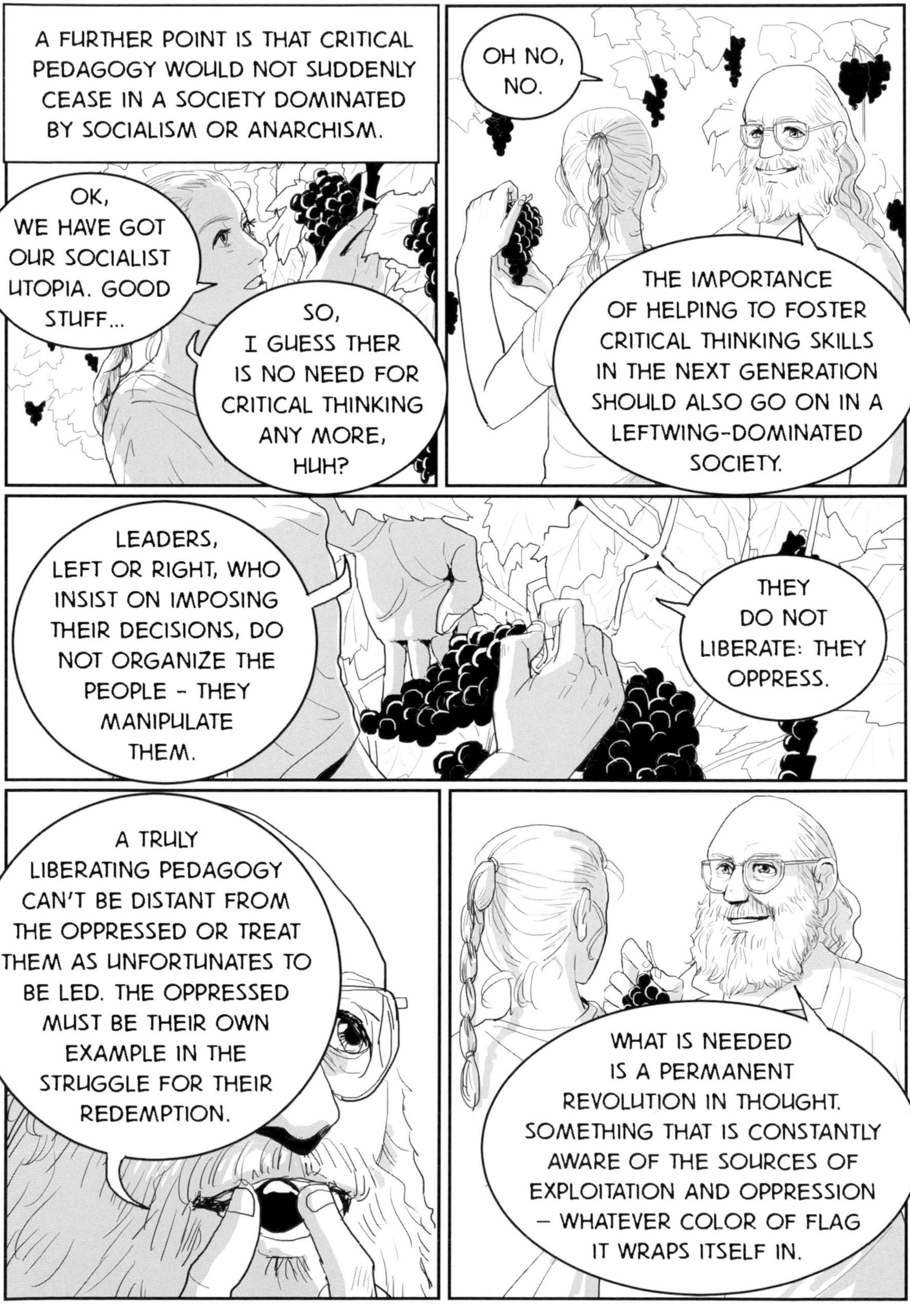
A FURTHER POINT IS THAT CRITICAL PEDAGOGY WOULD NOT SUDDENLY CEASE IN A SOCIETY DOMINATED BY SOCIALISM OR ANARCHISM.
OK, WE HAVE GOT OUR SOCIALIST UTOPIA. GOOD STUFF...
SO, I GUESS THER IS NO NEED FOR CRITICAL THINKING ANY MORE, HUH?
OH NO, NO.
THE IMPORTANCE OF HELPING TO FOSTER CRITICAL THINKING SKILLS IN THE NEXT GENERATION SHOULD ALSO GO ON IN A LEFTWING-DOMINATED SOCIETY.
LEADERS, LEFT OR RIGHT, WHO INSIST ON IMPOSING THEIR DECISIONS, DO NOT ORGANIZE THE PEOPLE - THEY MANIPULATE THEM.
THEY DO NOT LIBERATE: THEY OPPRESS.
A TRULY LIBERATING PEDAGOGY CAN'T BE DISTANT FROM THE OPPRESSED OR TREAT THEM AS UNFORTUNATES TO BE LED. THE OPPRESSED MUST BE THEIR OWN EXAMPLE IN THE STRUGGLE FOR THEIR REDEMPTION.
WHAT IS NEEDED IS A PERMANENT REVOLUTION IN THOUGHT. SOMETHING THAT IS CONSTANTLY AWARE OF THE SOURCES OF EXPLOITATION AND OPPRESSION – WHATEVER COLOR OF FLAG IT WRAPS ITSELF IN.

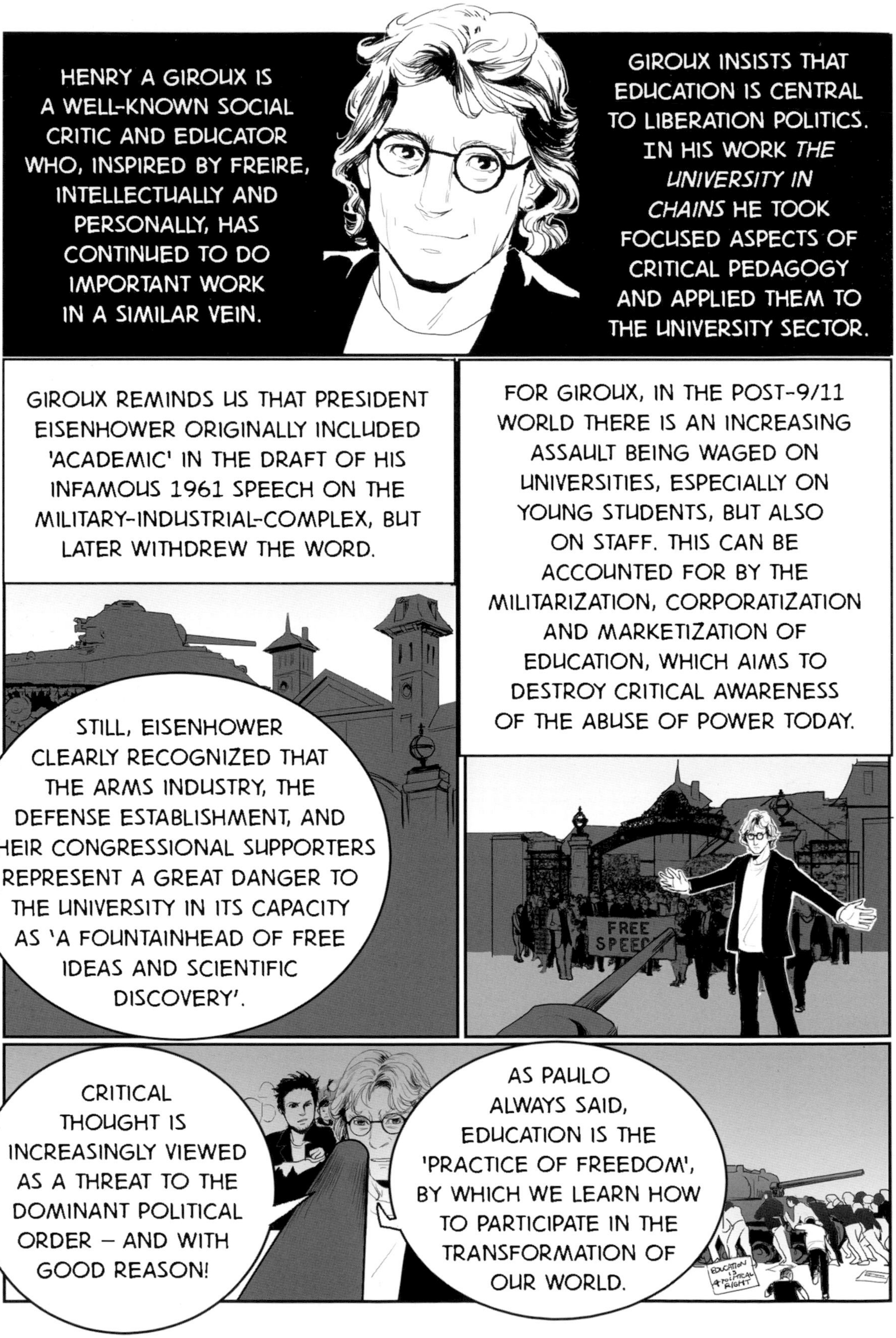
HENRY A GIROUX IS A WELL-KNOWN SOCIAL CRITIC AND EDUCATOR WHO, INSPIRED BY FREIRE, INTELLECTUALLY AND PERSONALLY, HAS CONTINUED TO DO IMPORTANT WORK IN A SIMILAR VEIN.
GIROUX INSISTS THAT EDUCATION IS CENTRAL TO LIBERATION POLITICS. IN HIS WORK *THE UNIVERSITY IN CHAINS* HE TOOK FOCUSED ASPECTS OF CRITICAL PEDAGOGY AND APPLIED THEM TO THE UNIVERSITY SECTOR.
GIROUX REMINDS US THAT PRESIDENT EISENHOWER ORIGINALLY INCLUDED 'ACADEMIC' IN THE DRAFT OF HIS INFAMOUS 1961 SPEECH ON THE MILITARY-INDUSTRIAL-COMPLEX, BUT LATER WITHDREW THE WORD.
STILL, EISENHOWER CLEARLY RECOGNIZED THAT THE ARMS INDUSTRY, THE DEFENSE ESTABLISHMENT, AND THEIR CONGRESSIONAL SUPPORTERS REPRESENT A GREAT DANGER TO THE UNIVERSITY IN ITS CAPACITY AS 'A FOUNTAINHEAD OF FREE IDEAS AND SCIENTIFIC DISCOVERY'.
FOR GIROUX, IN THE POST-9/11 WORLD THERE IS AN INCREASING ASSAULT BEING WAGED ON UNIVERSITIES, ESPECIALLY ON YOUNG STUDENTS, BUT ALSO ON STAFF. THIS CAN BE ACCOUNTED FOR BY THE MILITARIZATION, CORPORATIZATION AND MARKETIZATION OF EDUCATION, WHICH AIMS TO DESTROY CRITICAL AWARENESS OF THE ABUSE OF POWER TODAY.
CRITICAL THOUGHT IS INCREASINGLY VIEWED AS A THREAT TO THE DOMINANT POLITICAL ORDER – AND WITH GOOD REASON!
AS PAULO ALWAYS SAID, EDUCATION IS THE 'PRACTICE OF FREEDOM', BY WHICH WE LEARN HOW TO PARTICIPATE IN THE TRANSFORMATION OF OUR WORLD.

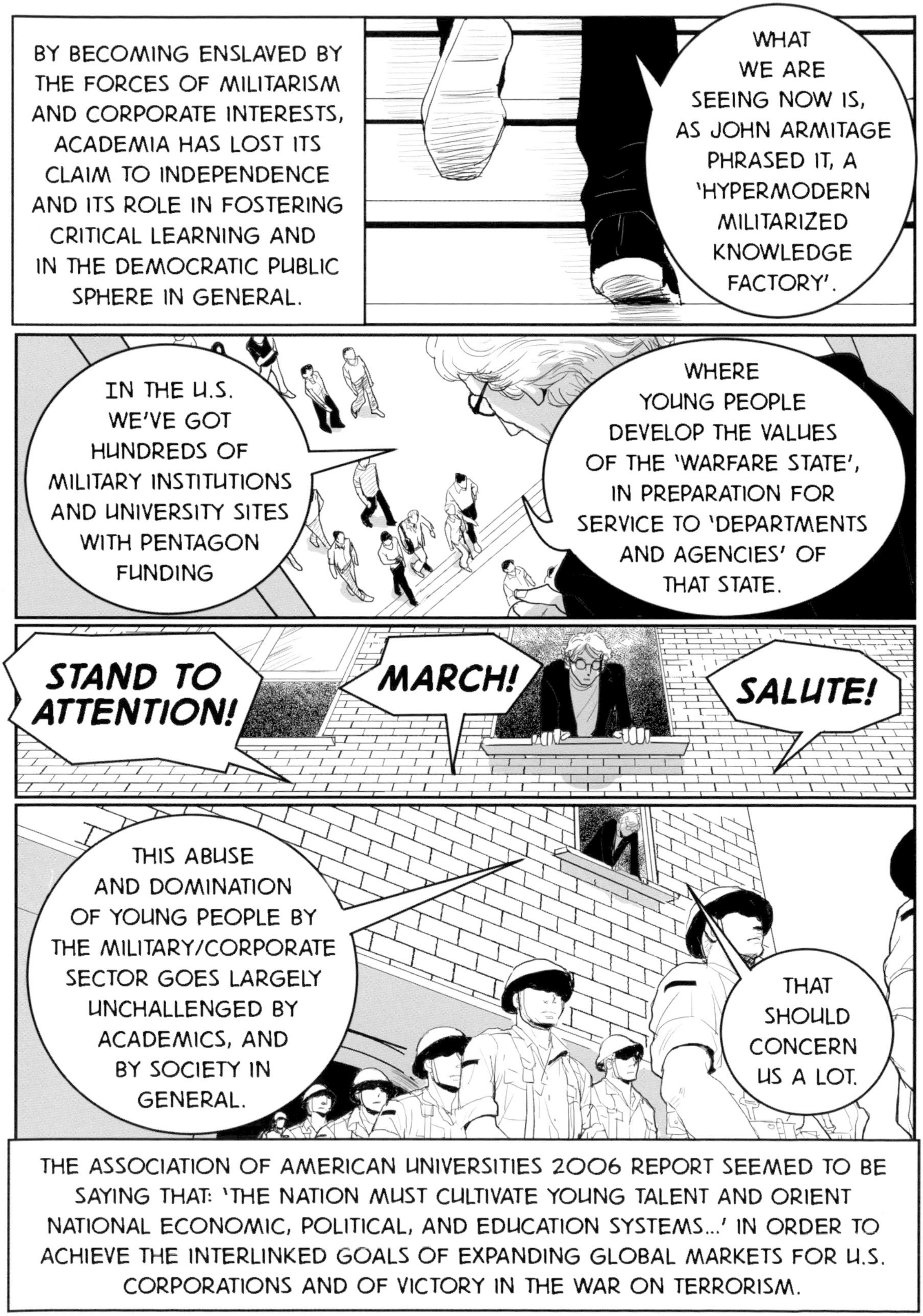
BY BECOMING ENSLAVED BY THE FORCES OF MILITARISM AND CORPORATE INTERESTS, ACADEMIA HAS LOST ITS CLAIM TO INDEPENDENCE AND ITS ROLE IN FOSTERING CRITICAL LEARNING AND IN THE DEMOCRATIC PUBLIC SPHERE IN GENERAL.
WHAT WE ARE SEEING NOW IS, AS JOHN ARMITAGE PHRASED IT, A 'HYPERMODERN MILITARIZED KNOWLEDGE FACTORY'.
IN THE U.S. WE'VE GOT HUNDREDS OF MILITARY INSTITUTIONS AND UNIVERSITY SITES WITH PENTAGON FUNDING
WHERE YOUNG PEOPLE DEVELOP THE VALUES OF THE 'WARFARE STATE', IN PREPARATION FOR SERVICE TO 'DEPARTMENTS AND AGENCIES' OF THAT STATE.
STAND TO ATTENTION!
MARCH!
SALUTE!
THIS ABUSE AND DOMINATION OF YOUNG PEOPLE BY THE MILITARY/CORPORATE SECTOR GOES LARGELY UNCHALLENGED BY ACADEMICS, AND BY SOCIETY IN GENERAL.
THAT SHOULD CONCERN US A LOT.
THE ASSOCIATION OF AMERICAN UNIVERSITIES 2006 REPORT SEEMED TO BE SAYING THAT: 'THE NATION MUST CULTIVATE YOUNG TALENT AND ORIENT NATIONAL ECONOMIC, POLITICAL, AND EDUCATION SYSTEMS...' IN ORDER TO ACHIEVE THE INTERLINKED GOALS OF EXPANDING GLOBAL MARKETS FOR U.S. CORPORATIONS AND OF VICTORY IN THE WAR ON TERRORISM.

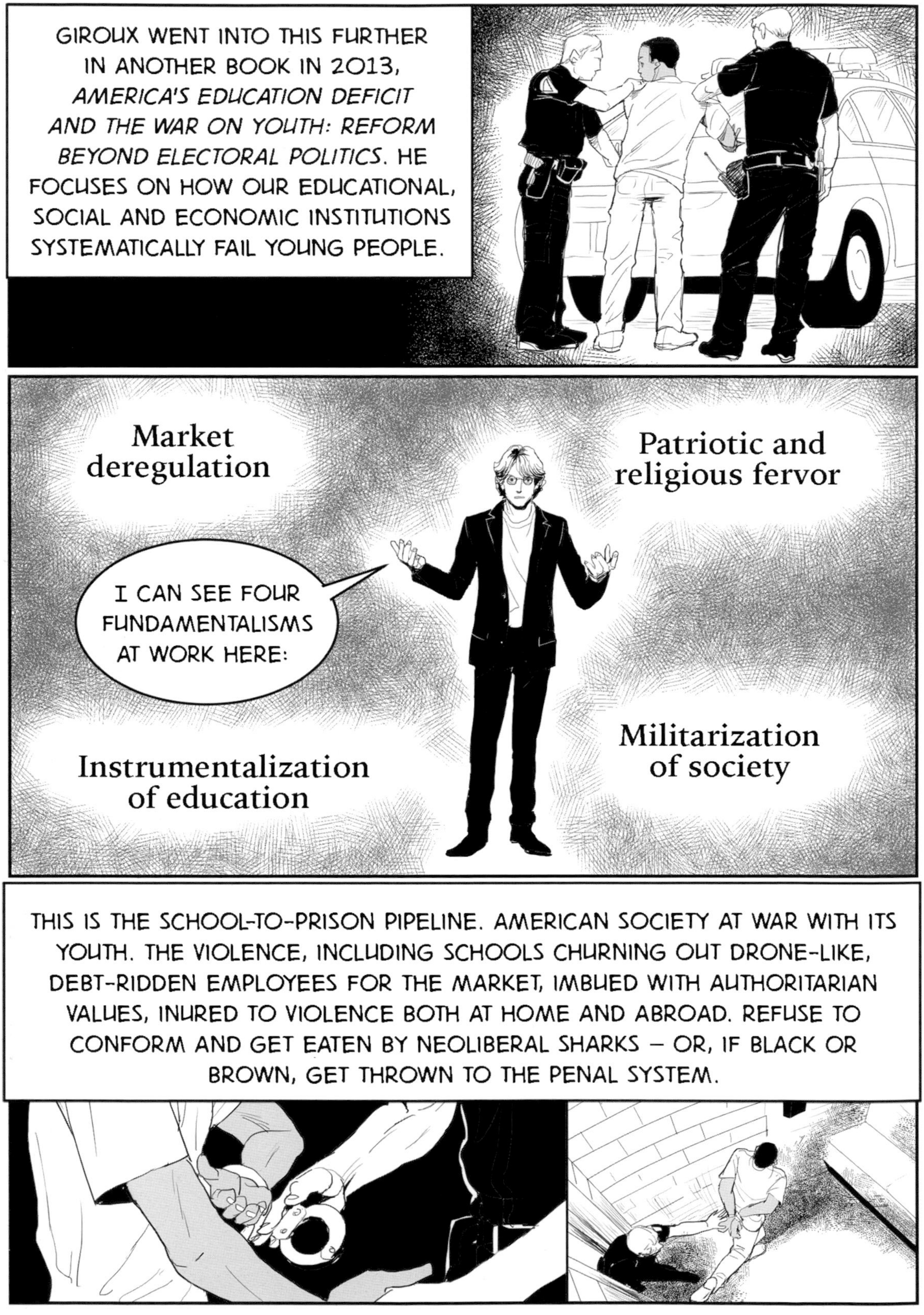
GIROUX WENT INTO THIS FURTHER IN ANOTHER BOOK IN 2013, *AMERICA'S EDUCATION DEFICIT AND THE WAR ON YOUTH: REFORM BEYOND ELECTORAL POLITICS*. HE FOCUSES ON HOW OUR EDUCATIONAL, SOCIAL AND ECONOMIC INSTITUTIONS SYSTEMATICALLY FAIL YOUNG PEOPLE.
I CAN SEE FOUR FUNDAMENTALISMS AT WORK HERE:
Market deregulation
Patriotic and religious fervor
Instrumentalization of education
Militarization of society
THIS IS THE SCHOOL-TO-PRISON PIPELINE. AMERICAN SOCIETY AT WAR WITH ITS YOUTH. THE VIOLENCE, INCLUDING SCHOOLS CHURNING OUT DRONE-LIKE, DEBT-RIDDEN EMPLOYEES FOR THE MARKET, IMBUED WITH AUTHORITARIAN VALUES, INURED TO VIOLENCE BOTH AT HOME AND ABROAD. REFUSE TO CONFORM AND GET EATEN BY NEOLIBERAL SHARKS – OR, IF BLACK OR BROWN, GET THROWN TO THE PENAL SYSTEM.

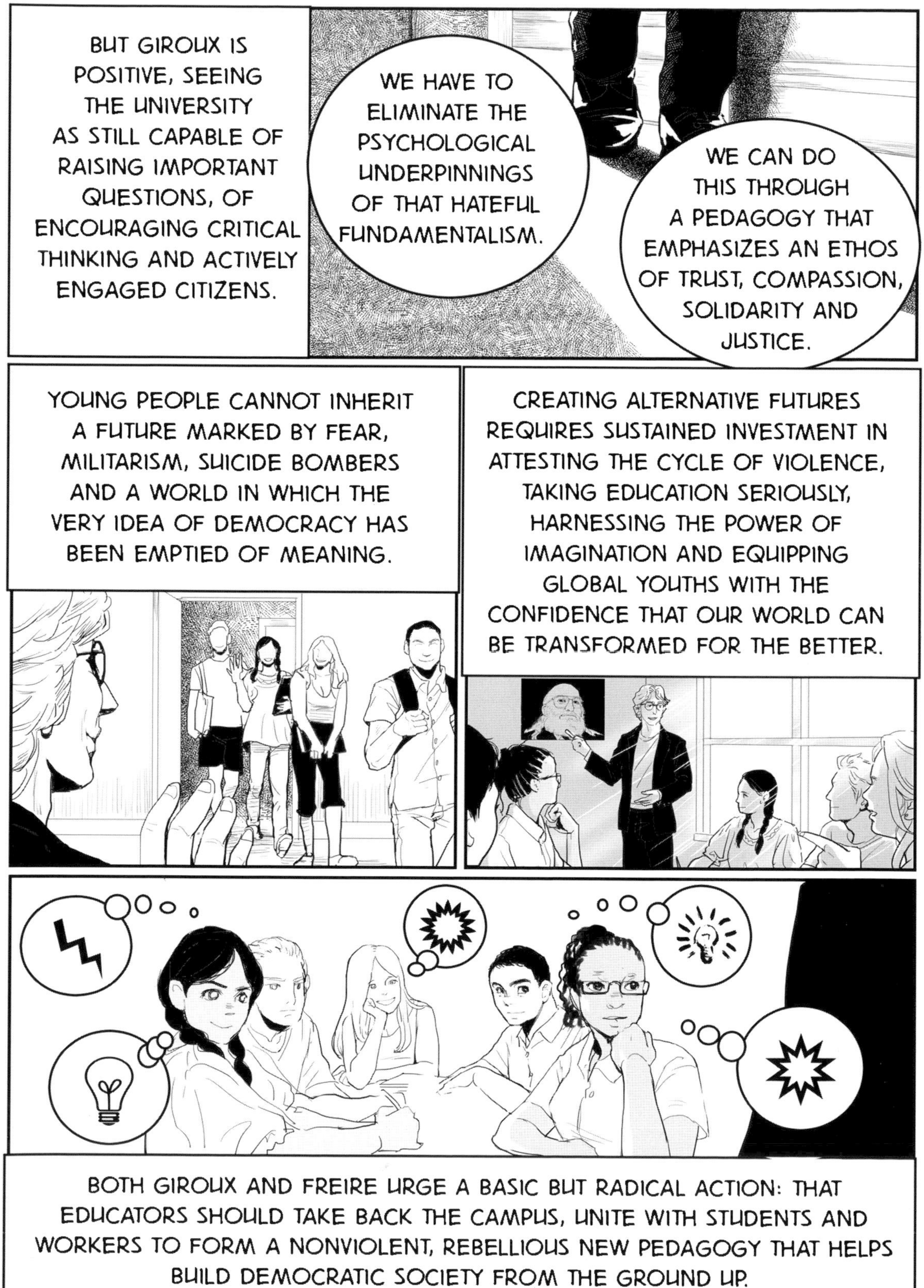
BUT GIROUX IS POSITIVE, SEEING THE UNIVERSITY AS STILL CAPABLE OF RAISING IMPORTANT QUESTIONS, OF ENCOURAGING CRITICAL THINKING AND ACTIVELY ENGAGED CITIZENS.
WE HAVE TO ELIMINATE THE PSYCHOLOGICAL UNDERPINNINGS OF THAT HATEFUL FUNDAMENTALISM.
WE CAN DO THIS THROUGH A PEDAGOGY THAT EMPHASIZES AN ETHOS OF TRUST, COMPASSION, SOLIDARITY AND JUSTICE.
YOUNG PEOPLE CANNOT INHERIT A FUTURE MARKED BY FEAR, MILITARISM, SUICIDE BOMBERS AND A WORLD IN WHICH THE VERY IDEA OF DEMOCRACY HAS BEEN EMPTIED OF MEANING.
CREATING ALTERNATIVE FUTURES REQUIRES SUSTAINED INVESTMENT IN ATTESTING THE CYCLE OF VIOLENCE, TAKING EDUCATION SERIOUSLY, HARNESSING THE POWER OF IMAGINATION AND EQUIPPING GLOBAL YOUTHS WITH THE CONFIDENCE THAT OUR WORLD CAN BE TRANSFORMED FOR THE BETTER.
BOTH GIROUX AND FREIRE URGE A BASIC BUT RADICAL ACTION: THAT EDUCATORS SHOULD TAKE BACK THE CAMPUS, UNITE WITH STUDENTS AND WORKERS TO FORM A NONVIOLENT, REBELLIOUS NEW PEDAGOGY THAT HELPS BUILD DEMOCRATIC SOCIETY FROM THE GROUND UP.

Michel Foucault

Society Must
be Defended

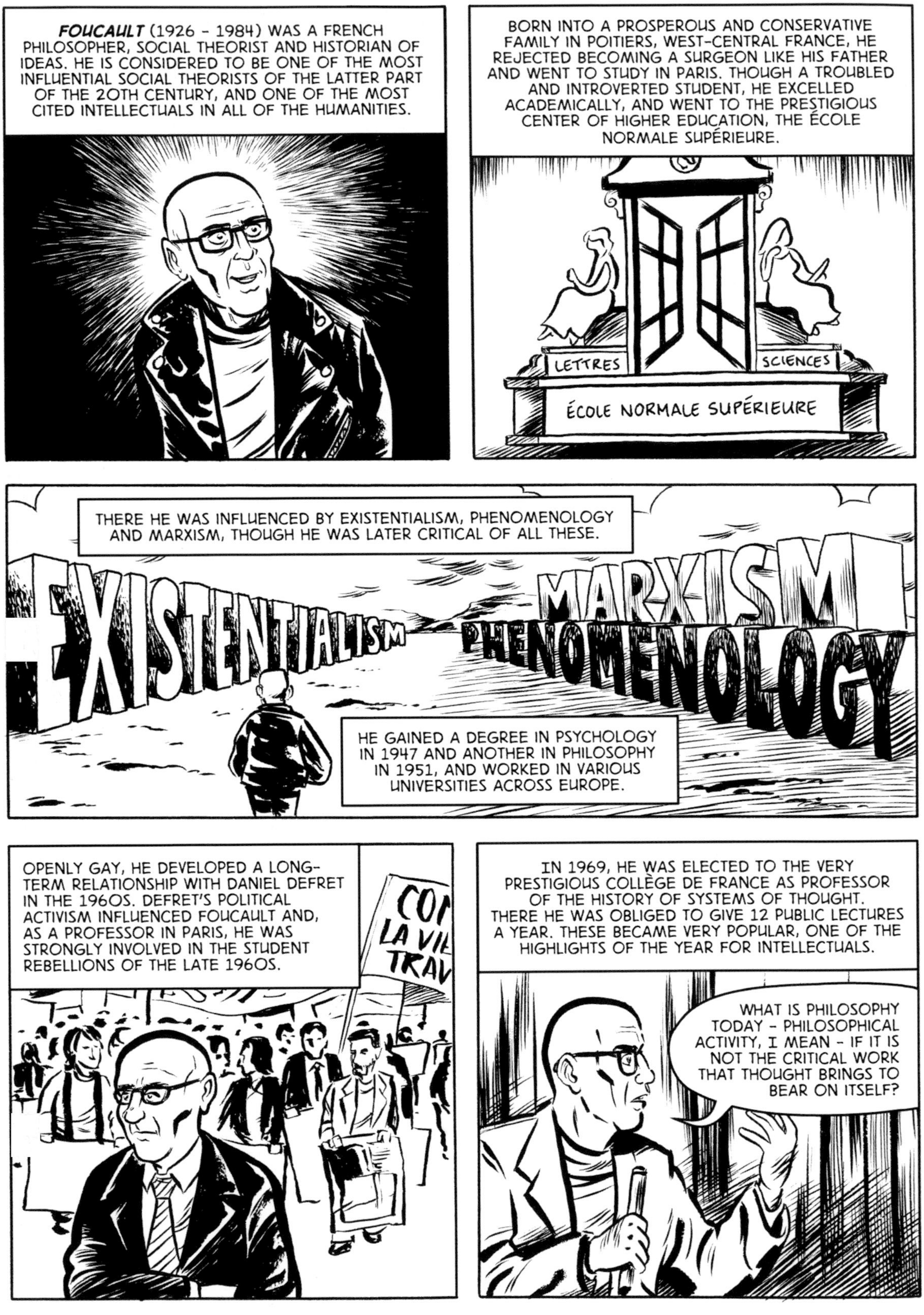
FOUCAULT (1926 – 1984) WAS A FRENCH PHILOSOPHER, SOCIAL THEORIST AND HISTORIAN OF IDEAS. HE IS CONSIDERED TO BE ONE OF THE MOST INFLUENTIAL SOCIAL THEORISTS OF THE LATTER PART OF THE 20TH CENTURY, AND ONE OF THE MOST CITED INTELLECTUALS IN ALL OF THE HUMANITIES.
BORN INTO A PROSPEROUS AND CONSERVATIVE FAMILY IN POITIERS, WEST-CENTRAL FRANCE, HE REJECTED BECOMING A SURGEON LIKE HIS FATHER AND WENT TO STUDY IN PARIS. THOUGH A TROUBLED AND INTROVERTED STUDENT, HE EXCELLED ACADEMICALLY, AND WENT TO THE PRESTIGIOUS CENTER OF HIGHER EDUCATION, THE ÉCOLE NORMALE SUPÉRIEURE.
LETTRES
SCIENCES
ÉCOLE NORMALE SUPÉRIEURE
THERE HE WAS INFLUENCED BY EXISTENTIALISM, PHENOMENOLOGY AND MARXISM, THOUGH HE WAS LATER CRITICAL OF ALL THESE.
EXISTENTIALISM
MARXISM
PHENOMENOLOGY
HE GAINED A DEGREE IN PSYCHOLOGY IN 1947 AND ANOTHER IN PHILOSOPHY IN 1951, AND WORKED IN VARIOUS UNIVERSITIES ACROSS EUROPE.
OPENLY GAY, HE DEVELOPED A LONG-TERM RELATIONSHIP WITH DANIEL DEFRET IN THE 1960S. DEFRET'S POLITICAL ACTIVISM INFLUENCED FOUCAULT AND, AS A PROFESSOR IN PARIS, HE WAS STRONGLY INVOLVED IN THE STUDENT REBELLIONS OF THE LATE 1960S.
IN 1969, HE WAS ELECTED TO THE VERY PRESTIGIOUS COLLÈGE DE FRANCE AS PROFESSOR OF THE HISTORY OF SYSTEMS OF THOUGHT. THERE HE WAS OBLIGED TO GIVE 12 PUBLIC LECTURES A YEAR. THESE BECAME VERY POPULAR, ONE OF THE HIGHLIGHTS OF THE YEAR FOR INTELLECTUALS.
WHAT IS PHILOSOPHY TODAY – PHILOSOPHICAL ACTIVITY, I MEAN – IF IT IS NOT THE CRITICAL WORK THAT THOUGHT BRINGS TO BEAR ON ITSELF?

HE GAVE AN ANONYMOUS INTERVIEW TO THE FRENCH NEWSPAPER *LE MONDE*, BECAUSE HE BELIEVED THAT WORK WITH HIS NAME ATTACHED WOULD NO LONGER BE JUDGED ON ITS CONTENT ALONE.

LISTEN TO THIS:

'I CAN'T HELP BUT DREAM ABOUT A KIND OF CRITICISM THAT WOULD TRY NOT TO JUDGE BUT TO BRING AN *OEUVRE*, A BOOK, A SENTENCE, AN IDEA TO LIFE...'

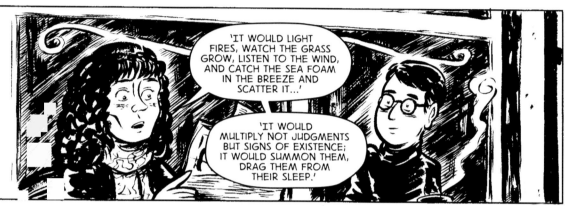

'IT WOULD LIGHT FIRES, WATCH THE GRASS GROW, LISTEN TO THE WIND, AND CATCH THE SEA FOAM IN THE BREEZE AND SCATTER IT...'

'IT WOULD MULTIPLY NOT JUDGMENTS BUT SIGNS OF EXISTENCE; IT WOULD SUMMON THEM, DRAG THEM FROM THEIR SLEEP.'

'PERHAPS IT WOULD INVENT THEM SOMETIMES – ALL THE BETTER. ALL THE BETTER.'

'CRITICISM THAT HANDS DOWN SENTENCES SENDS ME TO SLEEP...'

'I'D LIKE A CRITICISM OF SCINTILLATING LEAPS OF THE IMAGINATION. IT WOULD NOT BE SOVEREIGN OR DRESSED IN RED. IT WOULD BEAR THE LIGHTNING OF POSSIBLE STORMS.'

FANTASTIC!

MICHEL FOUCAULT: SOCIETY MUST BE DEFENDED

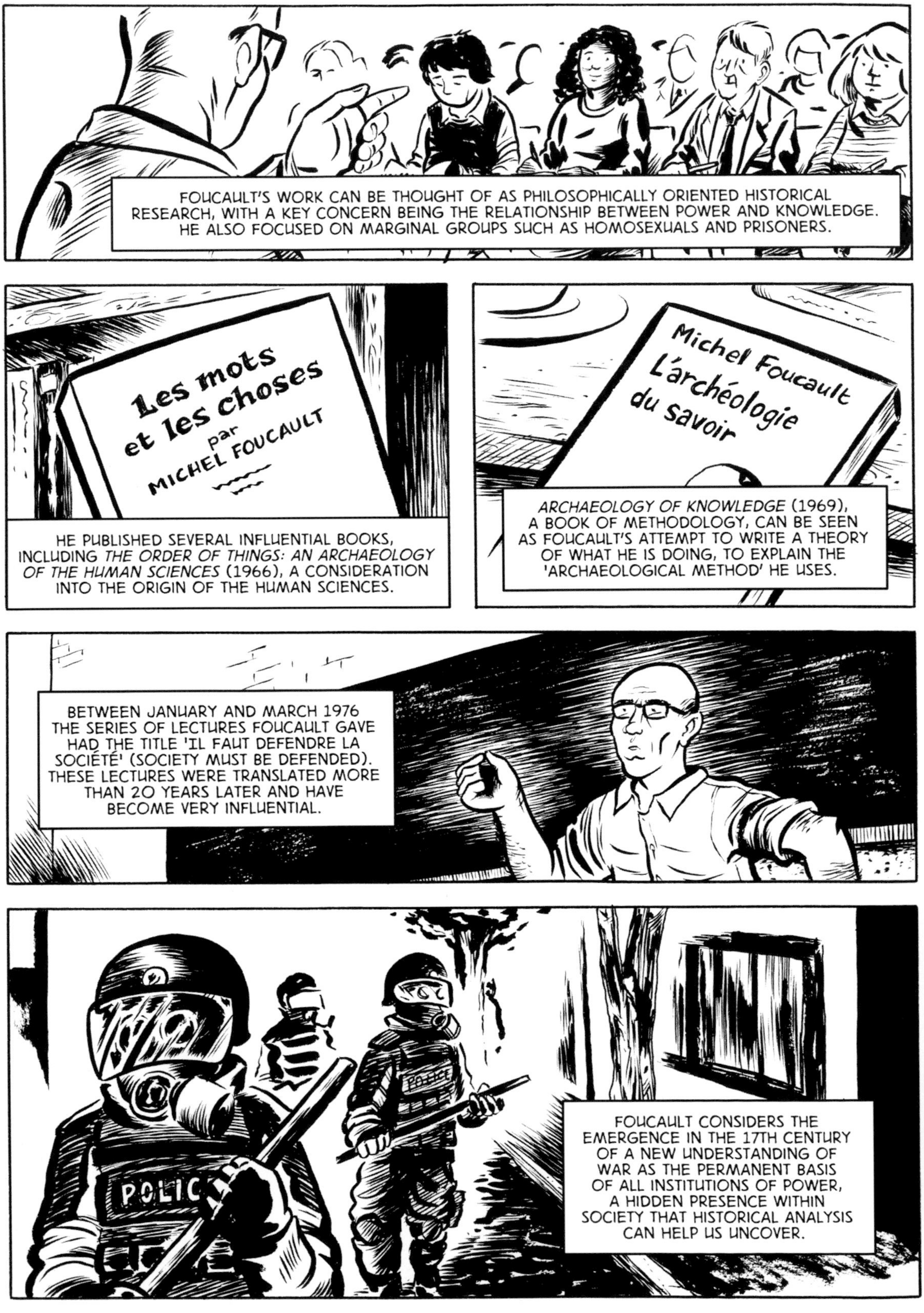
FOUCAULT'S WORK CAN BE THOUGHT OF AS PHILOSOPHICALLY ORIENTED HISTORICAL RESEARCH, WITH A KEY CONCERN BEING THE RELATIONSHIP BETWEEN POWER AND KNOWLEDGE. HE ALSO FOCUSED ON MARGINAL GROUPS SUCH AS HOMOSEXUALS AND PRISONERS.
Les mots et les choses par MICHEL FOUCAULT
HE PUBLISHED SEVERAL INFLUENTIAL BOOKS, INCLUDING *THE ORDER OF THINGS: AN ARCHAEOLOGY OF THE HUMAN SCIENCES* (1966), A CONSIDERATION INTO THE ORIGIN OF THE HUMAN SCIENCES.
Michel Foucault L'archéologie du savoir
ARCHAEOLOGY OF KNOWLEDGE (1969), A BOOK OF METHODOLOGY, CAN BE SEEN AS FOUCAULT'S ATTEMPT TO WRITE A THEORY OF WHAT HE IS DOING, TO EXPLAIN THE 'ARCHAEOLOGICAL METHOD' HE USES.
BETWEEN JANUARY AND MARCH 1976 THE SERIES OF LECTURES FOUCAULT GAVE HAD THE TITLE 'IL FAUT DEFENDRE LA SOCIÉTÉ' (SOCIETY MUST BE DEFENDED). THESE LECTURES WERE TRANSLATED MORE THAN 20 YEARS LATER AND HAVE BECOME VERY INFLUENTIAL.
POLIC
POLICE
FOUCAULT CONSIDERS THE EMERGENCE IN THE 17TH CENTURY OF A NEW UNDERSTANDING OF WAR AS THE PERMANENT BASIS OF ALL INSTITUTIONS OF POWER, A HIDDEN PRESENCE WITHIN SOCIETY THAT HISTORICAL ANALYSIS CAN HELP US UNCOVER.

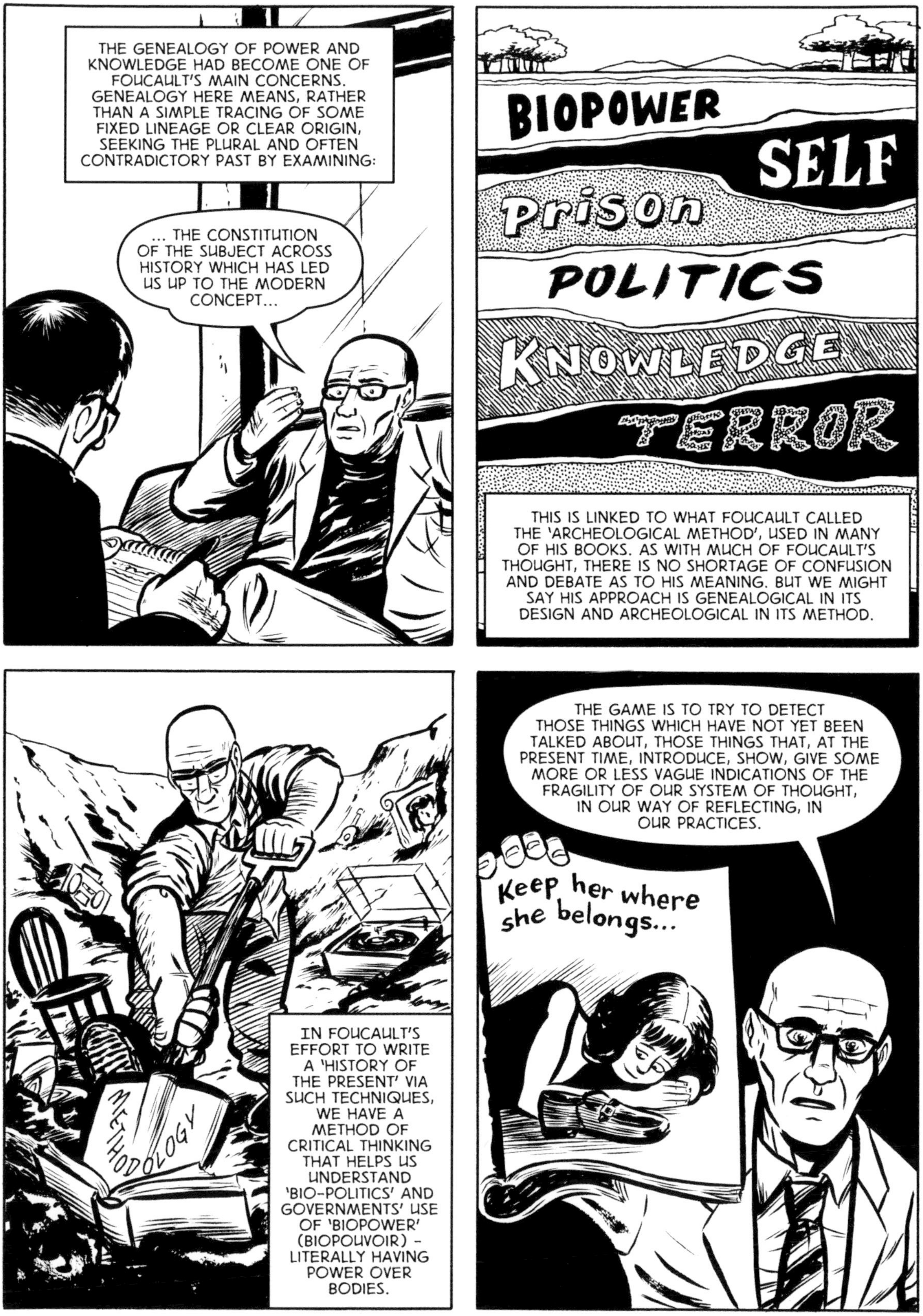

THE GENEALOGY OF POWER AND KNOWLEDGE HAD BECOME ONE OF FOUCAULT'S MAIN CONCERNS. GENEALOGY HERE MEANS, RATHER THAN A SIMPLE TRACING OF SOME FIXED LINEAGE OR CLEAR ORIGIN, SEEKING THE PLURAL AND OFTEN CONTRADICTORY PAST BY EXAMINING:
... THE CONSTITUTION OF THE SUBJECT ACROSS HISTORY WHICH HAS LED US UP TO THE MODERN CONCEPT...
BIOPOWER
SELF
Prison
POLITICS
KNOWLEDGE
TERROR
THIS IS LINKED TO WHAT FOUCAULT CALLED THE 'ARCHEOLOGICAL METHOD', USED IN MANY OF HIS BOOKS. AS WITH MUCH OF FOUCAULT'S THOUGHT, THERE IS NO SHORTAGE OF CONFUSION AND DEBATE AS TO HIS MEANING. BUT WE MIGHT SAY HIS APPROACH IS GENEALOGICAL IN ITS DESIGN AND ARCHEOLOGICAL IN ITS METHOD.
METHODOLOGY
IN FOUCAULT'S EFFORT TO WRITE A 'HISTORY OF THE PRESENT' VIA SUCH TECHNIQUES, WE HAVE A METHOD OF CRITICAL THINKING THAT HELPS US UNDERSTAND 'BIO-POLITICS' AND GOVERNMENTS' USE OF 'BIOPOWER' (BIOPOUVOIR) – LITERALLY HAVING POWER OVER BODIES.
THE GAME IS TO TRY TO DETECT THOSE THINGS WHICH HAVE NOT YET BEEN TALKED ABOUT, THOSE THINGS THAT, AT THE PRESENT TIME, INTRODUCE, SHOW, GIVE SOME MORE OR LESS VAGUE INDICATIONS OF THE FRAGILITY OF OUR SYSTEM OF THOUGHT, IN OUR WAY OF REFLECTING, IN OUR PRACTICES.
Keep her where she belongs...

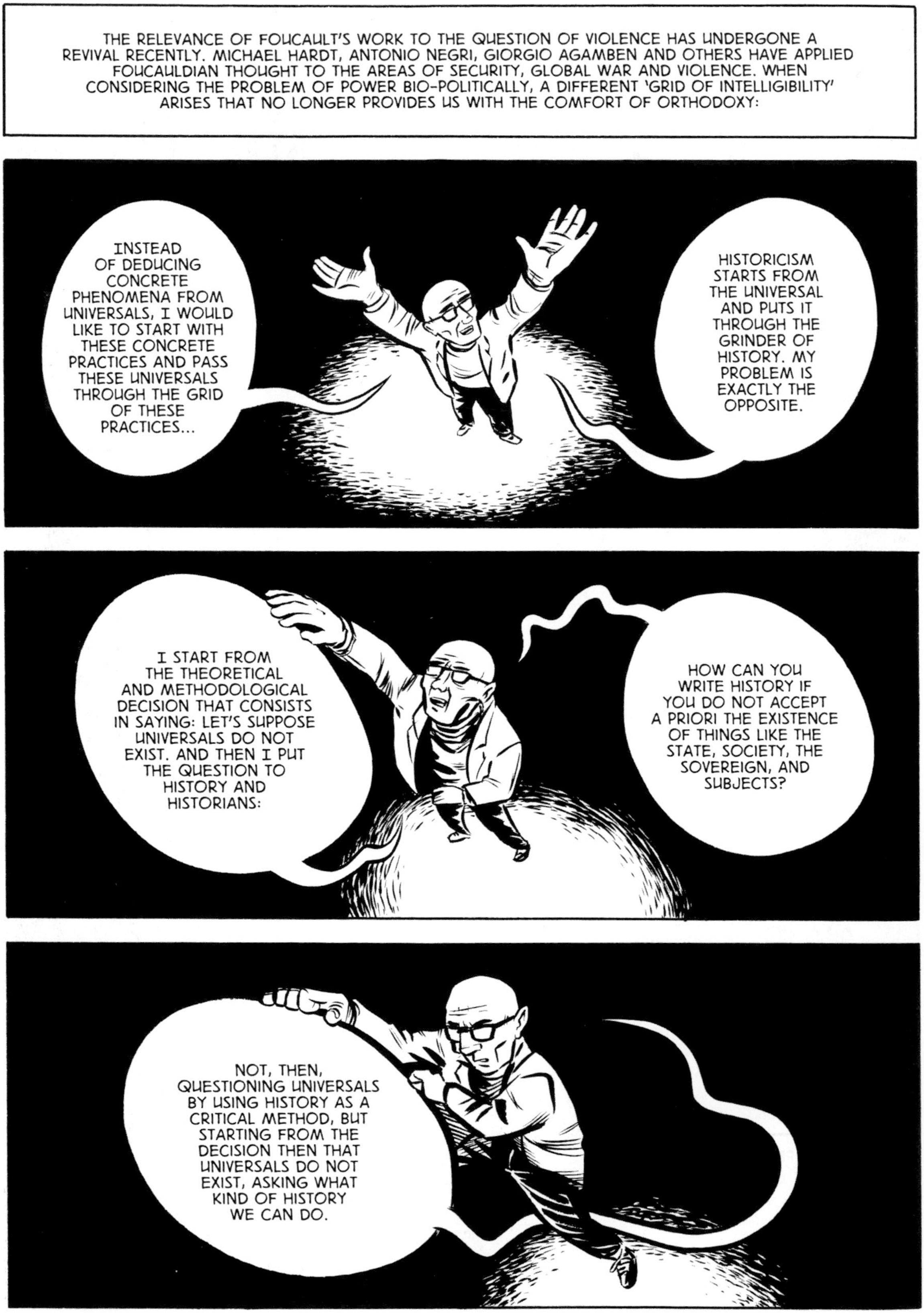
THE RELEVANCE OF FOUCAULT'S WORK TO THE QUESTION OF VIOLENCE HAS UNDERGONE A REVIVAL RECENTLY. MICHAEL HARDT, ANTONIO NEGRI, GIORGIO AGAMBEN AND OTHERS HAVE APPLIED FOUCAULDIAN THOUGHT TO THE AREAS OF SECURITY, GLOBAL WAR AND VIOLENCE. WHEN CONSIDERING THE PROBLEM OF POWER BIO-POLITICALLY, A DIFFERENT 'GRID OF INTELLIGIBILITY' ARISES THAT NO LONGER PROVIDES US WITH THE COMFORT OF ORTHODOXY:
INSTEAD OF DEDUCING CONCRETE PHENOMENA FROM UNIVERSALS, I WOULD LIKE TO START WITH THESE CONCRETE PRACTICES AND PASS THESE UNIVERSALS THROUGH THE GRID OF THESE PRACTICES...
HISTORICISM STARTS FROM THE UNIVERSAL AND PUTS IT THROUGH THE GRINDER OF HISTORY. MY PROBLEM IS EXACTLY THE OPPOSITE.
I START FROM THE THEORETICAL AND METHODOLOGICAL DECISION THAT CONSISTS IN SAYING: LET'S SUPPOSE UNIVERSALS DO NOT EXIST. AND THEN I PUT THE QUESTION TO HISTORY AND HISTORIANS:
HOW CAN YOU WRITE HISTORY IF YOU DO NOT ACCEPT A PRIORI THE EXISTENCE OF THINGS LIKE THE STATE, SOCIETY, THE SOVEREIGN, AND SUBJECTS?
NOT, THEN, QUESTIONING UNIVERSALS BY USING HISTORY AS A CRITICAL METHOD, BUT STARTING FROM THE DECISION THEN THAT UNIVERSALS DO NOT EXIST, ASKING WHAT KIND OF HISTORY WE CAN DO.

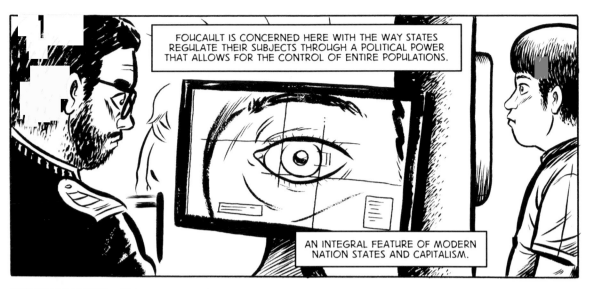

FOUCAULT IS CONCERNED HERE WITH THE WAY STATES REGULATE THEIR SUBJECTS THROUGH A POLITICAL POWER THAT ALLOWS FOR THE CONTROL OF ENTIRE POPULATIONS.

AN INTEGRAL FEATURE OF MODERN NATION STATES AND CAPITALISM.

BY BIOPOWER I MEAN THE SET OF MECHANISMS THROUGH WHICH THE BASIC BIOLOGICAL FEATURES OF THE HUMAN SPECIES BECAME THE OBJECT OF A POLITICAL STRATEGY, OF A GENERAL STRATEGY OF POWER.

IN THE 'SOCIETY MUST BE DEFENDED' LECTURE, FOUCAULT TAKES THE FAMOUS DICTUM OF THE EARLY 19TH-CENTURY PRUSSIAN GENERAL, CARL VON CLAUSEWITZ:

WAR IS A CONTINUATION OF POLITICS BY OTHER MEANS.

BUT FOUCAULT REVERSES THIS TO BECOME: 'POLITICS IS A CONTINUATION OF WAR BY OTHER MEANS.'

SO, WAR IS A PERMANENT FEATURE OF POLITICS AND THE IDEA OF THE LEGITIMACY OF POLITICAL SOVEREIGNTY IS A RUSE HIDING THAT WAR OF POLITICS, ESPECIALLY BETWEEN THE PRIVILEGED AND THE DISADVANTAGED.

THIS VIEW UNDERMINES OUR NORMAL CULTURAL HISTORIES THAT DEPEND ON NOTIONS OF INDIVIDUAL RIGHTS OR ON SECURITY THROUGH THE SOCIAL CONTRACT, OF THE SOVEREIGN/JURIDICAL MODEL.

FOUCAULT SEES IT AS:

CUTTING THE HEAD OFF THE KING!

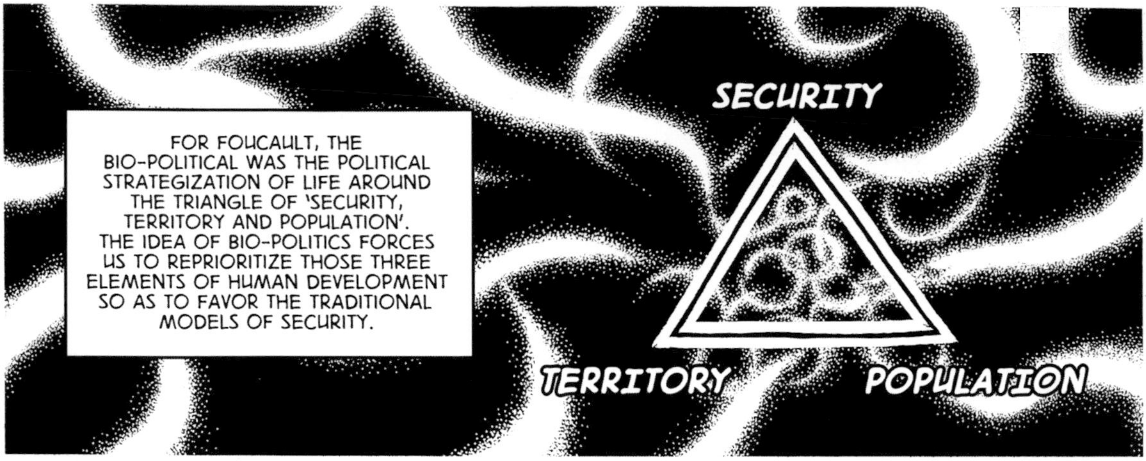
FOR FOUCAULT, THE BIO-POLITICAL WAS THE POLITICAL STRATEGIZATION OF LIFE AROUND THE TRIANGLE OF 'SECURITY, TERRITORY AND POPULATION'. THE IDEA OF BIO-POLITICS FORCES US TO REPRIORITIZE THOSE THREE ELEMENTS OF HUMAN DEVELOPMENT SO AS TO FAVOR THE TRADITIONAL MODELS OF SECURITY.
SECURITY
TERRITORY
POPULATION

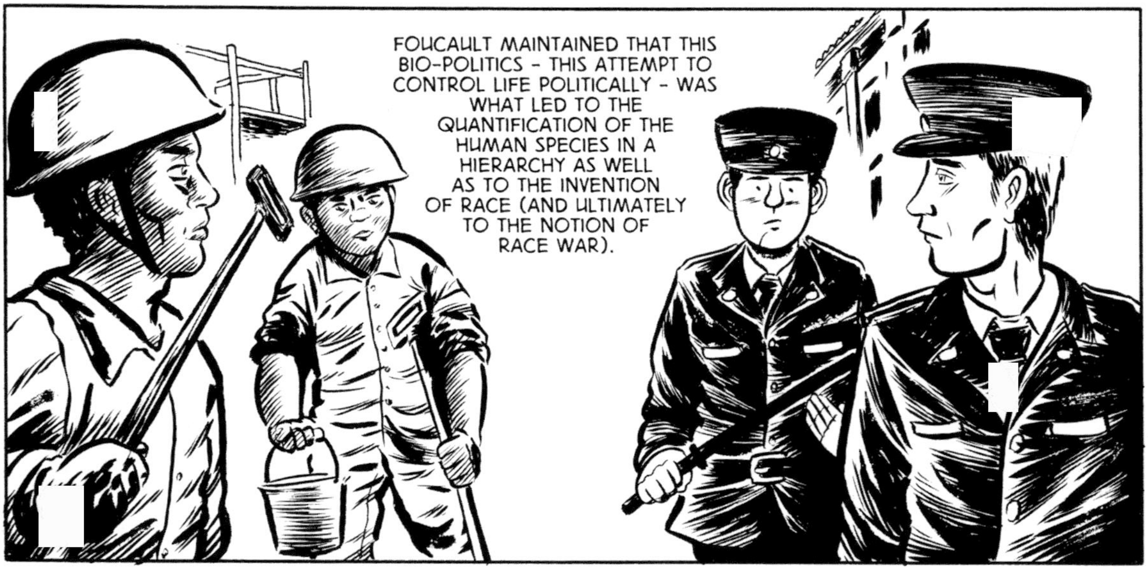
FOUCAULT MAINTAINED THAT THIS BIO-POLITICS - THIS ATTEMPT TO CONTROL LIFE POLITICALLY - WAS WHAT LED TO THE QUANTIFICATION OF THE HUMAN SPECIES IN A HIERARCHY AS WELL AS TO THE INVENTION OF RACE (AND ULTIMATELY TO THE NOTION OF RACE WAR).

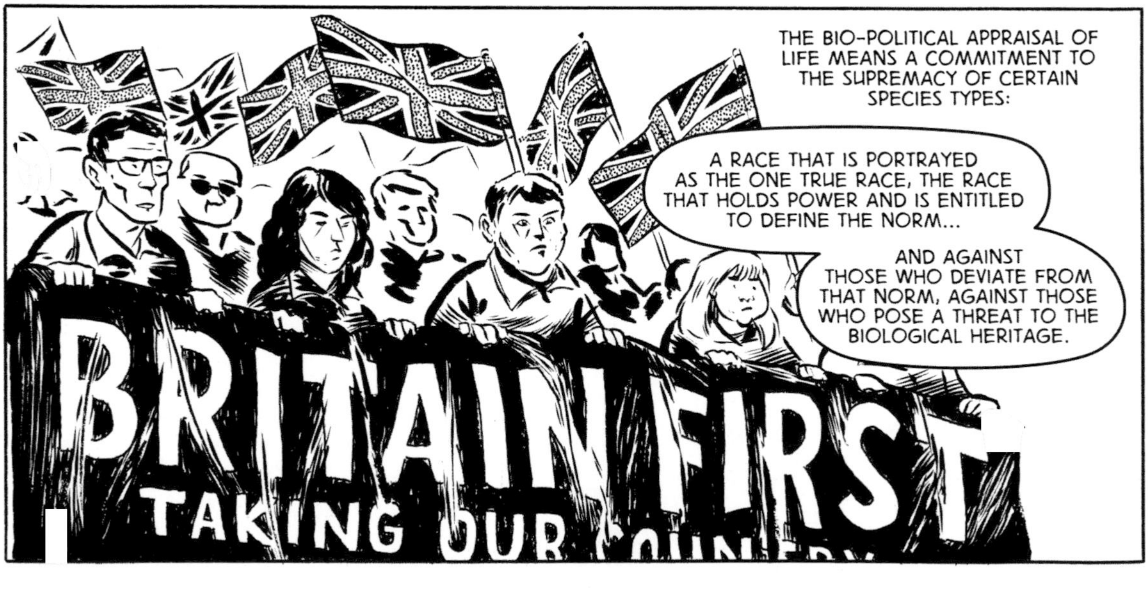
THE BIO-POLITICAL APPRAISAL OF LIFE MEANS A COMMITMENT TO THE SUPREMACY OF CERTAIN SPECIES TYPES:
A RACE THAT IS PORTRAYED AS THE ONE TRUE RACE, THE RACE THAT HOLDS POWER AND IS ENTITLED TO DEFINE THE NORM...
AND AGAINST THOSE WHO DEVIATE FROM THAT NORM, AGAINST THOSE WHO POSE A THREAT TO THE BIOLOGICAL HERITAGE.
BRITAIN FIRST
TAKING OUR

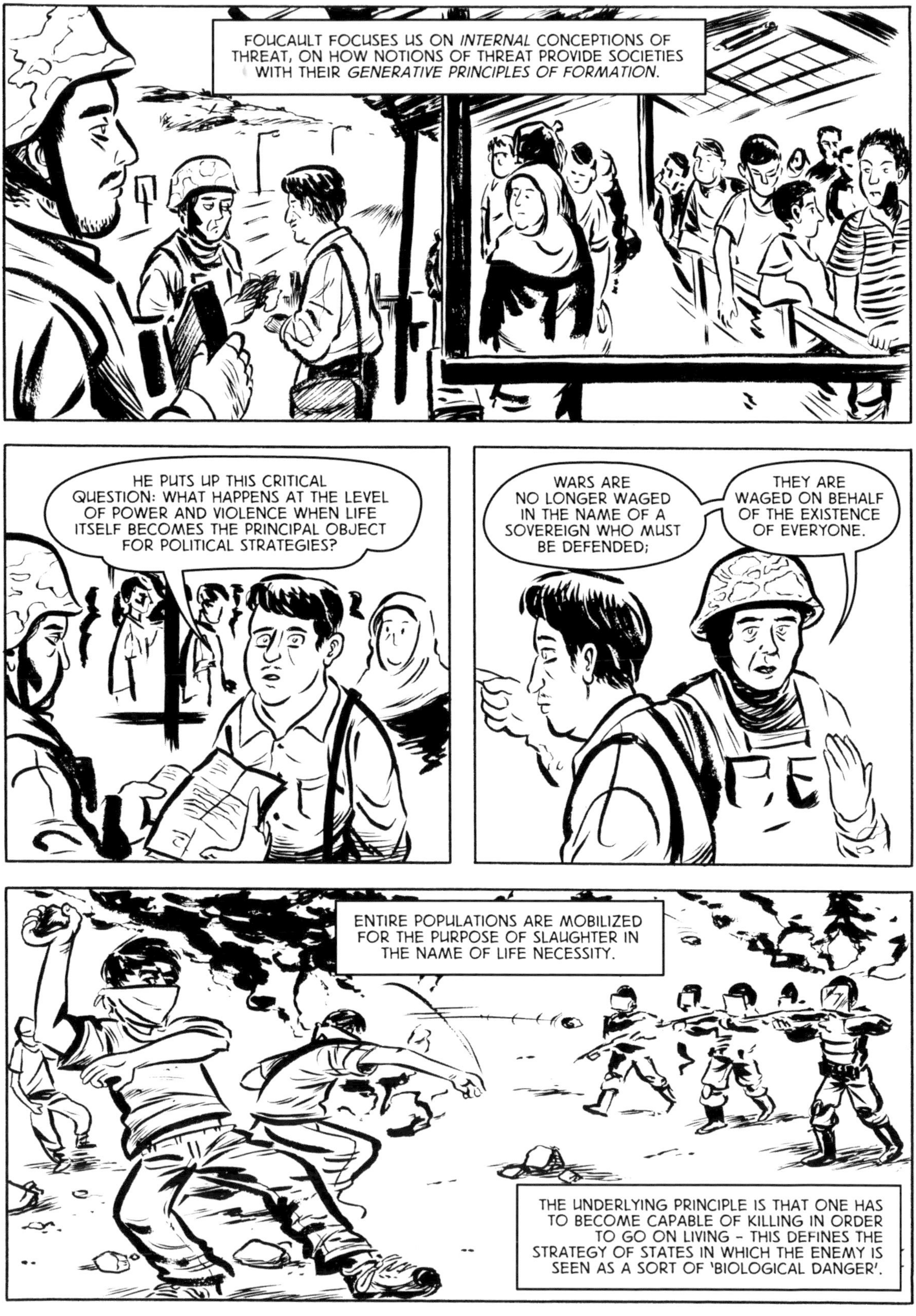
FOUCAULT FOCUSES US ON *INTERNAL* CONCEPTIONS OF THREAT, ON HOW NOTIONS OF THREAT PROVIDE SOCIETIES WITH THEIR *GENERATIVE PRINCIPLES OF FORMATION*.
HE PUTS UP THIS CRITICAL QUESTION: WHAT HAPPENS AT THE LEVEL OF POWER AND VIOLENCE WHEN LIFE ITSELF BECOMES THE PRINCIPAL OBJECT FOR POLITICAL STRATEGIES?
WARS ARE NO LONGER WAGED IN THE NAME OF A SOVEREIGN WHO MUST BE DEFENDED;
THEY ARE WAGED ON BEHALF OF THE EXISTENCE OF EVERYONE.
ENTIRE POPULATIONS ARE MOBILIZED FOR THE PURPOSE OF SLAUGHTER IN THE NAME OF LIFE NECESSITY.
THE UNDERLYING PRINCIPLE IS THAT ONE HAS TO BECOME CAPABLE OF KILLING IN ORDER TO GO ON LIVING – THIS DEFINES THE STRATEGY OF STATES IN WHICH THE ENEMY IS SEEN AS A SORT OF 'BIOLOGICAL DANGER'.

WHEN I SAY 'KILLING', I DO NOT MEAN SIMPLY MURDER, BUT ALSO EVERY FORM OF INDIRECT MURDER:

THE FACT OF EXPOSING SOMEONE TO DEATH, INCREASING THE RISK OF DEATH FOR SOME PEOPLE, OR, QUITE SIMPLY, POLITICAL DEATH, EXPULSION, REJECTION...

SUCH FIGURES AS STEVEN PINKER REASON THAT WE HAVE BECOME LESS WARLIKE BECAUSE OF OUR LIBERAL MATURITY, THAT LIBERALISM AND PEACE MARCH HAND IN HAND. BUT, THROUGH A FOUCAULDIAN LENS, WE MIGHT SAY THIS IS A MISREADING OF THE HISTORICAL RELATIONSHIPS BETWEEN LIBERALISM AND VIOLENCE AND IGNORES BIO-POLITICS.

JOHN GRAY NOTES:

THE IDEA THAT A NEW WORLD CAN BE CONSTRUCTED THROUGH THE RATIONAL APPLICATION OF FORCE IS PECULIARLY MODERN, ANIMATING IDEAS... OF RADICAL ENLIGHTENMENT THINKING.

DOWNPLAYING THIS TRADITION IS EXTREMELY IMPORTANT FOR LIBERAL HUMANISTS WHO REGARD THE CORE OF THE ENLIGHTENMENT AS A COMMITMENT TO RATIONALITY.

ACTUALLY, PROMINENT ENLIGHTENMENT FIGURES FAVORED VIOLENCE AS AN INSTRUMENT OF SOCIAL TRANSFORMATION.

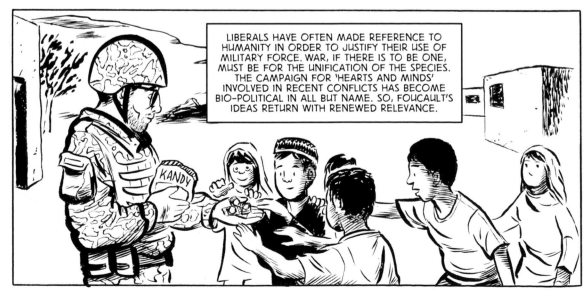

LIBERALS HAVE OFTEN MADE REFERENCE TO HUMANITY IN ORDER TO JUSTIFY THEIR USE OF MILITARY FORCE. WAR, IF THERE IS TO BE ONE, MUST BE FOR THE UNIFICATION OF THE SPECIES. THE CAMPAIGN FOR 'HEARTS AND MINDS' INVOLVED IN RECENT CONFLICTS HAS BECOME BIO-POLITICAL IN ALL BUT NAME. SO, FOUCAULT'S IDEAS RETURN WITH RENEWED RELEVANCE.

PORTRAITS OF VIOLENCE

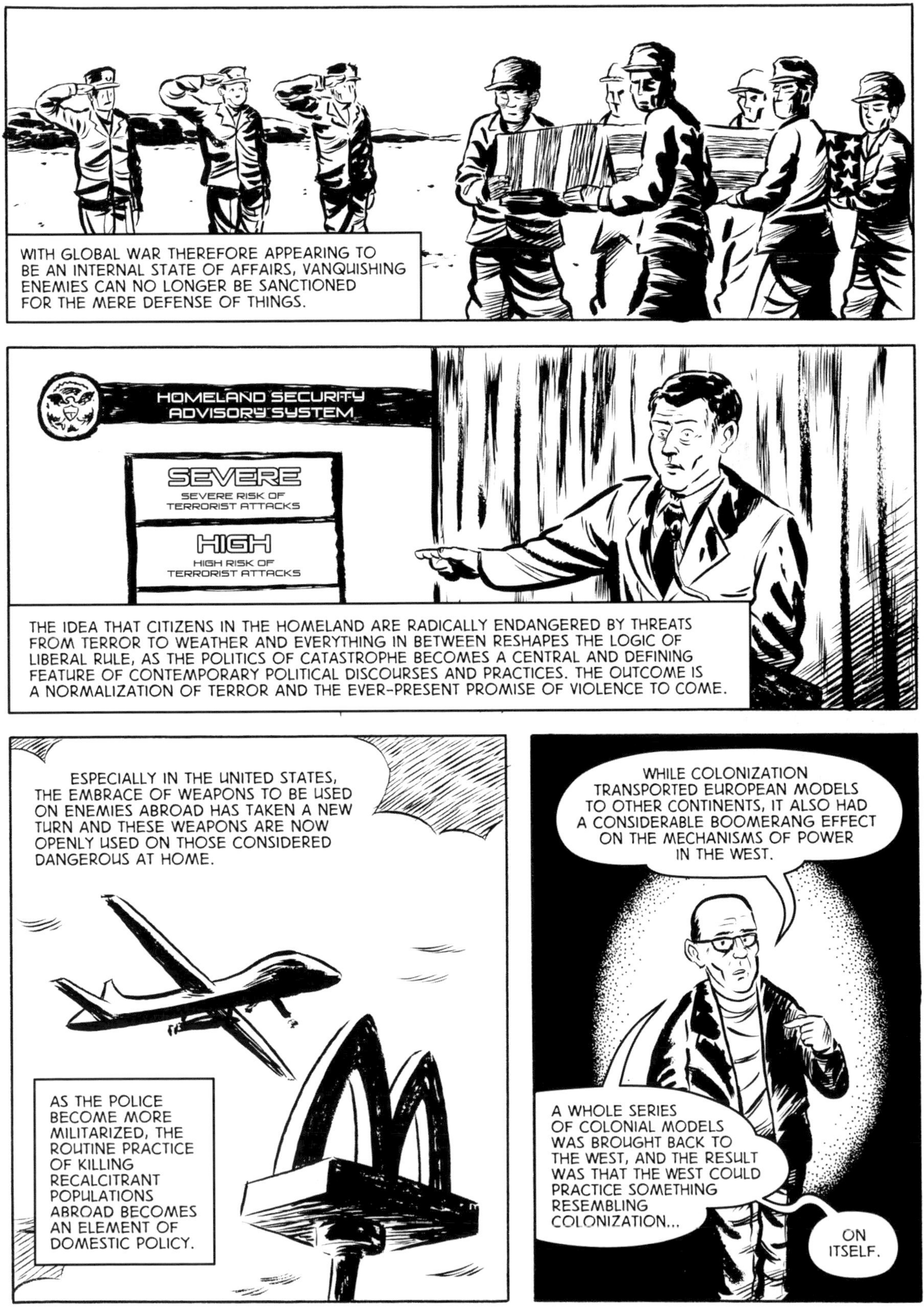
WITH GLOBAL WAR THEREFORE APPEARING TO BE AN INTERNAL STATE OF AFFAIRS, VANQUISHING ENEMIES CAN NO LONGER BE SANCTIONED FOR THE MERE DEFENSE OF THINGS.
HOMELAND SECURITY ADVISORY SYSTEM
SEVERE
SEVERE RISK OF TERRORIST ATTACKS
HIGH
HIGH RISK OF TERRORIST ATTACKS
THE IDEA THAT CITIZENS IN THE HOMELAND ARE RADICALLY ENDANGERED BY THREATS FROM TERROR TO WEATHER AND EVERYTHING IN BETWEEN RESHAPES THE LOGIC OF LIBERAL RULE, AS THE POLITICS OF CATASTROPHE BECOMES A CENTRAL AND DEFINING FEATURE OF CONTEMPORARY POLITICAL DISCOURSES AND PRACTICES. THE OUTCOME IS A NORMALIZATION OF TERROR AND THE EVER-PRESENT PROMISE OF VIOLENCE TO COME.
ESPECIALLY IN THE UNITED STATES, THE EMBRACE OF WEAPONS TO BE USED ON ENEMIES ABROAD HAS TAKEN A NEW TURN AND THESE WEAPONS ARE NOW OPENLY USED ON THOSE CONSIDERED DANGEROUS AT HOME.
AS THE POLICE BECOME MORE MILITARIZED, THE ROUTINE PRACTICE OF KILLING RECALCITRANT POPULATIONS ABROAD BECOMES AN ELEMENT OF DOMESTIC POLICY.
WHILE COLONIZATION TRANSPORTED EUROPEAN MODELS TO OTHER CONTINENTS, IT ALSO HAD A CONSIDERABLE BOOMERANG EFFECT ON THE MECHANISMS OF POWER IN THE WEST.
A WHOLE SERIES OF COLONIAL MODELS WAS BROUGHT BACK TO THE WEST, AND THE RESULT WAS THAT THE WEST COULD PRACTICE SOMETHING RESEMBLING COLONIZATION...
ON ITSELF.

Edward Said

Orientalism

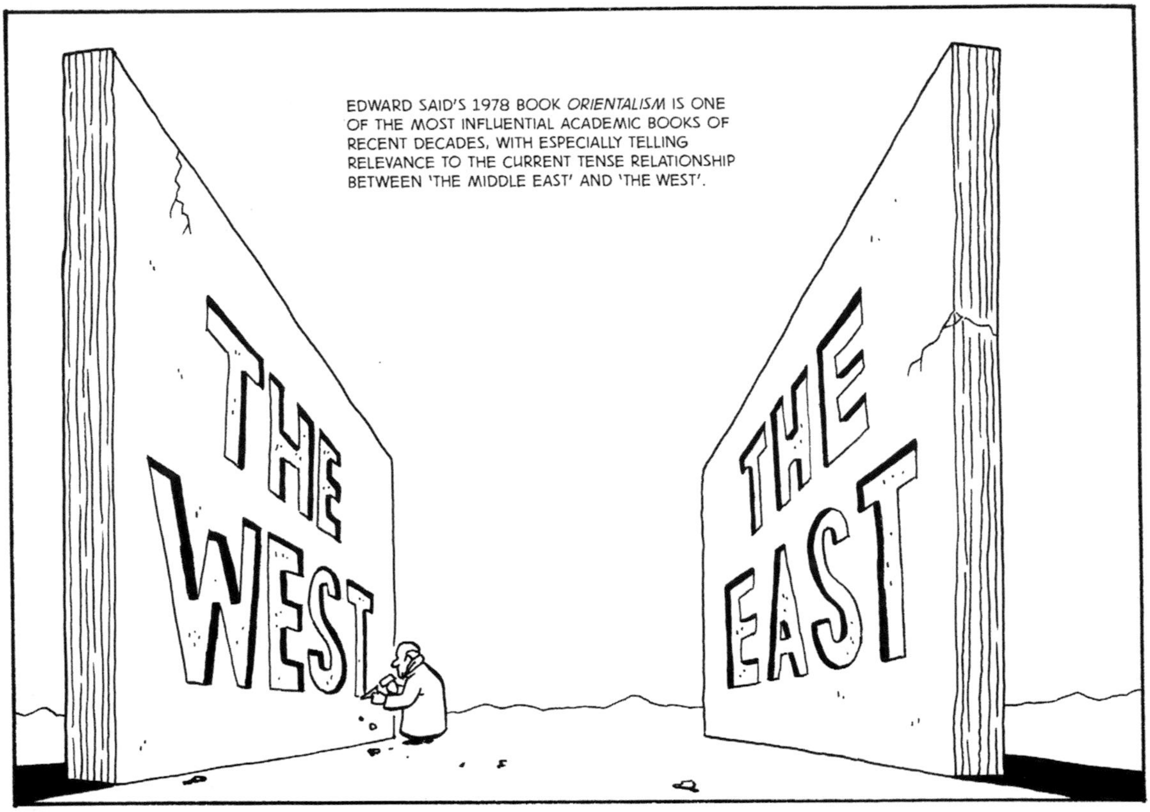
EDWARD SAID'S 1978 BOOK *ORIENTALISM* IS ONE OF THE MOST INFLUENTIAL ACADEMIC BOOKS OF RECENT DECADES, WITH ESPECIALLY TELLING RELEVANCE TO THE CURRENT TENSE RELATIONSHIP BETWEEN 'THE MIDDLE EAST' AND 'THE WEST'.
THE WEST
THE EAST

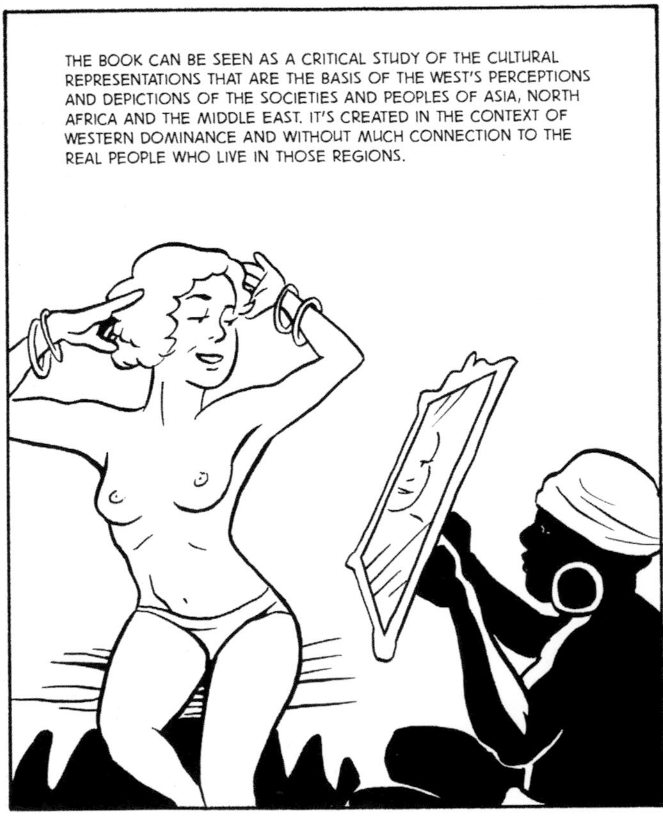
THE BOOK CAN BE SEEN AS A CRITICAL STUDY OF THE CULTURAL REPRESENTATIONS THAT ARE THE BASIS OF THE WEST'S PERCEPTIONS AND DEPICTIONS OF THE SOCIETIES AND PEOPLES OF ASIA, NORTH AFRICA AND THE MIDDLE EAST. IT'S CREATED IN THE CONTEXT OF WESTERN DOMINANCE AND WITHOUT MUCH CONNECTION TO THE REAL PEOPLE WHO LIVE IN THOSE REGIONS.

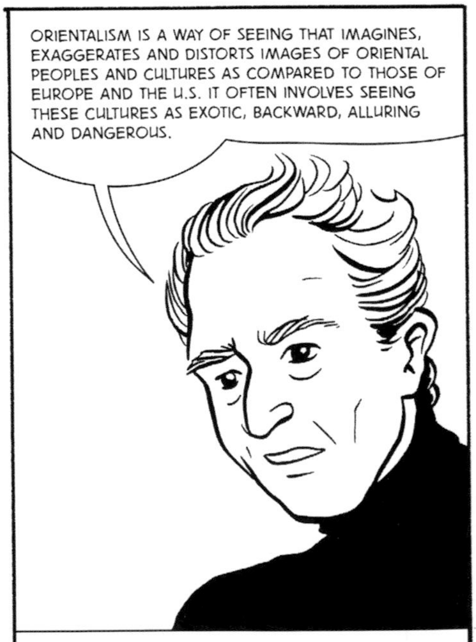
ORIENTALISM IS A WAY OF SEEING THAT IMAGINES, EXAGGERATES AND DISTORTS IMAGES OF ORIENTAL PEOPLES AND CULTURES AS COMPARED TO THOSE OF EUROPE AND THE U.S. IT OFTEN INVOLVES SEEING THESE CULTURES AS EXOTIC, BACKWARD, ALLURING AND DANGEROUS.
ACCORDING TO SAID, ORIENTALISM DATES FROM THE PERIOD OF EUROPEAN ENLIGHTENMENT AND COLONIZATION. IT PROVIDED A RATIONALIZATION FOR COLONIALISM BASED ON A SELF-SERVING IMAGE OF SUPREMACY IN WHICH 'THE WEST' CONSTRUCTED 'THE EAST' AS NOT JUST DIFFERENT BUT INFERIOR, AND THEREFORE IN NEED OF WESTERN 'RESCUE'.

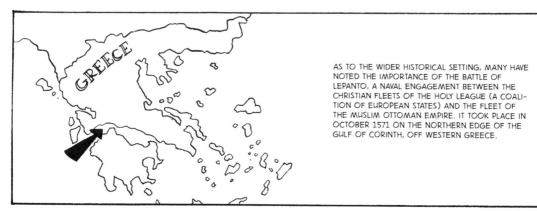

AS TO THE WIDER HISTORICAL SETTING, MANY HAVE NOTED THE IMPORTANCE OF THE BATTLE OF LEPANTO, A NAVAL ENGAGEMENT BETWEEN THE CHRISTIAN FLEETS OF THE HOLY LEAGUE (A COALITION OF EUROPEAN STATES) AND THE FLEET OF THE MUSLIM OTTOMAN EMPIRE. IT TOOK PLACE IN OCTOBER 1571 ON THE NORTHERN EDGE OF THE GULF OF CORINTH, OFF WESTERN GREECE.

IT WAS AN OVERWHELMING DEFEAT FOR THE OTTOMANS. THIS HAS BEEN SEEN BY SOME AS ONE OF THE MAJOR BATTLES IN HISTORY, SIGNALLING THE BEGINNING OF THE END OF THE 'EASTERN THREAT' AND THE RISE OF 'THE WEST' AS THE STRONGER SOURCE OF POWER.

THE SPANISH AUTHOR, MIGUEL DE CERVANTES, WAS IN THE BATTLE AND WAS BADLY WOUNDED. HIS *DON QUIXOTE* IS OFTEN READ AS A FORM OF RESISTANCE TO WESTERN RATIONALITY AND REASON.

THE EVENT WAS SEEN AT THE TIME IN RELIGIOUS TERMS, AS AN ACT OF DIVINE WILL, BOLSTERING CHRISTIANS' CONFIDENCE AND DENTING THAT OF SOME MUSLIMS:

THE IMPERIAL FLEET ENCOUNTERED THE FLEET OF THE WRETCHED INFIDELS... AND THE WILL OF GOD TURNED ANOTHER WAY.

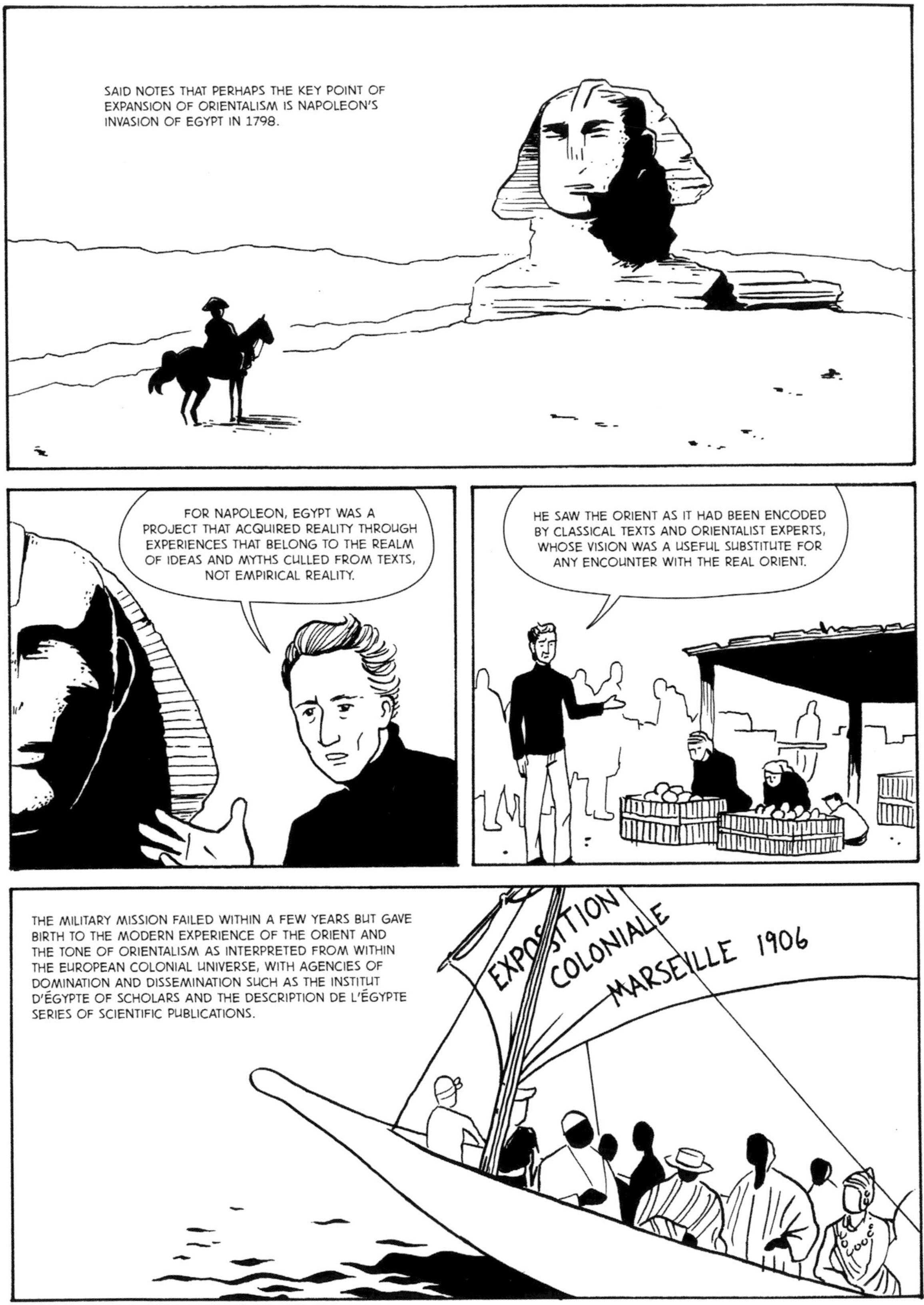
SAID NOTES THAT PERHAPS THE KEY POINT OF EXPANSION OF ORIENTALISM IS NAPOLEON'S INVASION OF EGYPT IN 1798.
FOR NAPOLEON, EGYPT WAS A PROJECT THAT ACQUIRED REALITY THROUGH EXPERIENCES THAT BELONG TO THE REALM OF IDEAS AND MYTHS CULLED FROM TEXTS, NOT EMPIRICAL REALITY.
HE SAW THE ORIENT AS IT HAD BEEN ENCODED BY CLASSICAL TEXTS AND ORIENTALIST EXPERTS, WHOSE VISION WAS A USEFUL SUBSTITUTE FOR ANY ENCOUNTER WITH THE REAL ORIENT.
THE MILITARY MISSION FAILED WITHIN A FEW YEARS BUT GAVE BIRTH TO THE MODERN EXPERIENCE OF THE ORIENT AND THE TONE OF ORIENTALISM AS INTERPRETED FROM WITHIN THE EUROPEAN COLONIAL UNIVERSE, WITH AGENCIES OF DOMINATION AND DISSEMINATION SUCH AS THE INSTITUT D'ÉGYPTE OF SCHOLARS AND THE DESCRIPTION DE L'ÉGYPTE SERIES OF SCIENTIFIC PUBLICATIONS.
EXPOSITION COLONIALE MARSEILLE 1906

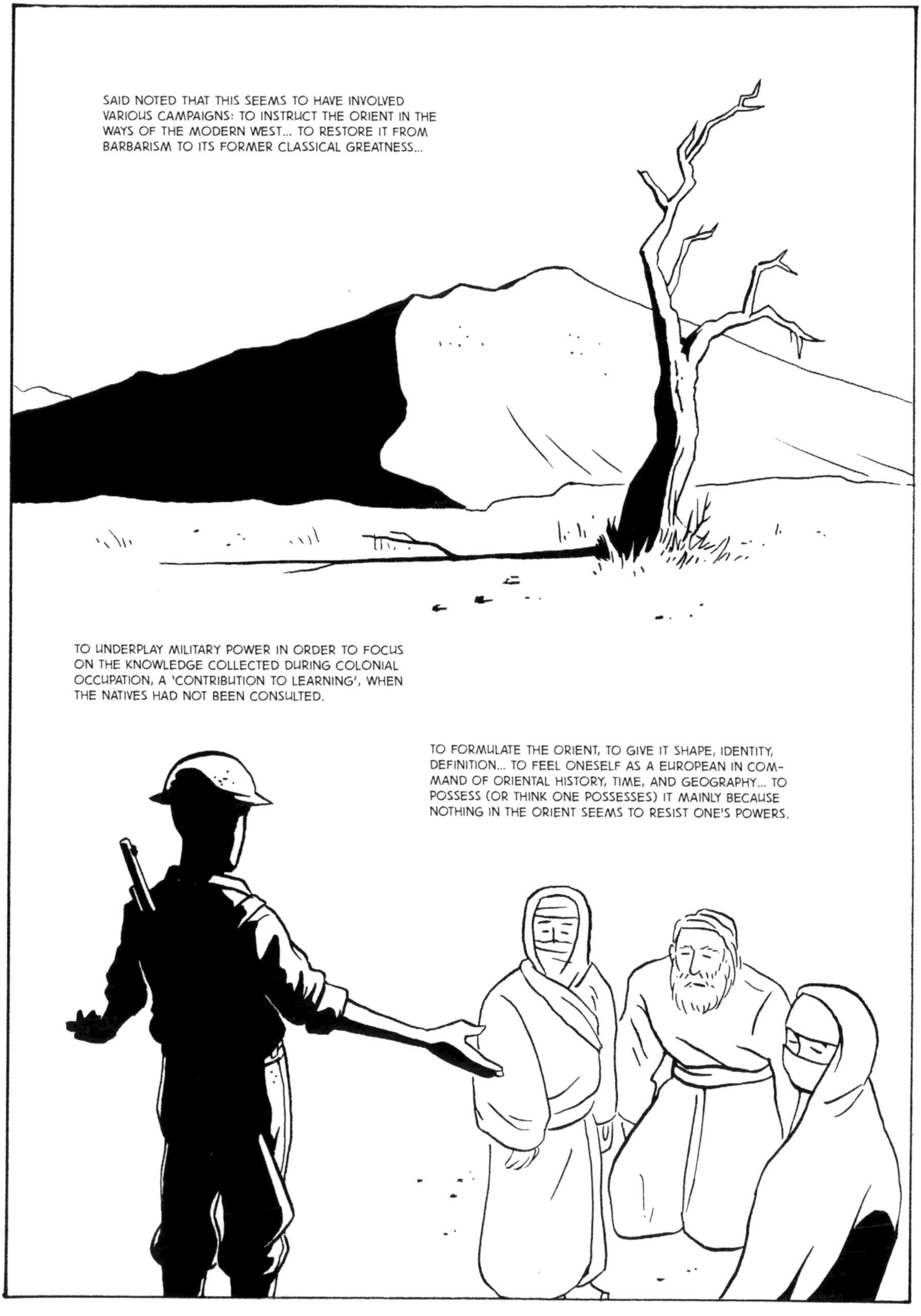
SAID NOTED THAT THIS SEEMS TO HAVE INVOLVED VARIOUS CAMPAIGNS: TO INSTRUCT THE ORIENT IN THE WAYS OF THE MODERN WEST... TO RESTORE IT FROM BARBARISM TO ITS FORMER CLASSICAL GREATNESS...
TO UNDERPLAY MILITARY POWER IN ORDER TO FOCUS ON THE KNOWLEDGE COLLECTED DURING COLONIAL OCCUPATION, A 'CONTRIBUTION TO LEARNING', WHEN THE NATIVES HAD NOT BEEN CONSULTED.
TO FORMULATE THE ORIENT, TO GIVE IT SHAPE, IDENTITY, DEFINITION... TO FEEL ONESELF AS A EUROPEAN IN COMMAND OF ORIENTAL HISTORY, TIME, AND GEOGRAPHY... TO POSSESS (OR THINK ONE POSSESSES) IT MAINLY BECAUSE NOTHING IN THE ORIENT SEEMS TO RESIST ONE'S POWERS.

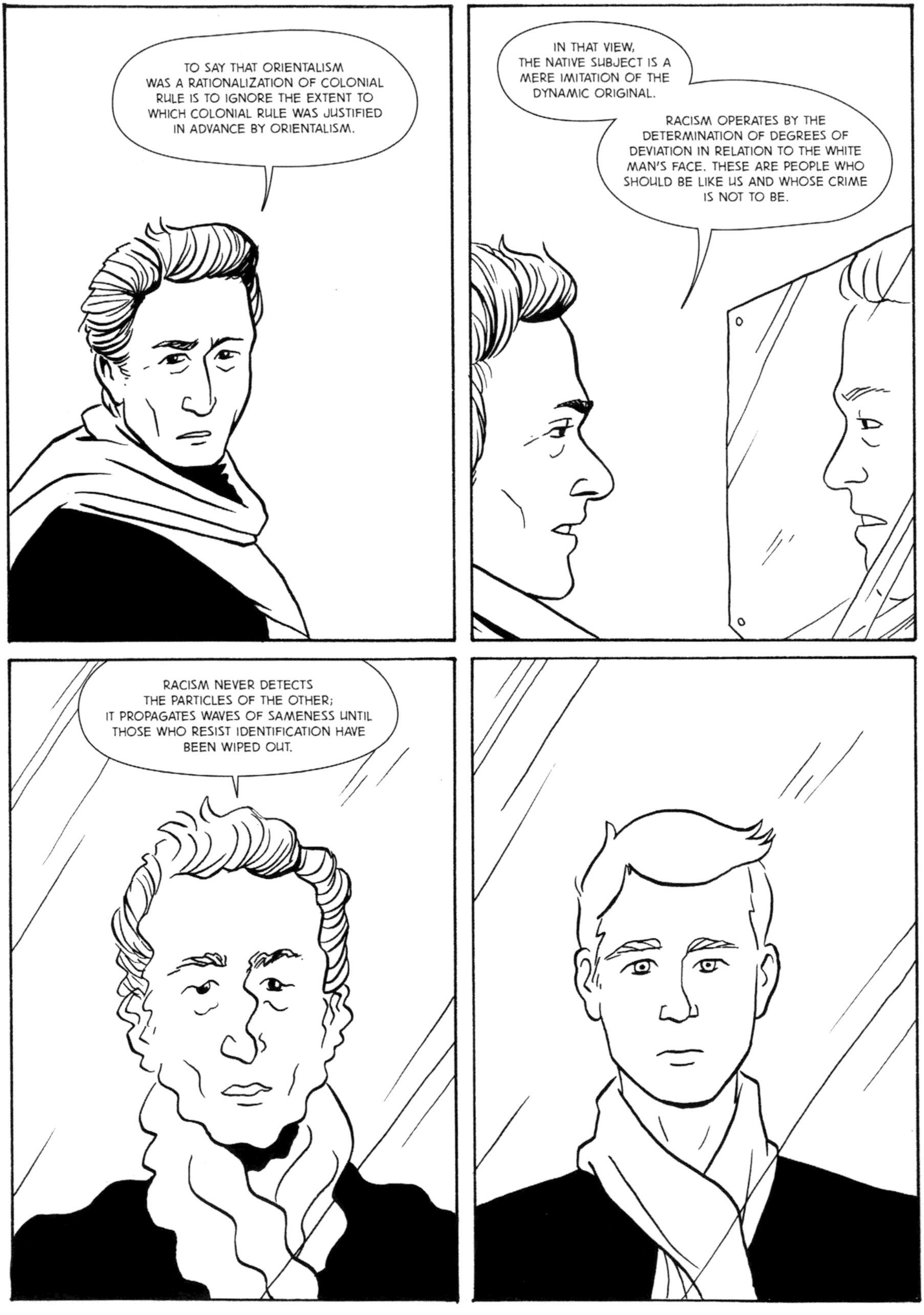
TO SAY THAT ORIENTALISM WAS A RATIONALIZATION OF COLONIAL RULE IS TO IGNORE THE EXTENT TO WHICH COLONIAL RULE WAS JUSTIFIED IN ADVANCE BY ORIENTALISM.
IN THAT VIEW, THE NATIVE SUBJECT IS A MERE IMITATION OF THE DYNAMIC ORIGINAL.
RACISM OPERATES BY THE DETERMINATION OF DEGREES OF DEVIATION IN RELATION TO THE WHITE MAN'S FACE. THESE ARE PEOPLE WHO SHOULD BE LIKE US AND WHOSE CRIME IS NOT TO BE.
RACISM NEVER DETECTS THE PARTICLES OF THE OTHER; IT PROPAGATES WAVES OF SAMENESS UNTIL THOSE WHO RESIST IDENTIFICATION HAVE BEEN WIPED OUT.

FOR SAID, ORIENTALISM OFFERS A NEW WAY TO READ THE VIOLENCE OF HISTORY AND COLONIALISM FROM THE PERSPECTIVE OF 'PEOPLE'. ORIENTALISM WAS A SYSTEM OF HUMAN DIVISION, WITH WHITE, EUROPEAN CHRISTIANS BEING, OF COURSE, AT THE TOP. THERE WAS A NOTABLE DIVISION BETWEEN 'BARBARIANS' (THOSE WHO CAN BE KILLED) AND 'NOBLE SAVAGES' WHO CAN BE REDEEMED, MEANING THAT WITH THE CORRECT METHODS OF INCORPORATION THEY COULD BECOME LIKE US. THIS ENABLED THE POPULATIONS OF DIFFERENCE TO BE INCLUDED AND GOVERNED UNDER A 'SCIENTIFIC DISCIPLINE', ALONG WITH OTHER PEOPLES VARIOUSLY DESIGNATED AS BACKWARD, UNCIVILIZED, RETARDED.

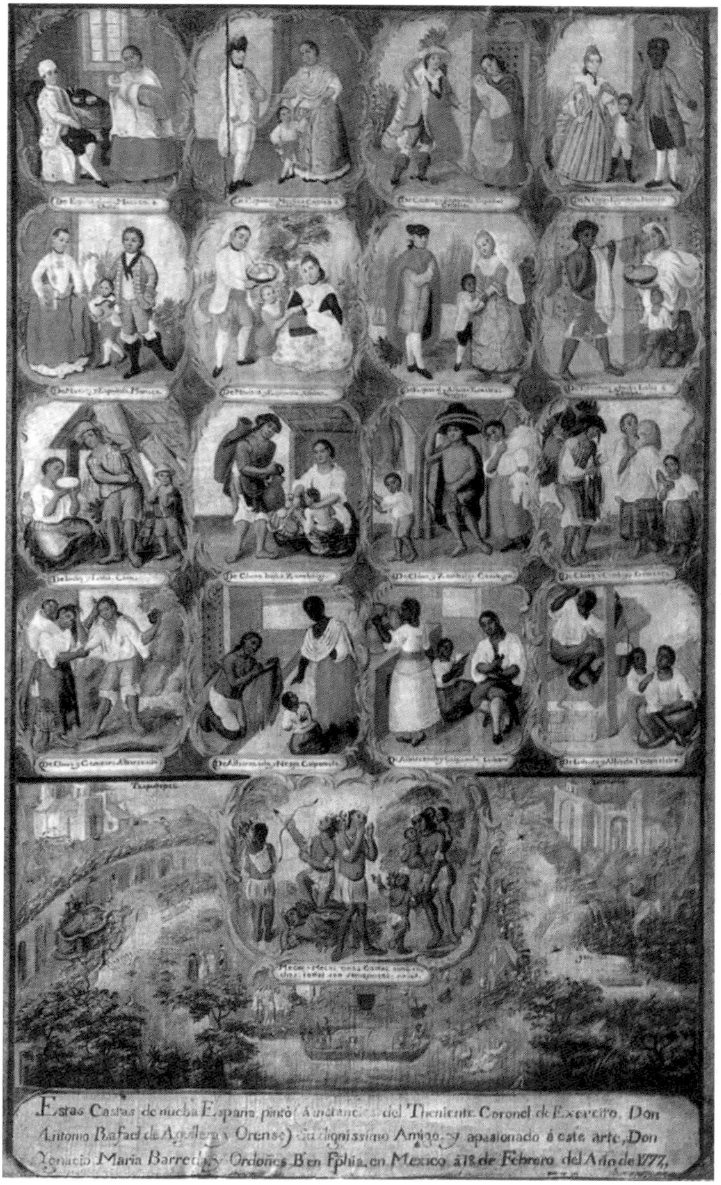

Estas Castas de nueba España pintó
del Theniente Coronel de Exercito, Don
Antonio Rafael de Aguilera y Orense) su dignissimo Amigo, y apasionado á este arte, Don
Ygnacio Maria Barreda, y Ordoñes B en Fphia, en Mexico á 18 de Febrero del Año de 1777,

LATE 18TH CENTURY MEXICAN CASTE PAINTING BY IGNACIO MARIA BARREDA

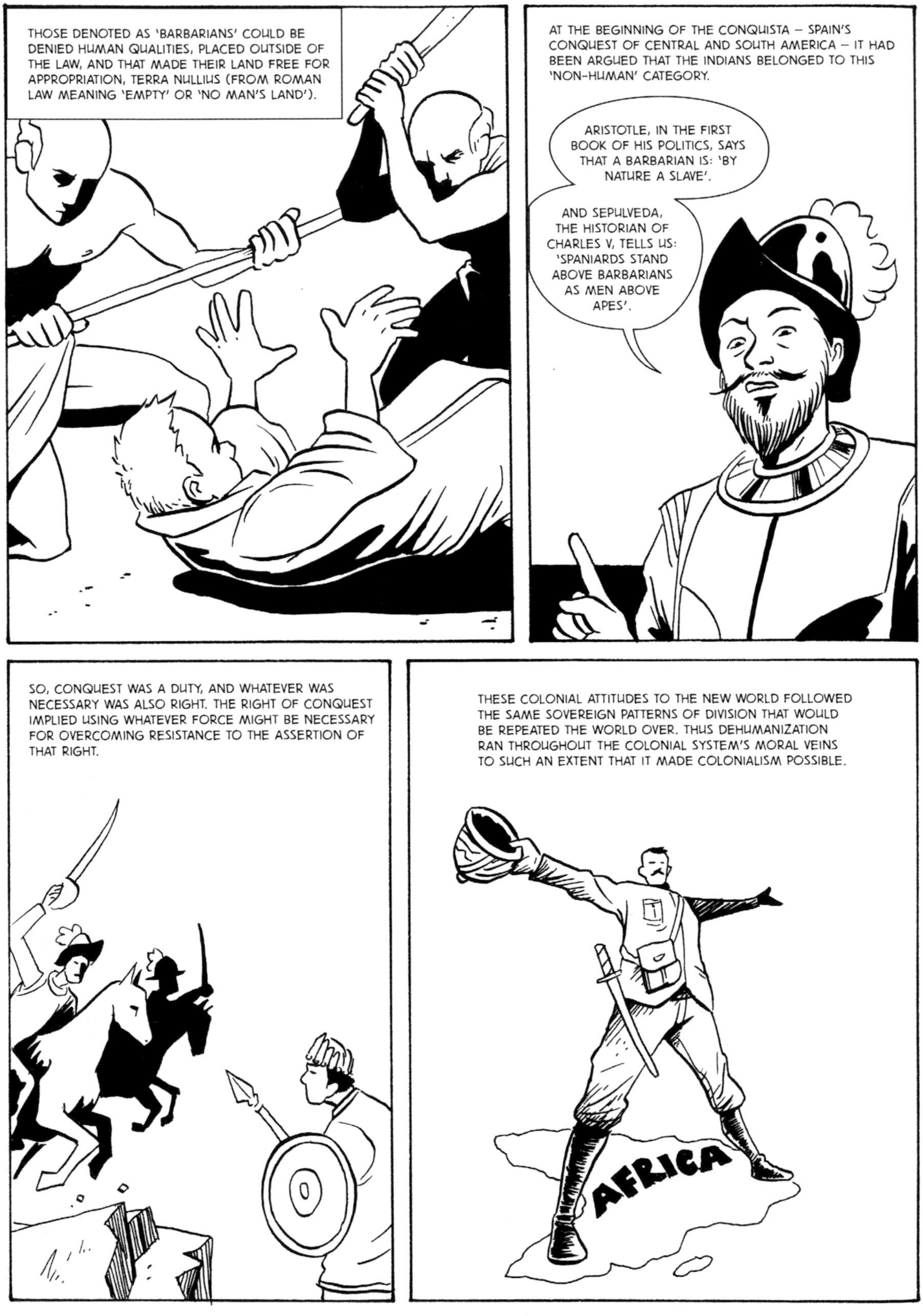
THOSE DENOTED AS 'BARBARIANS' COULD BE DENIED HUMAN QUALITIES, PLACED OUTSIDE OF THE LAW, AND THAT MADE THEIR LAND FREE FOR APPROPRIATION, TERRA NULLIUS (FROM ROMAN LAW MEANING 'EMPTY' OR 'NO MAN'S LAND').
AT THE BEGINNING OF THE CONQUISTA – SPAIN'S CONQUEST OF CENTRAL AND SOUTH AMERICA – IT HAD BEEN ARGUED THAT THE INDIANS BELONGED TO THIS 'NON-HUMAN' CATEGORY.
ARISTOTLE, IN THE FIRST BOOK OF HIS POLITICS, SAYS THAT A BARBARIAN IS: 'BY NATURE A SLAVE'.
AND SEPULVEDA, THE HISTORIAN OF CHARLES V, TELLS US: 'SPANIARDS STAND ABOVE BARBARIANS AS MEN ABOVE APES'.
SO, CONQUEST WAS A DUTY, AND WHATEVER WAS NECESSARY WAS ALSO RIGHT. THE RIGHT OF CONQUEST IMPLIED USING WHATEVER FORCE MIGHT BE NECESSARY FOR OVERCOMING RESISTANCE TO THE ASSERTION OF THAT RIGHT.
THESE COLONIAL ATTITUDES TO THE NEW WORLD FOLLOWED THE SAME SOVEREIGN PATTERNS OF DIVISION THAT WOULD BE REPEATED THE WORLD OVER. THUS DEHUMANIZATION RAN THROUGHOUT THE COLONIAL SYSTEM'S MORAL VEINS TO SUCH AN EXTENT THAT IT MADE COLONIALISM POSSIBLE.
AFRICA

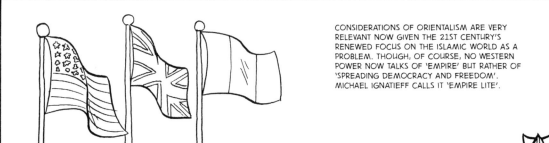

CONSIDERATIONS OF ORIENTALISM ARE VERY RELEVANT NOW GIVEN THE 21ST CENTURY'S RENEWED FOCUS ON THE ISLAMIC WORLD AS A PROBLEM. THOUGH, OF COURSE, NO WESTERN POWER NOW TALKS OF 'EMPIRE' BUT RATHER OF 'SPREADING DEMOCRACY AND FREEDOM'. MICHAEL IGNATIEFF CALLS IT 'EMPIRE LITE'.

WE'RE GONNA FREE THE HELL OUT OF YOU

THE MIDDLE EAST

BUT EVERY SINGLE EMPIRE HAS SAID THAT IT IS NOT LIKE ALL THE OTHERS, THAT ITS CIRCUMSTANCES ARE SPECIAL, THAT IT HAS A MISSION TO BRING ORDER AND DEMOCRACY, AND THAT IT USES FORCE ONLY AS A LAST RESORT.

AND, AS IF ONE SHOULDN'T TRUST THE EVIDENCE OF ONE'S EYES WATCHING THE DESTRUCTION, MISERY AND DEATH BROUGHT BY THE LATEST MILITARY CAMPAIGN, THERE IS ALWAYS A CHORUS OF MEDIA TRUMPETING HIGH IDEALS OF 'PROGRESS' AND ITS 'CIVILIZING MISSION'.

MEDIA-INFLUENCED CONSIDERATIONS ABOUT EXTERNAL AND INTERNAL THREATS CAN BEEN SEEN AS SOCIAL CONTESTS INVOLVING ISSUES SUCH AS CULTURAL IDENTITY, SECURITY, A 'CLASH OF CIVILIZATIONS', ECONOMY, IMMIGRATION, THE LEGITIMIZATION OF VIOLENCE, AND THE DIRECTION OF FOREIGN POLICY. ALL OF THESE ARE OFTEN HIGHLY INFLUENCED BY AN ORIENTALIST MINDSET.

ILLEGAL IS A CRIME

EDWARD SAID: ORIENTALISM

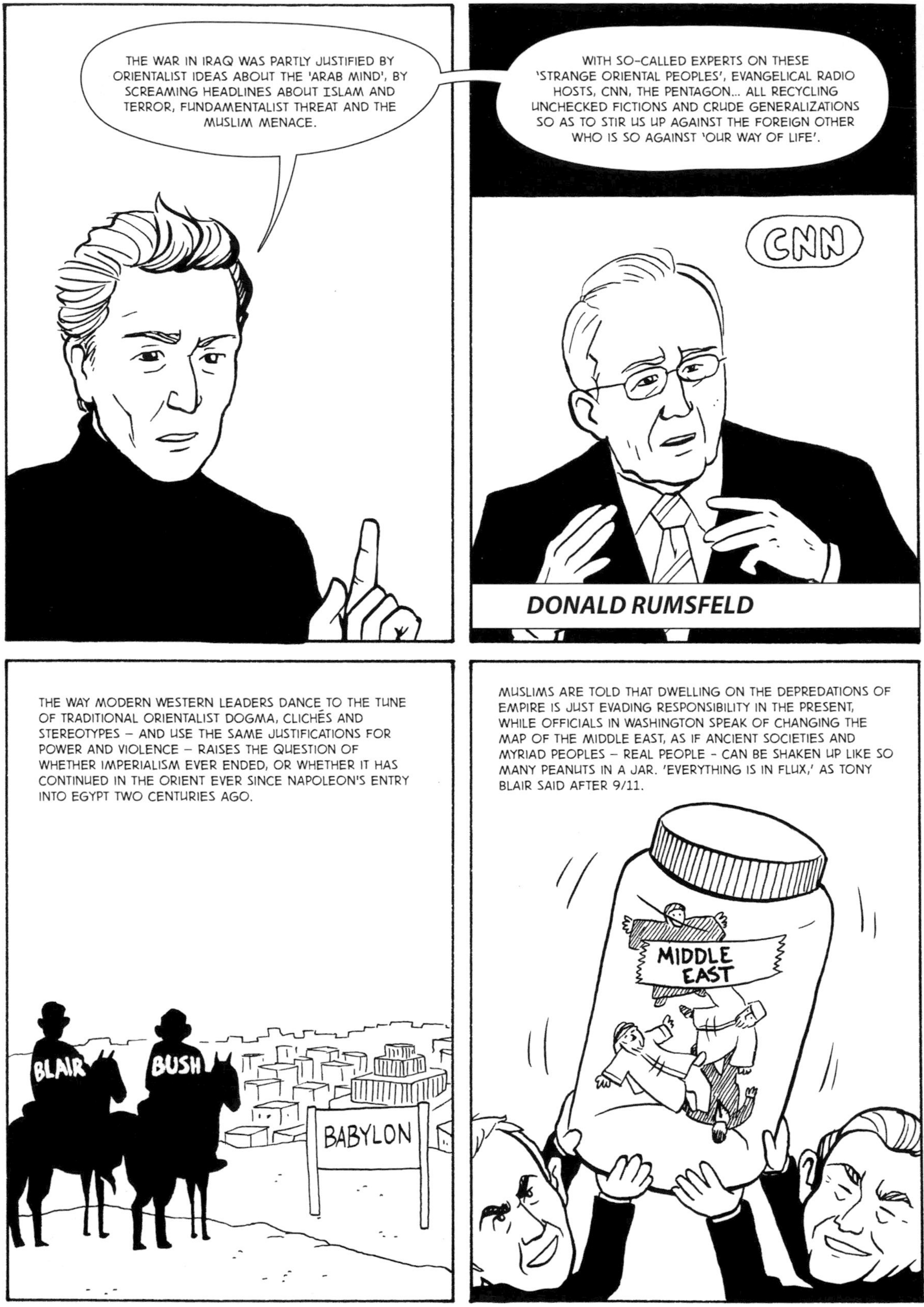
THE WAR IN IRAQ WAS PARTLY JUSTIFIED BY ORIENTALIST IDEAS ABOUT THE 'ARAB MIND', BY SCREAMING HEADLINES ABOUT ISLAM AND TERROR, FUNDAMENTALIST THREAT AND THE MUSLIM MENACE.
WITH SO-CALLED EXPERTS ON THESE 'STRANGE ORIENTAL PEOPLES', EVANGELICAL RADIO HOSTS, CNN, THE PENTAGON... ALL RECYCLING UNCHECKED FICTIONS AND CRUDE GENERALIZATIONS SO AS TO STIR US UP AGAINST THE FOREIGN OTHER WHO IS SO AGAINST 'OUR WAY OF LIFE'.
CNN
DONALD RUMSFELD
THE WAY MODERN WESTERN LEADERS DANCE TO THE TUNE OF TRADITIONAL ORIENTALIST DOGMA, CLICHÉS AND STEREOTYPES – AND USE THE SAME JUSTIFICATIONS FOR POWER AND VIOLENCE – RAISES THE QUESTION OF WHETHER IMPERIALISM EVER ENDED, OR WHETHER IT HAS CONTINUED IN THE ORIENT EVER SINCE NAPOLEON'S ENTRY INTO EGYPT TWO CENTURIES AGO.
BLAIR
BUSH
BABYLON
MUSLIMS ARE TOLD THAT DWELLING ON THE DEPREDATIONS OF EMPIRE IS JUST EVADING RESPONSIBILITY IN THE PRESENT, WHILE OFFICIALS IN WASHINGTON SPEAK OF CHANGING THE MAP OF THE MIDDLE EAST, AS IF ANCIENT SOCIETIES AND MYRIAD PEOPLES – REAL PEOPLE – CAN BE SHAKEN UP LIKE SO MANY PEANUTS IN A JAR. 'EVERYTHING IS IN FLUX,' AS TONY BLAIR SAID AFTER 9/11.
MIDDLE EAST

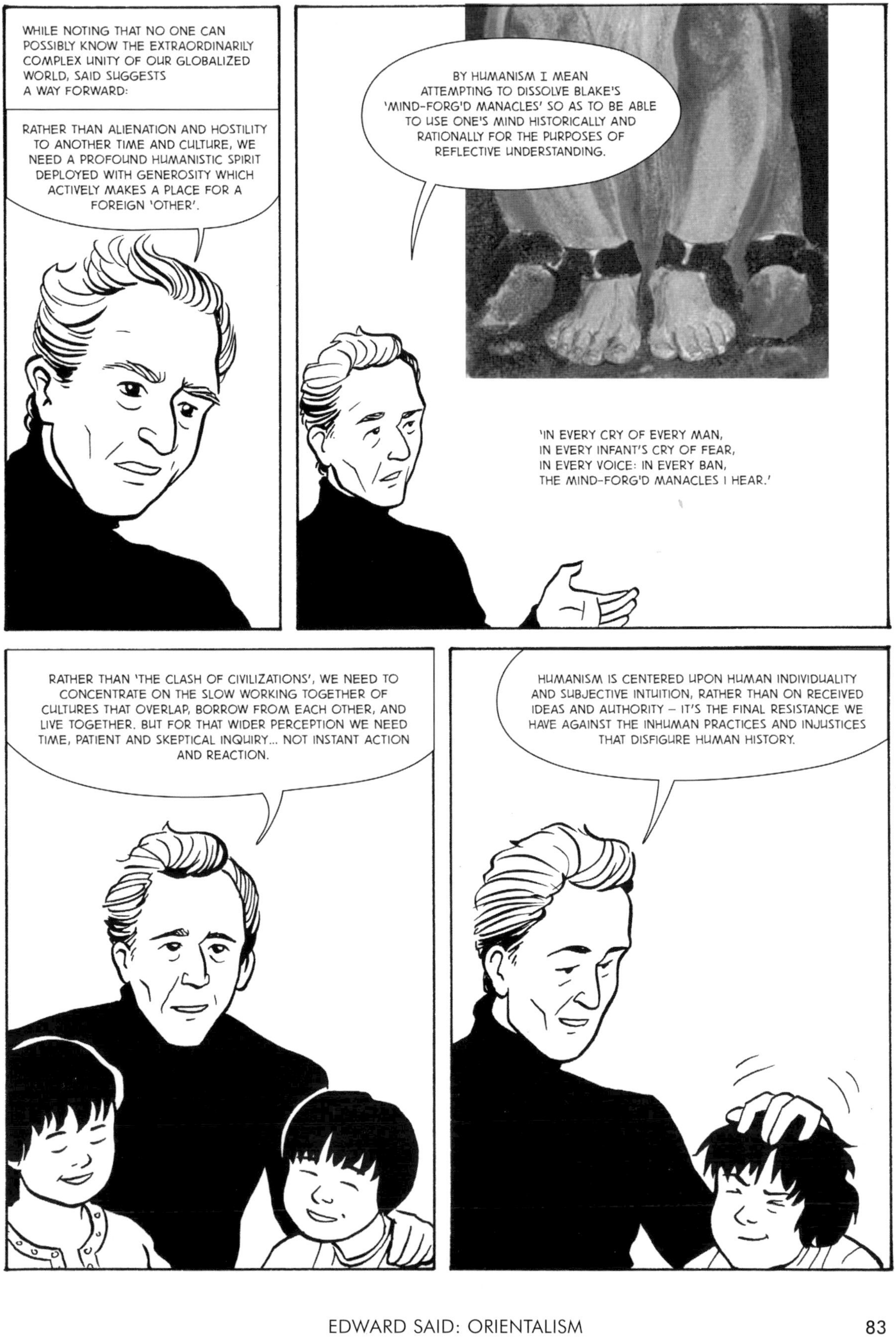
WHILE NOTING THAT NO ONE CAN POSSIBLY KNOW THE EXTRAORDINARILY COMPLEX UNITY OF OUR GLOBALIZED WORLD, SAID SUGGESTS A WAY FORWARD:
RATHER THAN ALIENATION AND HOSTILITY TO ANOTHER TIME AND CULTURE, WE NEED A PROFOUND HUMANISTIC SPIRIT DEPLOYED WITH GENEROSITY WHICH ACTIVELY MAKES A PLACE FOR A FOREIGN 'OTHER'.
BY HUMANISM I MEAN ATTEMPTING TO DISSOLVE BLAKE'S 'MIND-FORG'D MANACLES' SO AS TO BE ABLE TO USE ONE'S MIND HISTORICALLY AND RATIONALLY FOR THE PURPOSES OF REFLECTIVE UNDERSTANDING.
'IN EVERY CRY OF EVERY MAN,
IN EVERY INFANT'S CRY OF FEAR,
IN EVERY VOICE: IN EVERY BAN,
THE MIND-FORG'D MANACLES I HEAR.'
RATHER THAN 'THE CLASH OF CIVILIZATIONS', WE NEED TO CONCENTRATE ON THE SLOW WORKING TOGETHER OF CULTURES THAT OVERLAP, BORROW FROM EACH OTHER, AND LIVE TOGETHER. BUT FOR THAT WIDER PERCEPTION WE NEED TIME, PATIENT AND SKEPTICAL INQUIRY... NOT INSTANT ACTION AND REACTION.
HUMANISM IS CENTERED UPON HUMAN INDIVIDUALITY AND SUBJECTIVE INTUITION, RATHER THAN ON RECEIVED IDEAS AND AUTHORITY – IT'S THE FINAL RESISTANCE WE HAVE AGAINST THE INHUMAN PRACTICES AND INJUSTICES THAT DISFIGURE HUMAN HISTORY.

Susan Sontag

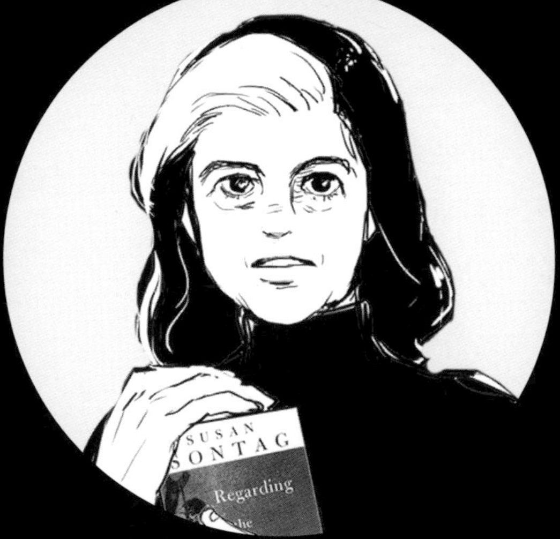
SUSAN
SONTAG
Regarding

Regarding the Pain of Others

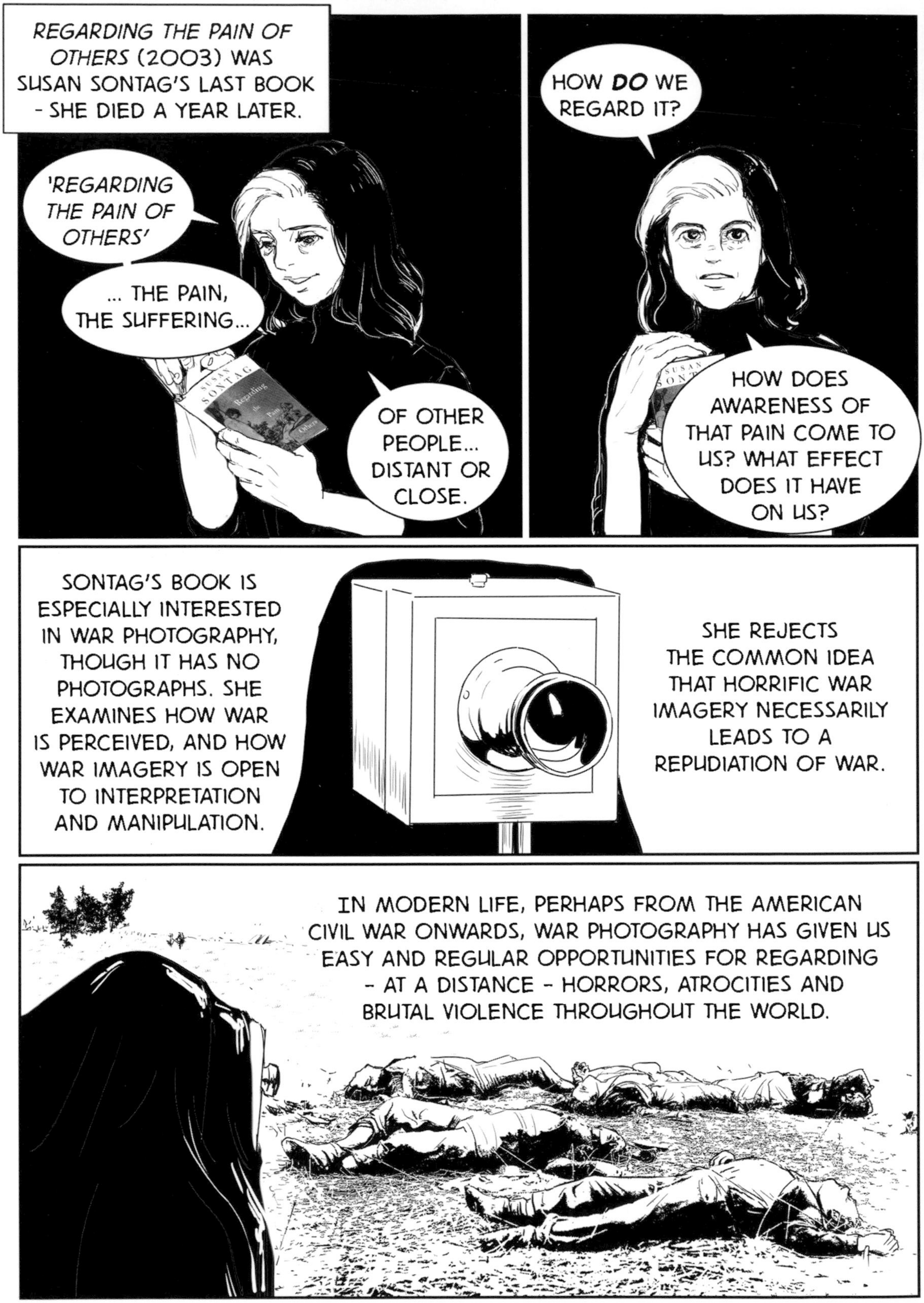
REGARDING THE PAIN OF OTHERS (2003) WAS SUSAN SONTAG'S LAST BOOK - SHE DIED A YEAR LATER.
'REGARDING THE PAIN OF OTHERS'
... THE PAIN, THE SUFFERING...
OF OTHER PEOPLE... DISTANT OR CLOSE.
HOW **DO** WE REGARD IT?
HOW DOES AWARENESS OF THAT PAIN COME TO US? WHAT EFFECT DOES IT HAVE ON US?
SONTAG'S BOOK IS ESPECIALLY INTERESTED IN WAR PHOTOGRAPHY, THOUGH IT HAS NO PHOTOGRAPHS. SHE EXAMINES HOW WAR IS PERCEIVED, AND HOW WAR IMAGERY IS OPEN TO INTERPRETATION AND MANIPULATION.
SHE REJECTS THE COMMON IDEA THAT HORRIFIC WAR IMAGERY NECESSARILY LEADS TO A REPUDIATION OF WAR.
IN MODERN LIFE, PERHAPS FROM THE AMERICAN CIVIL WAR ONWARDS, WAR PHOTOGRAPHY HAS GIVEN US EASY AND REGULAR OPPORTUNITIES FOR REGARDING - AT A DISTANCE - HORRORS, ATROCITIES AND BRUTAL VIOLENCE THROUGHOUT THE WORLD.

SONTAG TAKES AS HER STARTING POINT ONE OF THE THREE QUESTIONS CONSIDERED BY VIRGINIA WOOLF IN HER BOOK *THREE GUINEAS* (1938):

WRITTEN WHEN THE FASCISTS AND ANARCHISTS WERE CLASHING IN SPAIN, WOOLF REPLIES TO THE QUESTION ASKED BY A BARRISTER BY SAYING THAT A REALLY TRUTHFUL DIALOGUE MAY NOT BE POSSIBLE BETWEEN THEM. BECAUSE, EVEN THOUGH THEY ARE OF THE SAME CLASS, SHE IS A WOMAN AND THE BARRISTER IS A MAN.

HOW IN YOUR OPINION ARE WE TO PREVENT WAR?

MEN MAKE WAR. MOST MEN LIKE WAR, SINCE FOR MEN THERE IS 'SOME GLORY, SOME NECESSITY, SOME SATISFACTION IN FIGHTING' THAT MOST WOMEN DO NOT FEEL OR ENJOY.

YET SHE CONSIDERS THAT A SHARED 'WE' IS POSSIBLE WHEN OBSERVING THE HORRENDOUS PHOTOGRAPHS FROM SPAIN.

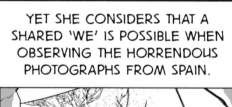

THE PICTURES THAT CAUSED US TO FEEL THE SAME EMOTIONS – YOU CALLED THEM 'HORROR AND DISGUST'; WE CALLED THEM HORROR AND DISGUST.

NO 'WE' SHOULD BE TAKEN FOR GRANTED WHEN THE SUBJECT IS LOOKING AT OTHER PEOPLE'S PAIN.

WHAT DOES IT MEAN TO CARE ABOUT THE SUFFERINGS OF PEOPLE IN FAR-OFF CONFLICTS?

WHAT ROLE DO IMAGES OF SUFFERING PLAY IN OUR LIVES?

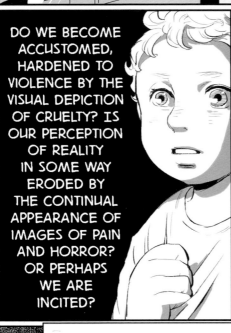

DO WE BECOME ACCUSTOMED, HARDENED TO VIOLENCE BY THE VISUAL DEPICTION OF CRUELTY? IS OUR PERCEPTION OF REALITY IN SOME WAY ERODED BY THE CONTINUAL APPEARANCE OF IMAGES OF PAIN AND HORROR? OR PERHAPS WE ARE INCITED?

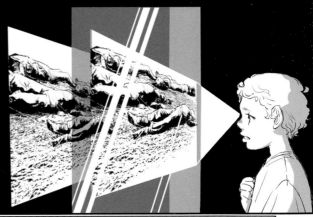

IMAGES MAKE EVENTS SEEM REAL TO US, BUT SONTAG REMINDS US THAT IMAGES ARE FIRST FILTERED THROUGH IMAGE-TAKERS, AND THAT A PHOTO'S MEANING IS BASED ON INTERPRETATION, CONTEXT AND EXPERIENCE.

SHE ALSO ATTACKS THE MEDIA WHO DENIGRATE THE REALITY OF WAR, WHO SELF-CENSOR FOR THE SAKE OF 'GOOD TASTE', AND GOVERNMENTS THAT USE IMAGES TO PUT A POSITIVE FACE ON UNPOPULAR WARS AND SUPPRESS THOSE WHO ARE CRITICAL.

PORTRAITS OF VIOLENCE

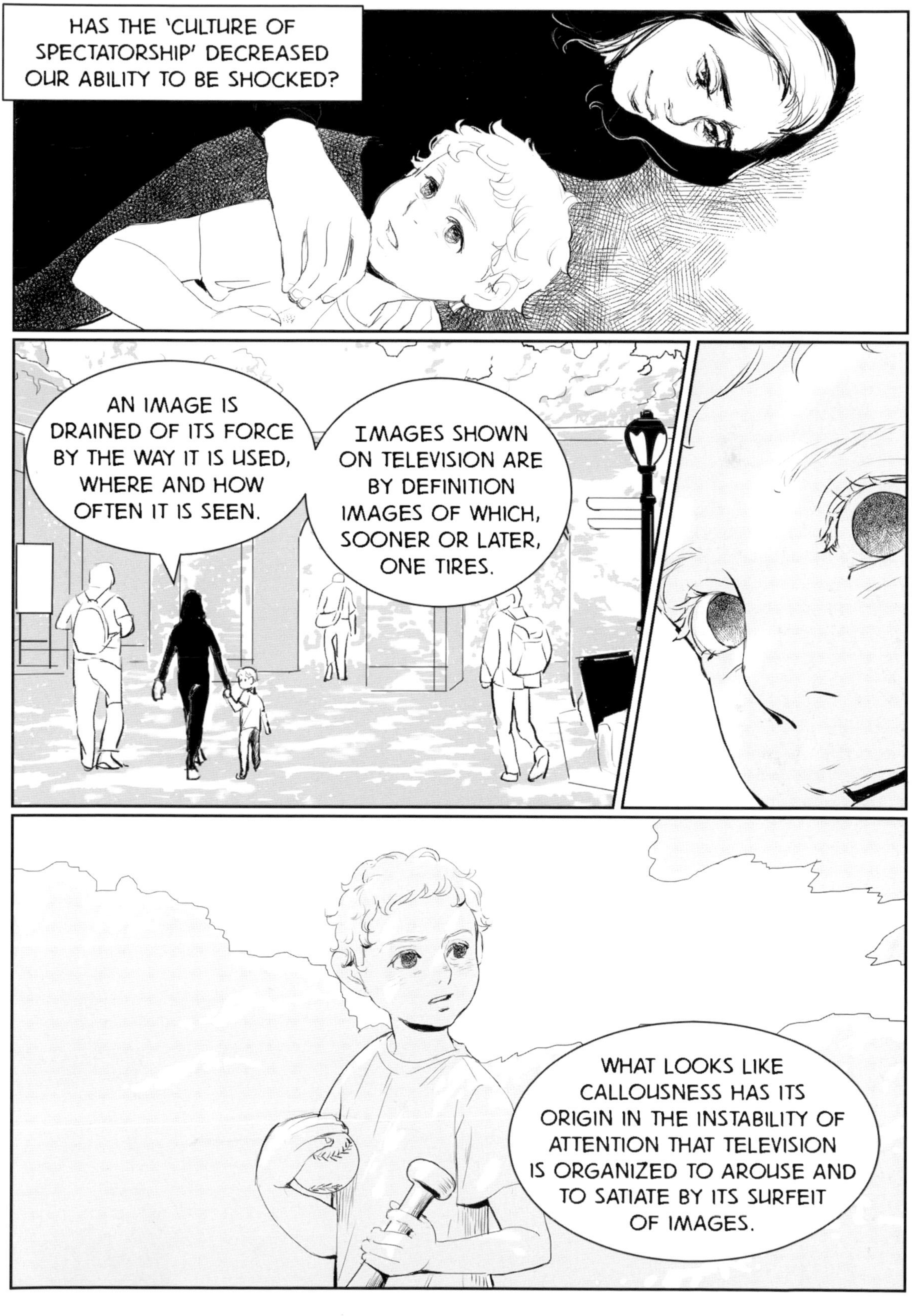
HAS THE 'CULTURE OF SPECTATORSHIP' DECREASED OUR ABILITY TO BE SHOCKED?
AN IMAGE IS DRAINED OF ITS FORCE BY THE WAY IT IS USED, WHERE AND HOW OFTEN IT IS SEEN.
IMAGES SHOWN ON TELEVISION ARE BY DEFINITION IMAGES OF WHICH, SOONER OR LATER, ONE TIRES.
WHAT LOOKS LIKE CALLOUSNESS HAS ITS ORIGIN IN THE INSTABILITY OF ATTENTION THAT TELEVISION IS ORGANIZED TO AROUSE AND TO SATIATE BY ITS SURFEIT OF IMAGES.

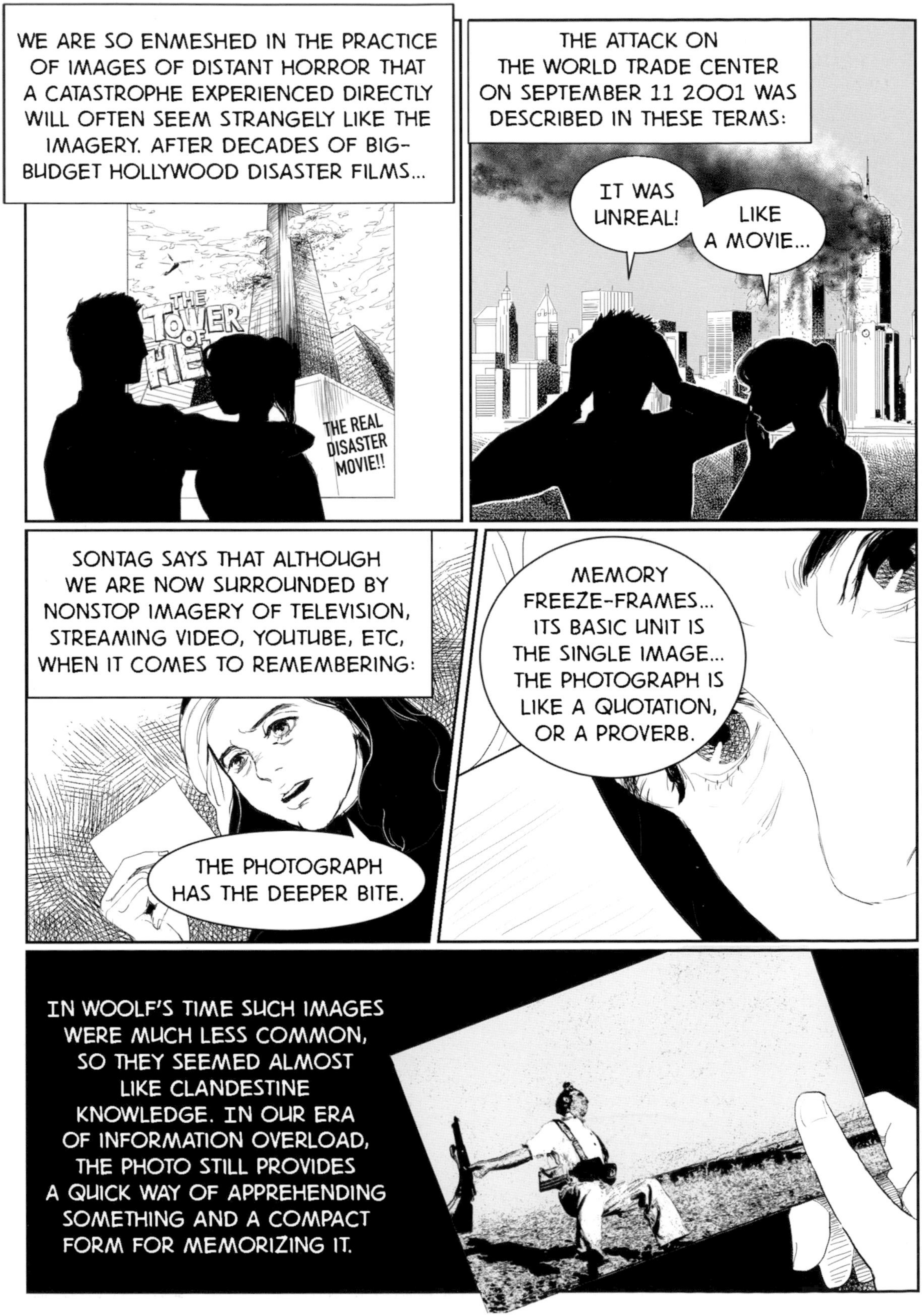
WE ARE SO ENMESHED IN THE PRACTICE OF IMAGES OF DISTANT HORROR THAT A CATASTROPHE EXPERIENCED DIRECTLY WILL OFTEN SEEM STRANGELY LIKE THE IMAGERY. AFTER DECADES OF BIG-BUDGET HOLLYWOOD DISASTER FILMS...
THE TOWER OF HE
THE REAL DISASTER MOVIE!!
THE ATTACK ON THE WORLD TRADE CENTER ON SEPTEMBER 11 2001 WAS DESCRIBED IN THESE TERMS:
IT WAS UNREAL!
LIKE A MOVIE...
SONTAG SAYS THAT ALTHOUGH WE ARE NOW SURROUNDED BY NONSTOP IMAGERY OF TELEVISION, STREAMING VIDEO, YOUTUBE, ETC, WHEN IT COMES TO REMEMBERING:
THE PHOTOGRAPH HAS THE DEEPER BITE.
MEMORY FREEZE-FRAMES... ITS BASIC UNIT IS THE SINGLE IMAGE... THE PHOTOGRAPH IS LIKE A QUOTATION, OR A PROVERB.
IN WOOLF'S TIME SUCH IMAGES WERE MUCH LESS COMMON, SO THEY SEEMED ALMOST LIKE CLANDESTINE KNOWLEDGE. IN OUR ERA OF INFORMATION OVERLOAD, THE PHOTO STILL PROVIDES A QUICK WAY OF APPREHENDING SOMETHING AND A COMPACT FORM FOR MEMORIZING IT.

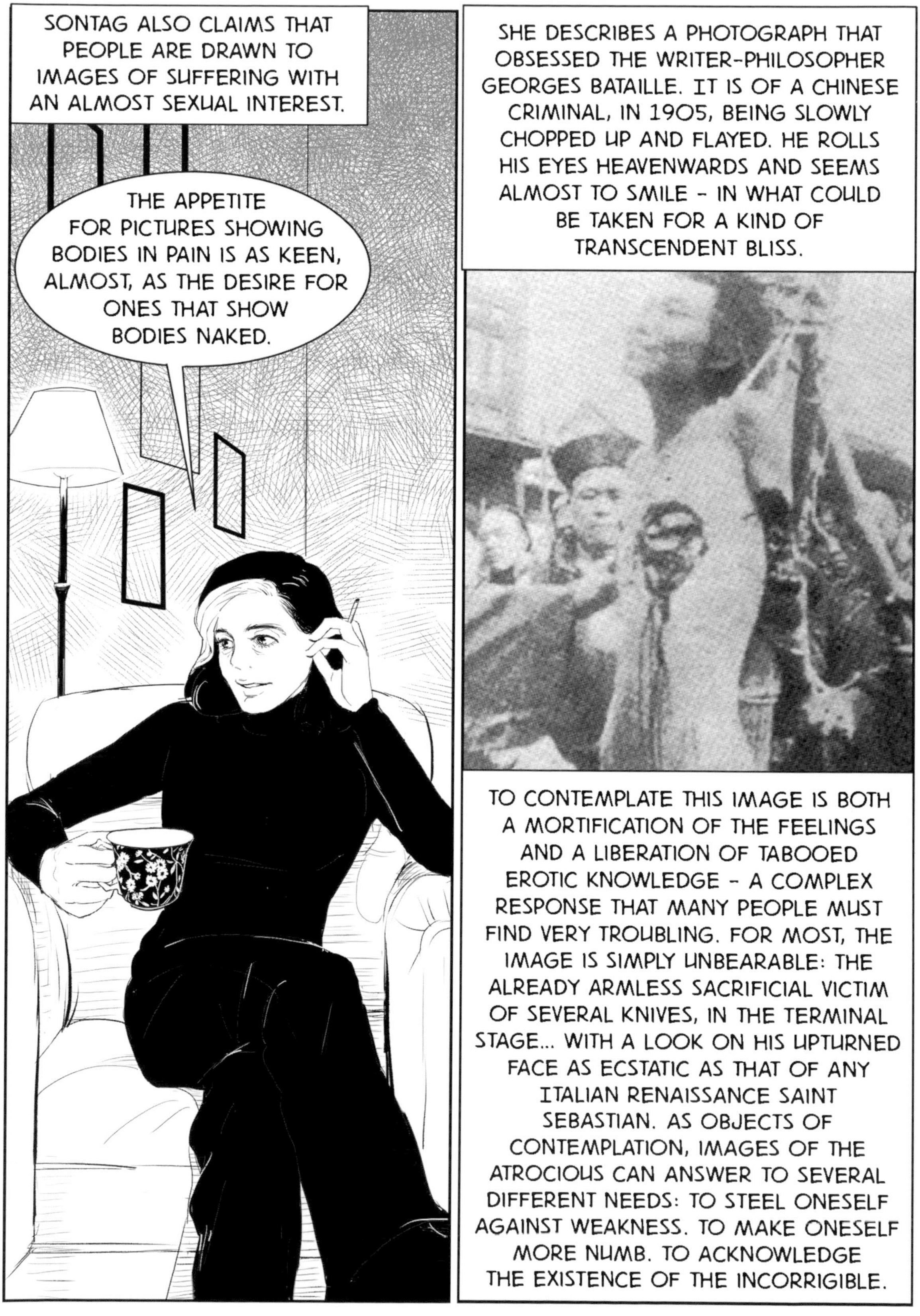
SONTAG ALSO CLAIMS THAT PEOPLE ARE DRAWN TO IMAGES OF SUFFERING WITH AN ALMOST SEXUAL INTEREST.
THE APPETITE FOR PICTURES SHOWING BODIES IN PAIN IS AS KEEN, ALMOST, AS THE DESIRE FOR ONES THAT SHOW BODIES NAKED.
SHE DESCRIBES A PHOTOGRAPH THAT OBSESSED THE WRITER-PHILOSOPHER GEORGES BATAILLE. IT IS OF A CHINESE CRIMINAL, IN 1905, BEING SLOWLY CHOPPED UP AND FLAYED. HE ROLLS HIS EYES HEAVENWARDS AND SEEMS ALMOST TO SMILE – IN WHAT COULD BE TAKEN FOR A KIND OF TRANSCENDENT BLISS.
TO CONTEMPLATE THIS IMAGE IS BOTH A MORTIFICATION OF THE FEELINGS AND A LIBERATION OF TABOOED EROTIC KNOWLEDGE – A COMPLEX RESPONSE THAT MANY PEOPLE MUST FIND VERY TROUBLING. FOR MOST, THE IMAGE IS SIMPLY UNBEARABLE: THE ALREADY ARMLESS SACRIFICIAL VICTIM OF SEVERAL KNIVES, IN THE TERMINAL STAGE... WITH A LOOK ON HIS UPTURNED FACE AS ECSTATIC AS THAT OF ANY ITALIAN RENAISSANCE SAINT SEBASTIAN. AS OBJECTS OF CONTEMPLATION, IMAGES OF THE ATROCIOUS CAN ANSWER TO SEVERAL DIFFERENT NEEDS: TO STEEL ONESELF AGAINST WEAKNESS. TO MAKE ONESELF MORE NUMB. TO ACKNOWLEDGE THE EXISTENCE OF THE INCORRIGIBLE.

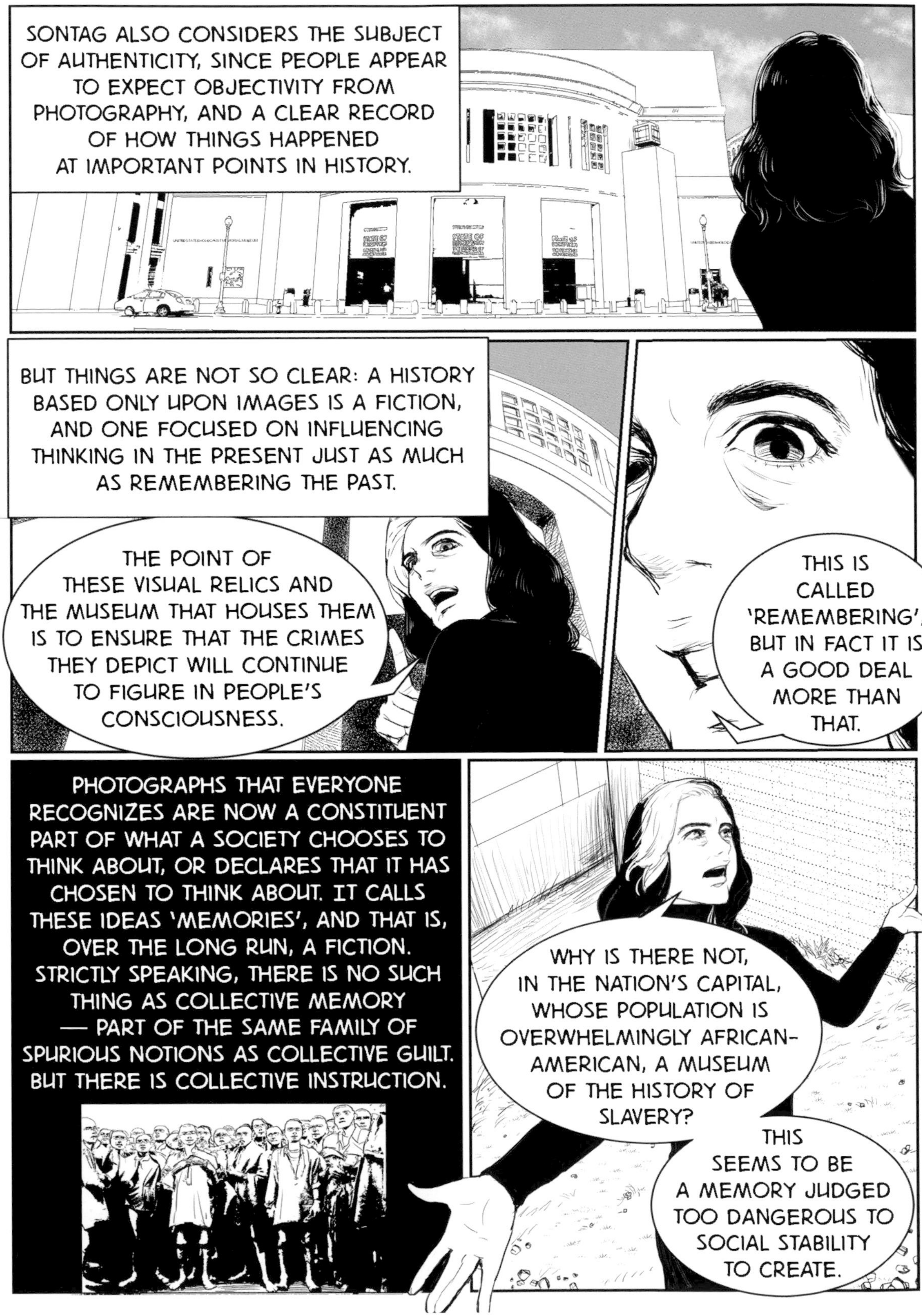

SONTAG ALSO CONSIDERS THE SUBJECT OF AUTHENTICITY, SINCE PEOPLE APPEAR TO EXPECT OBJECTIVITY FROM PHOTOGRAPHY, AND A CLEAR RECORD OF HOW THINGS HAPPENED AT IMPORTANT POINTS IN HISTORY.
BUT THINGS ARE NOT SO CLEAR: A HISTORY BASED ONLY UPON IMAGES IS A FICTION, AND ONE FOCUSED ON INFLUENCING THINKING IN THE PRESENT JUST AS MUCH AS REMEMBERING THE PAST.
THE POINT OF THESE VISUAL RELICS AND THE MUSEUM THAT HOUSES THEM IS TO ENSURE THAT THE CRIMES THEY DEPICT WILL CONTINUE TO FIGURE IN PEOPLE'S CONSCIOUSNESS.
THIS IS CALLED 'REMEMBERING', BUT IN FACT IT IS A GOOD DEAL MORE THAN THAT.
PHOTOGRAPHS THAT EVERYONE RECOGNIZES ARE NOW A CONSTITUENT PART OF WHAT A SOCIETY CHOOSES TO THINK ABOUT, OR DECLARES THAT IT HAS CHOSEN TO THINK ABOUT. IT CALLS THESE IDEAS 'MEMORIES', AND THAT IS, OVER THE LONG RUN, A FICTION. STRICTLY SPEAKING, THERE IS NO SUCH THING AS COLLECTIVE MEMORY — PART OF THE SAME FAMILY OF SPURIOUS NOTIONS AS COLLECTIVE GUILT. BUT THERE IS COLLECTIVE INSTRUCTION.
WHY IS THERE NOT, IN THE NATION'S CAPITAL, WHOSE POPULATION IS OVERWHELMINGLY AFRICAN-AMERICAN, A MUSEUM OF THE HISTORY OF SLAVERY?
THIS SEEMS TO BE A MEMORY JUDGED TOO DANGEROUS TO SOCIAL STABILITY TO CREATE.

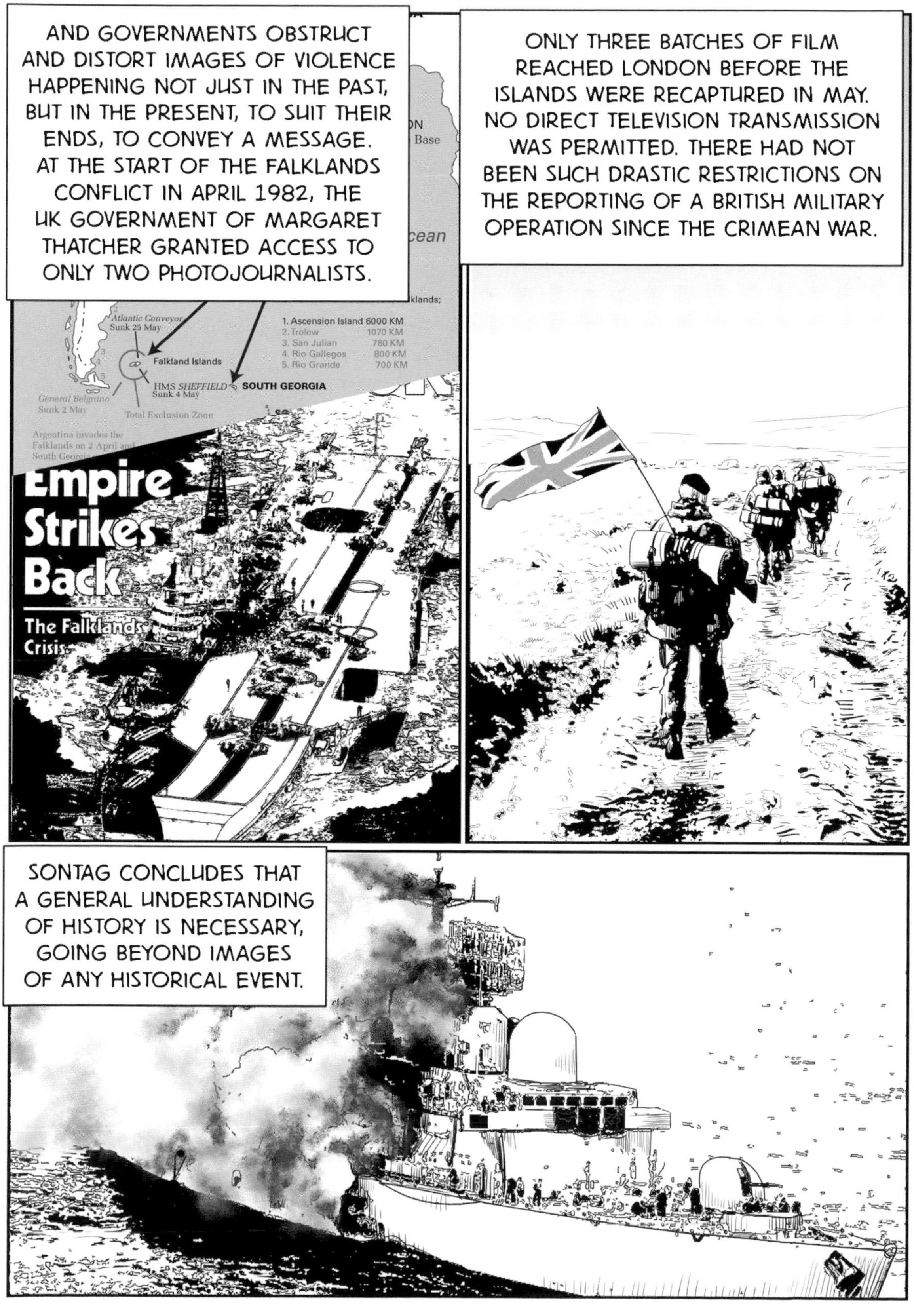
AND GOVERNMENTS OBSTRUCT AND DISTORT IMAGES OF VIOLENCE HAPPENING NOT JUST IN THE PAST, BUT IN THE PRESENT, TO SUIT THEIR ENDS, TO CONVEY A MESSAGE. AT THE START OF THE FALKLANDS CONFLICT IN APRIL 1982, THE UK GOVERNMENT OF MARGARET THATCHER GRANTED ACCESS TO ONLY TWO PHOTOJOURNALISTS.
Atlantic Conveyor Sunk 25 May
Falkland Islands
HMS SHEFFIELD Sunk 4 May
SOUTH GEORGIA
General Belgrano Sunk 2 May
Total Exclusion Zone
1. Ascension Island 6000 KM
2. Trelew 1070 KM
3. San Julian 780 KM
4. Rio Gallegos 800 KM
5. Rio Grande 700 KM
Argentina invades the
Falklands on 2 April and
Empire Strikes Back
The Falklands Crisis
ONLY THREE BATCHES OF FILM REACHED LONDON BEFORE THE ISLANDS WERE RECAPTURED IN MAY. NO DIRECT TELEVISION TRANSMISSION WAS PERMITTED. THERE HAD NOT BEEN SUCH DRASTIC RESTRICTIONS ON THE REPORTING OF A BRITISH MILITARY OPERATION SINCE THE CRIMEAN WAR.
SONTAG CONCLUDES THAT A GENERAL UNDERSTANDING OF HISTORY IS NECESSARY, GOING BEYOND IMAGES OF ANY HISTORICAL EVENT.

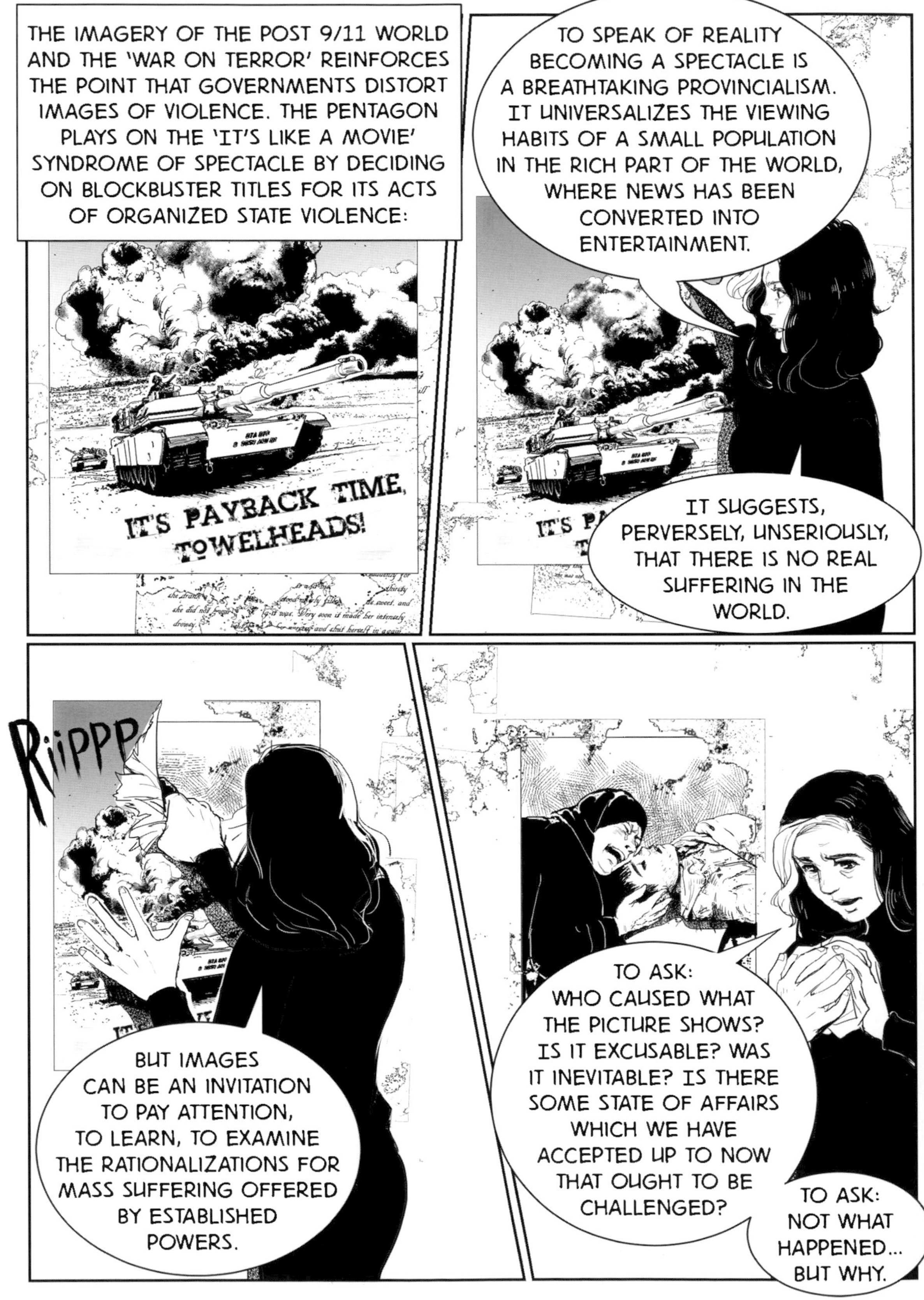
THE IMAGERY OF THE POST 9/11 WORLD AND THE 'WAR ON TERROR' REINFORCES THE POINT THAT GOVERNMENTS DISTORT IMAGES OF VIOLENCE. THE PENTAGON PLAYS ON THE 'IT'S LIKE A MOVIE' SYNDROME OF SPECTACLE BY DECIDING ON BLOCKBUSTER TITLES FOR ITS ACTS OF ORGANIZED STATE VIOLENCE:
IT'S PAYBACK TIME, TOWELHEADS!
TO SPEAK OF REALITY BECOMING A SPECTACLE IS A BREATHTAKING PROVINCIALISM. IT UNIVERSALIZES THE VIEWING HABITS OF A SMALL POPULATION IN THE RICH PART OF THE WORLD, WHERE NEWS HAS BEEN CONVERTED INTO ENTERTAINMENT.
IT SUGGESTS, PERVERSELY, UNSERIOUSLY, THAT THERE IS NO REAL SUFFERING IN THE WORLD.
RIIPPP
BUT IMAGES CAN BE AN INVITATION TO PAY ATTENTION, TO LEARN, TO EXAMINE THE RATIONALIZATIONS FOR MASS SUFFERING OFFERED BY ESTABLISHED POWERS.
TO ASK: WHO CAUSED WHAT THE PICTURE SHOWS? IS IT EXCUSABLE? WAS IT INEVITABLE? IS THERE SOME STATE OF AFFAIRS WHICH WE HAVE ACCEPTED UP TO NOW THAT OUGHT TO BE CHALLENGED?
TO ASK: NOT WHAT HAPPENED... BUT WHY.

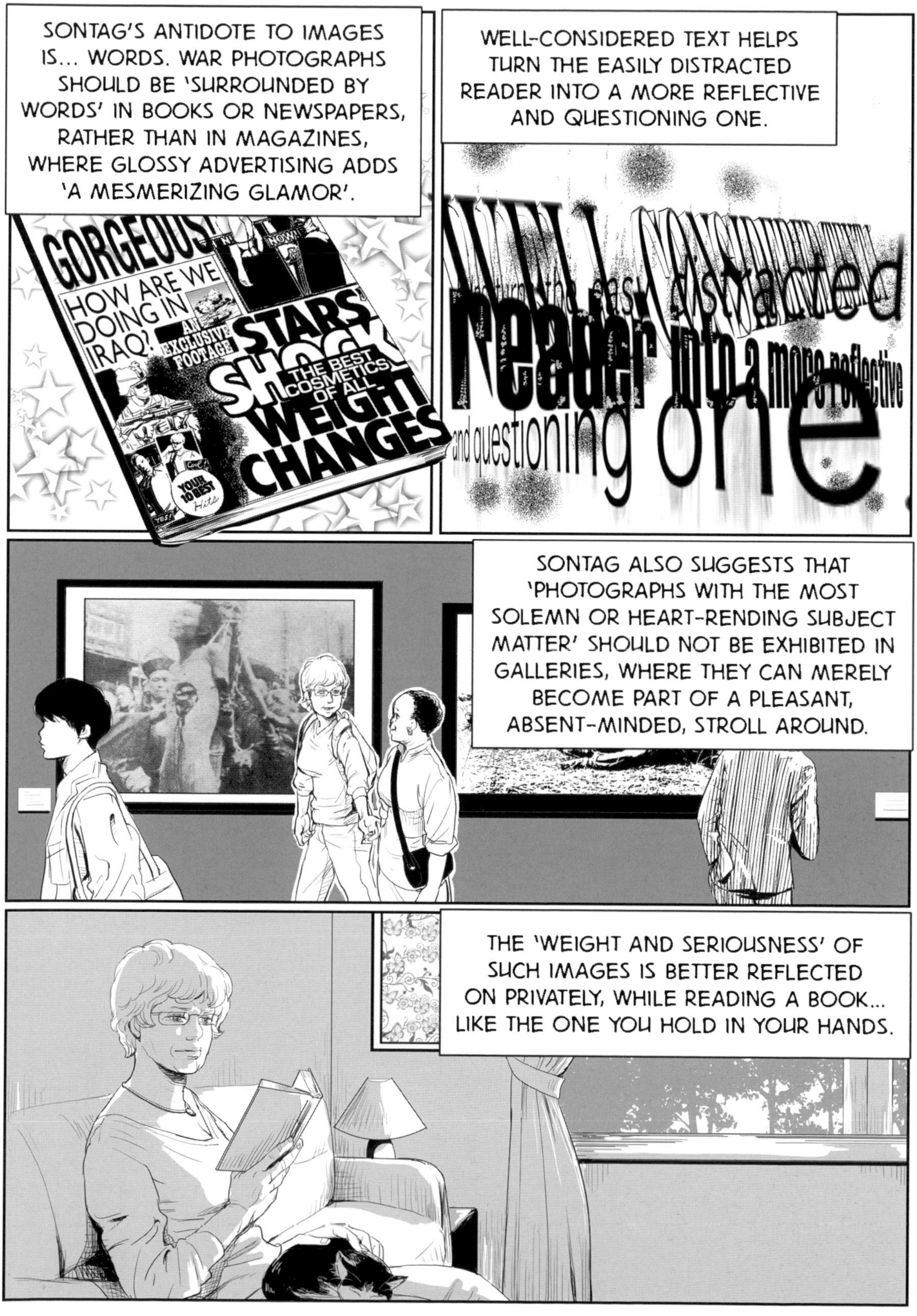
SONTAG'S ANTIDOTE TO IMAGES IS... WORDS. WAR PHOTOGRAPHS SHOULD BE 'SURROUNDED BY WORDS' IN BOOKS OR NEWSPAPERS, RATHER THAN IN MAGAZINES, WHERE GLOSSY ADVERTISING ADDS 'A MESMERIZING GLAMOR'.
GORGEOUS!
HOW ARE WE DOING IN IRAQ?
AN EXCLUSIVE FOOTAGE
STARS SHOCK
THE BEST COSMETICS OF ALL
WEIGHT CHANGES
YOUR 10 BEST Hits
WELL-CONSIDERED TEXT HELPS TURN THE EASILY DISTRACTED READER INTO A MORE REFLECTIVE AND QUESTIONING ONE.
distracted
reader into a more reflective
and questioning one.
SONTAG ALSO SUGGESTS THAT 'PHOTOGRAPHS WITH THE MOST SOLEMN OR HEART-RENDING SUBJECT MATTER' SHOULD NOT BE EXHIBITED IN GALLERIES, WHERE THEY CAN MERELY BECOME PART OF A PLEASANT, ABSENT-MINDED, STROLL AROUND.
THE 'WEIGHT AND SERIOUSNESS' OF SUCH IMAGES IS BETTER REFLECTED ON PRIVATELY, WHILE READING A BOOK... LIKE THE ONE YOU HOLD IN YOUR HANDS.

Noam Chomsky

Manufacturing
Consent

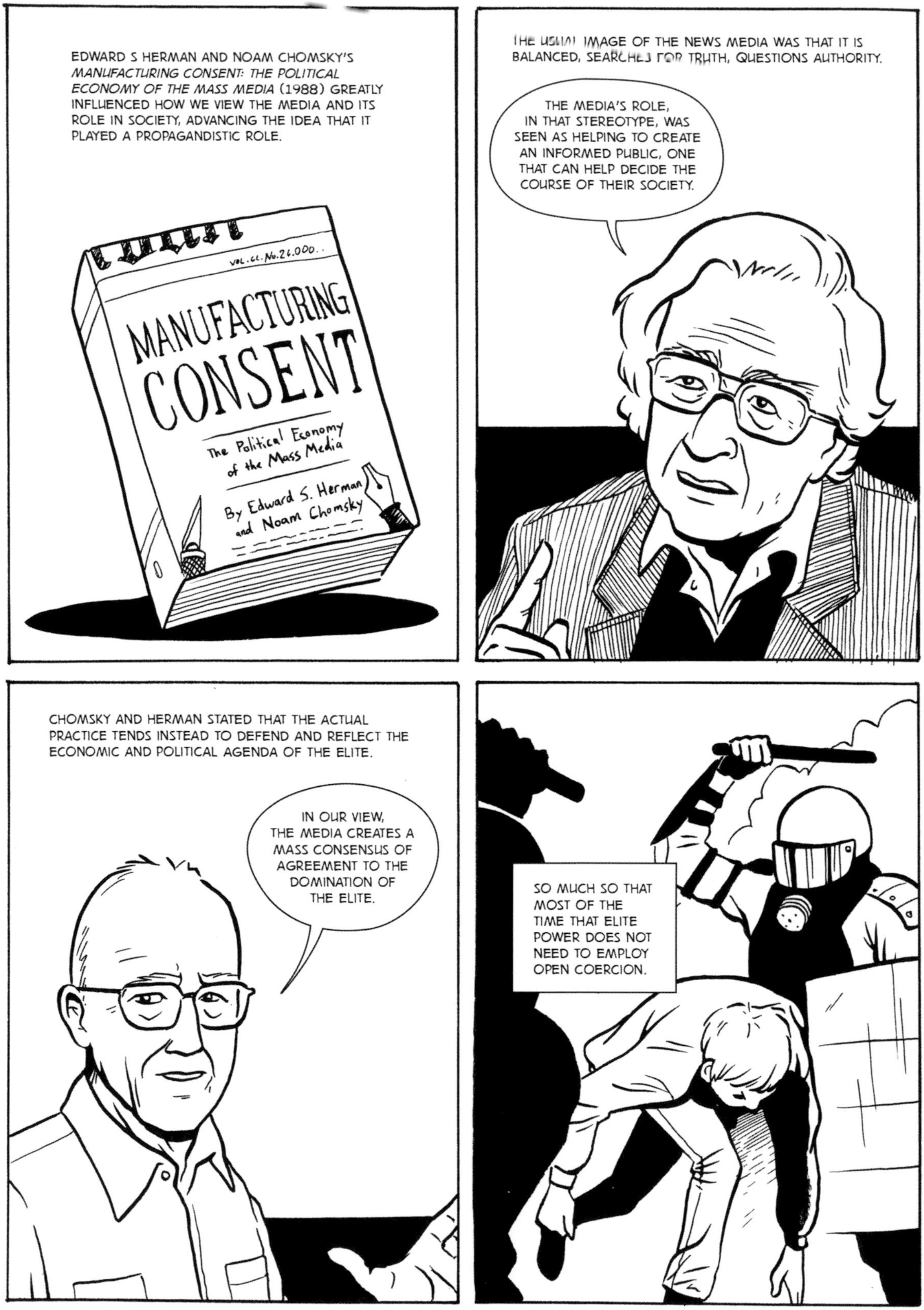
EDWARD S HERMAN AND NOAM CHOMSKY'S *MANUFACTURING CONSENT: THE POLITICAL ECONOMY OF THE MASS MEDIA* (1988) GREATLY INFLUENCED HOW WE VIEW THE MEDIA AND ITS ROLE IN SOCIETY, ADVANCING THE IDEA THAT IT PLAYED A PROPAGANDISTIC ROLE.
VOL. CC. No. 26.000.
MANUFACTURING CONSENT
The Political Economy of the Mass Media
By Edward S. Herman and Noam Chomsky
THE USUAL IMAGE OF THE NEWS MEDIA WAS THAT IT IS BALANCED, SEARCHES FOR TRUTH, QUESTIONS AUTHORITY.
THE MEDIA'S ROLE, IN THAT STEREOTYPE, WAS SEEN AS HELPING TO CREATE AN INFORMED PUBLIC, ONE THAT CAN HELP DECIDE THE COURSE OF THEIR SOCIETY.
CHOMSKY AND HERMAN STATED THAT THE ACTUAL PRACTICE TENDS INSTEAD TO DEFEND AND REFLECT THE ECONOMIC AND POLITICAL AGENDA OF THE ELITE.
IN OUR VIEW, THE MEDIA CREATES A MASS CONSENSUS OF AGREEMENT TO THE DOMINATION OF THE ELITE.
SO MUCH SO THAT MOST OF THE TIME THAT ELITE POWER DOES NOT NEED TO EMPLOY OPEN COERCION.

MANY PEOPLE, ESPECIALLY RIGHTWINGERS, THINK THE MEDIA ACTUALLY HAS LIBERAL BIAS. WHAT ABOUT THAT?

IT'S USEFUL TO THE ELITE THAT PEOPLE THINK THAT — AS IT MAKES SOCIETY SEEM FAIR, BALANCED, WITH A VOICE FOR ALTERNATIVES. BUT THE ACTUAL PRACTICE IS FAR FROM THAT.

MAINSTREAM MEDIA MAY SOMETIMES GIVE A LIBERAL SLANT ON WHAT THE DOMINANT ELITE IS DOING, BUT THEY WILL NOT QUESTION THE BASIC NATURE OF THAT DOMINATION OR CONSIDER ALTERNATIVES.

THIS MODEL OF 'DOMINATION BEHIND A FAÇADE OF FREEDOM' WORKS BETTER FOR THE ELITE THAN THE OVERT 'IN YOUR FACE DOMINATION' OF PLACES LIKE NAZI GERMANY.

I THINK ANY DICTATOR WOULD ADMIRE THE UNIFORMITY AND OBEDIENCE OF THE U.S. MEDIA.

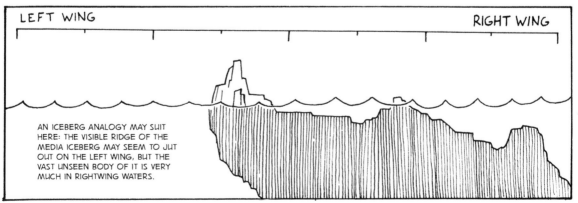

LEFT WING

RIGHT WING

AN ICEBERG ANALOGY MAY SUIT HERE: THE VISIBLE RIDGE OF THE MEDIA ICEBERG MAY SEEM TO JUT OUT ON THE LEFT WING, BUT THE VAST UNSEEN BODY OF IT IS VERY MUCH IN RIGHTWING WATERS.

THIS INSULTS THE INTELLIGENCE OF THE READER. THERE IS NO HIDDEN GROUP OF PEOPLE MANIPULATING THE MEDIA.

THOSE WORKING IN THE MEDIA ARE OFTEN WELL MEANING, AND THINK THEMSELVES OBJECTIVE, OR FREE FROM ELITE INTERFERENCE. BUT THEY OPERATE WITHIN A FRAMEWORK THAT CONSTRAINS THEM.

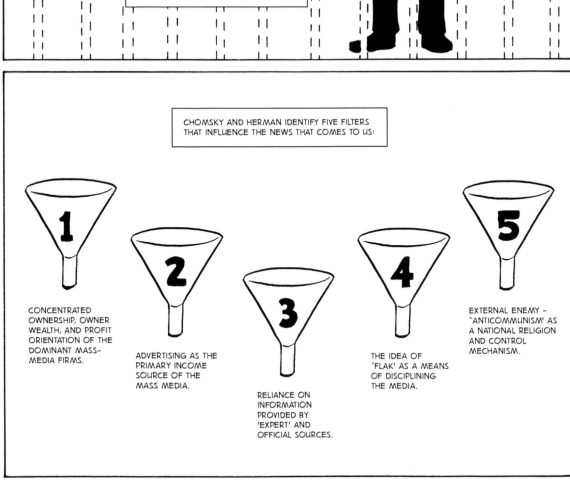

CHOMSKY AND HERMAN IDENTIFY FIVE FILTERS THAT INFLUENCE THE NEWS THAT COMES TO US:

1 CONCENTRATED OWNERSHIP, OWNER WEALTH, AND PROFIT ORIENTATION OF THE DOMINANT MASS-MEDIA FIRMS.

2 ADVERTISING AS THE PRIMARY INCOME SOURCE OF THE MASS MEDIA.

3 RELIANCE ON INFORMATION PROVIDED BY 'EXPERT' AND OFFICIAL SOURCES.

4 THE IDEA OF `FLAK' AS A MEANS OF DISCIPLINING THE MEDIA.

5 EXTERNAL ENEMY – `ANTICOMMUNISM' AS A NATIONAL RELIGION AND CONTROL MECHANISM.

PORTRAITS OF VIOLENCE

AS TO THE FIRST: GIVEN THAT BIG CORPORATE MEDIA GROUPS SHARE COMMON ECONOMIC AND POWER INTERESTS WITH OTHER ELITE GROUPS, IT BENEFITS THEM TO HELP MAINTAIN AN ECONOMIC AND POLITICAL CLIMATE THAT IS CONDUCIVE TO CONTINUING THEIR PROFIT AND POWER. WHY, THEN, IN THEIR NEWSPAPERS AND TV NEWS, WOULD THEY BE CRITICAL OF POLICIES THAT DIRECTLY BENEFIT THEM?

THE POWERFUL OWNERSHIP WEBS ARE FACTUAL:

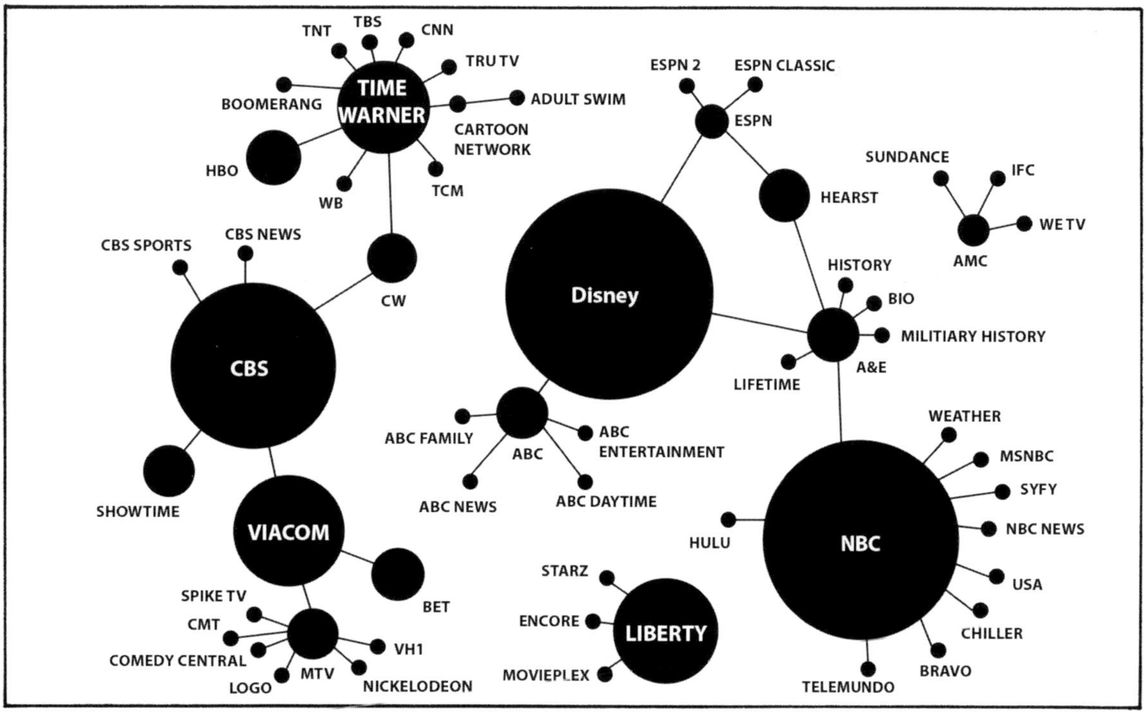
TIME WARNER
TNT
TBS
CNN
TRU TV
ADULT SWIM
CARTOON NETWORK
TCM
WB
HBO
BOOMERANG
CW
CBS
CBS SPORTS
CBS NEWS
SHOWTIME
VIACOM
BET
MTV
SPIKE TV
CMT
COMEDY CENTRAL
LOGO
VH1
NICKELODEON
Disney
ESPN
ESPN 2
ESPN CLASSIC
HEARST
ABC
ABC FAMILY
ABC ENTERTAINMENT
ABC NEWS
ABC DAYTIME
A&E
HISTORY
BIO
MILITIARY HISTORY
LIFETIME
AMC
SUNDANCE
IFC
WE TV
NBC
WEATHER
MSNBC
SYFY
NBC NEWS
USA
CHILLER
BRAVO
TELEMUNDO
HULU
LIBERTY
STARZ
ENCORE
MOVIEPLEX

AND SINCE THE 1980S THIS HAS BECOME EVEN MORE CONCENTRATED TO JUST A FEW GIANT CORPORATIONS:

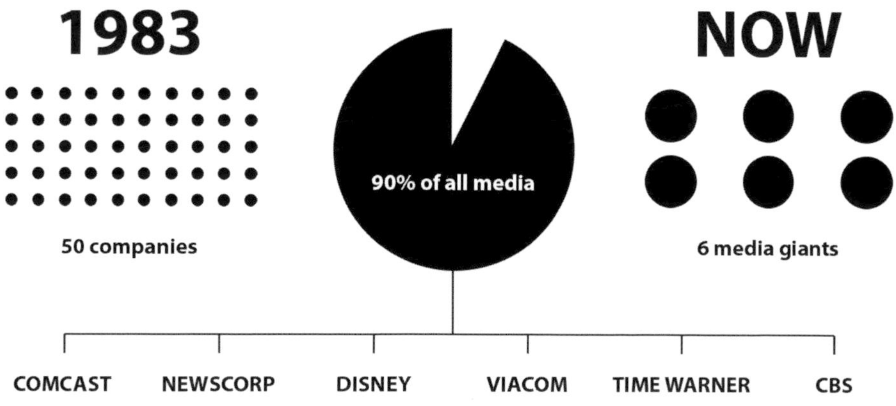
1983
50 companies
90% of all media
NOW
6 media giants
COMCAST
NEWSCORP
DISNEY
VIACOM
TIME WARNER
CBS

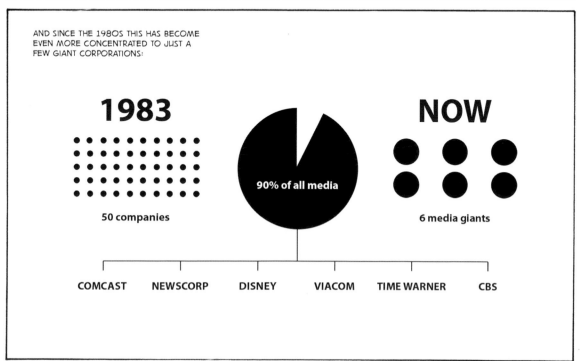

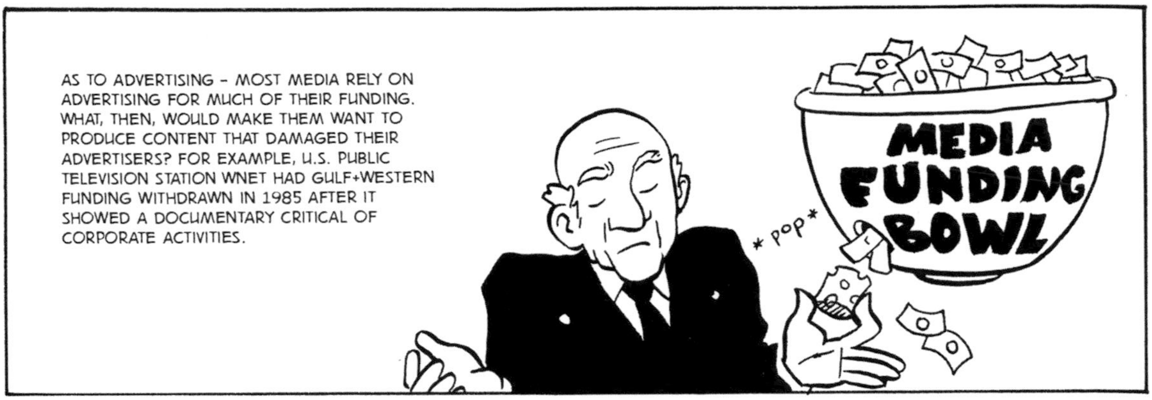
AS TO ADVERTISING - MOST MEDIA RELY ON ADVERTISING FOR MUCH OF THEIR FUNDING. WHAT, THEN, WOULD MAKE THEM WANT TO PRODUCE CONTENT THAT DAMAGED THEIR ADVERTISERS? FOR EXAMPLE, U.S. PUBLIC TELEVISION STATION WNET HAD GULF+WESTERN FUNDING WITHDRAWN IN 1985 AFTER IT SHOWED A DOCUMENTARY CRITICAL OF CORPORATE ACTIVITIES.
MEDIA FUNDING BOWL
pop

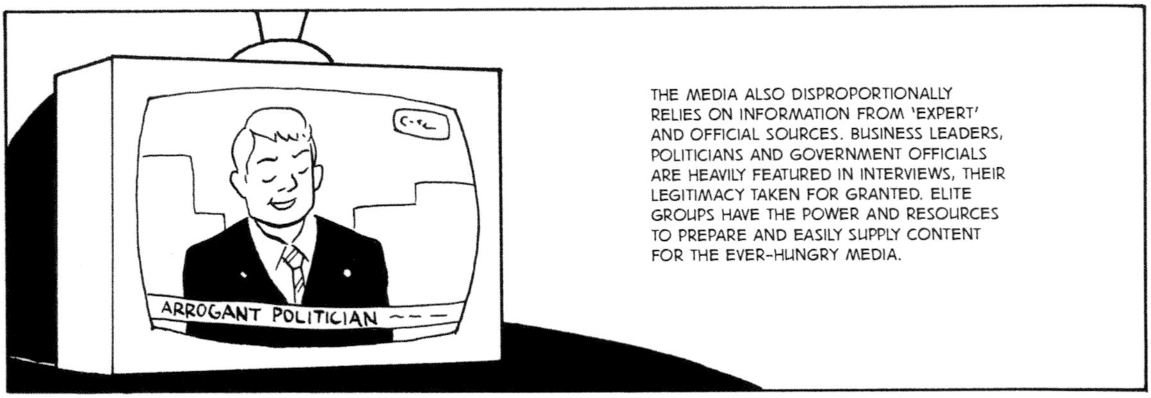
ARROGANT POLITICIAN
THE MEDIA ALSO DISPROPORTIONALLY RELIES ON INFORMATION FROM 'EXPERT' AND OFFICIAL SOURCES. BUSINESS LEADERS, POLITICIANS AND GOVERNMENT OFFICIALS ARE HEAVILY FEATURED IN INTERVIEWS, THEIR LEGITIMACY TAKEN FOR GRANTED. ELITE GROUPS HAVE THE POWER AND RESOURCES TO PREPARE AND EASILY SUPPLY CONTENT FOR THE EVER-HUNGRY MEDIA.

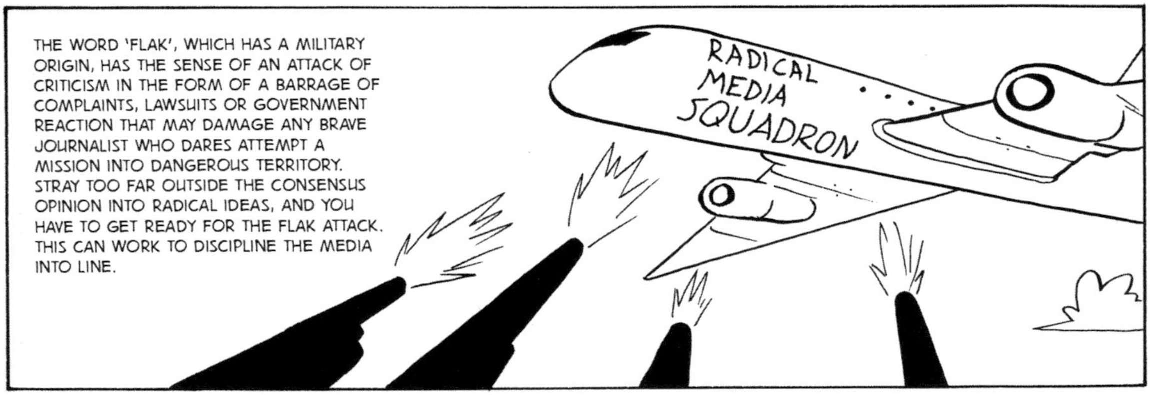
THE WORD 'FLAK', WHICH HAS A MILITARY ORIGIN, HAS THE SENSE OF AN ATTACK OF CRITICISM IN THE FORM OF A BARRAGE OF COMPLAINTS, LAWSUITS OR GOVERNMENT REACTION THAT MAY DAMAGE ANY BRAVE JOURNALIST WHO DARES ATTEMPT A MISSION INTO DANGEROUS TERRITORY. STRAY TOO FAR OUTSIDE THE CONSENSUS OPINION INTO RADICAL IDEAS, AND YOU HAVE TO GET READY FOR THE FLAK ATTACK. THIS CAN WORK TO DISCIPLINE THE MEDIA INTO LINE.
RADICAL MEDIA SQUADRON

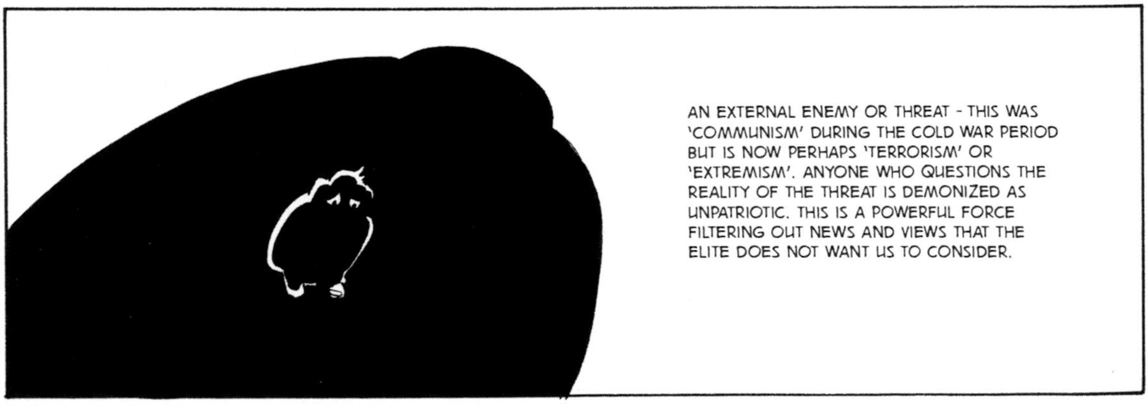
AN EXTERNAL ENEMY OR THREAT - THIS WAS 'COMMUNISM' DURING THE COLD WAR PERIOD BUT IS NOW PERHAPS 'TERRORISM' OR 'EXTREMISM'. ANYONE WHO QUESTIONS THE REALITY OF THE THREAT IS DEMONIZED AS UNPATRIOTIC. THIS IS A POWERFUL FORCE FILTERING OUT NEWS AND VIEWS THAT THE ELITE DOES NOT WANT US TO CONSIDER.

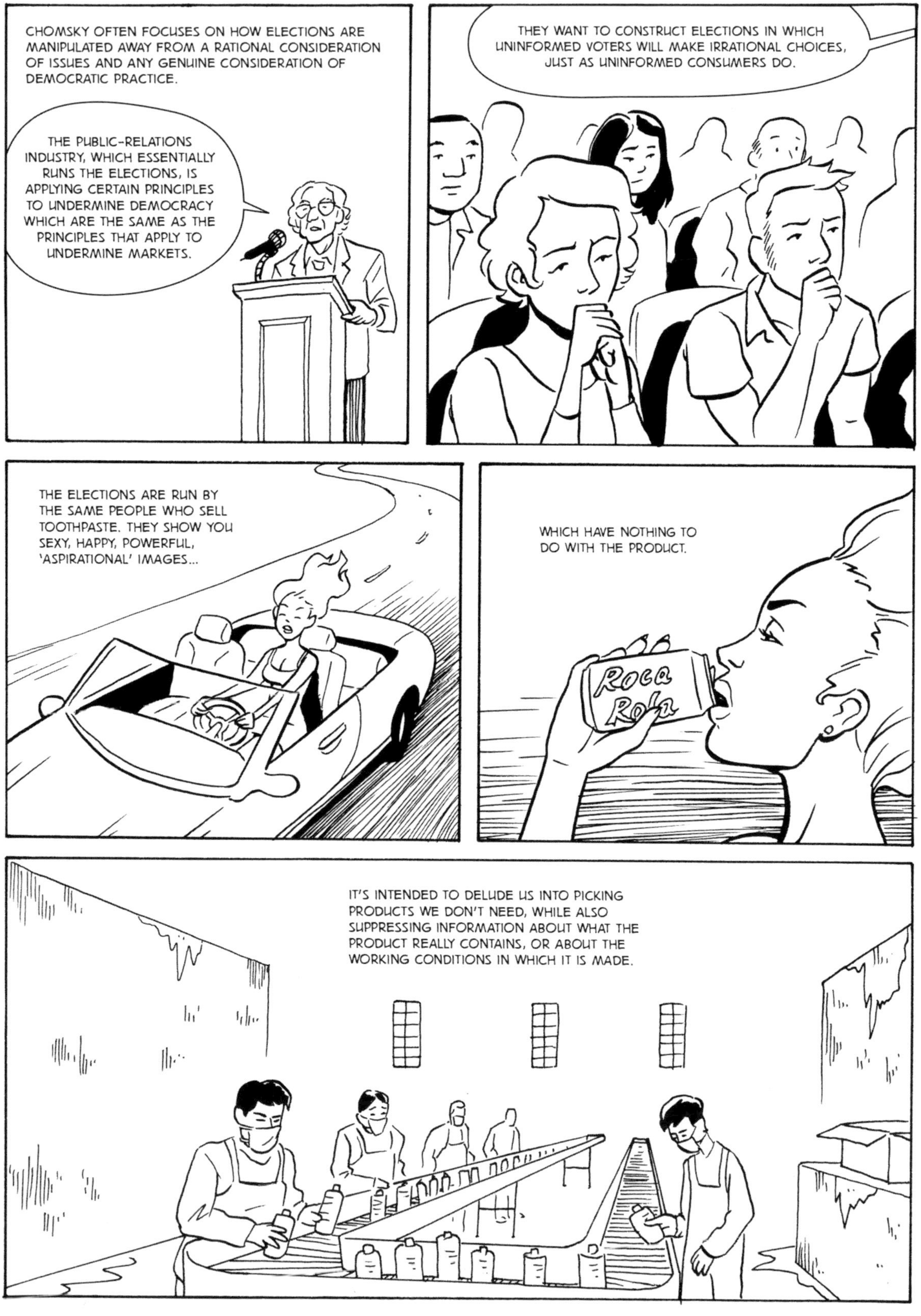
CHOMSKY OFTEN FOCUSES ON HOW ELECTIONS ARE MANIPULATED AWAY FROM A RATIONAL CONSIDERATION OF ISSUES AND ANY GENUINE CONSIDERATION OF DEMOCRATIC PRACTICE.
THE PUBLIC-RELATIONS INDUSTRY, WHICH ESSENTIALLY RUNS THE ELECTIONS, IS APPLYING CERTAIN PRINCIPLES TO UNDERMINE DEMOCRACY WHICH ARE THE SAME AS THE PRINCIPLES THAT APPLY TO UNDERMINE MARKETS.
THEY WANT TO CONSTRUCT ELECTIONS IN WHICH UNINFORMED VOTERS WILL MAKE IRRATIONAL CHOICES, JUST AS UNINFORMED CONSUMERS DO.
THE ELECTIONS ARE RUN BY THE SAME PEOPLE WHO SELL TOOTHPASTE. THEY SHOW YOU SEXY, HAPPY, POWERFUL, 'ASPIRATIONAL' IMAGES...
WHICH HAVE NOTHING TO DO WITH THE PRODUCT.
Roca Rola
IT'S INTENDED TO DELUDE US INTO PICKING PRODUCTS WE DON'T NEED, WHILE ALSO SUPPRESSING INFORMATION ABOUT WHAT THE PRODUCT REALLY CONTAINS, OR ABOUT THE WORKING CONDITIONS IN WHICH IT IS MADE.

UNINFORMED CONSUMERS AND UNINFORMED VOTERS LEAD TO THE ELITE ALWAYS GETTING ITS WAY. A PRIME EXAMPLE WAS THE FRAUDULENT U.S. PRESIDENTIAL ELECTION OF GEORGE W BUSH IN 2000 WHERE, DESPITE THE EVIDENT VOTE RIGGING IN MIAMI WHICH MAY HAVE PUT THE WRONG PERSON INTO THE WHITE HOUSE, THE MEDIA WAS SOON CRYING OUT:

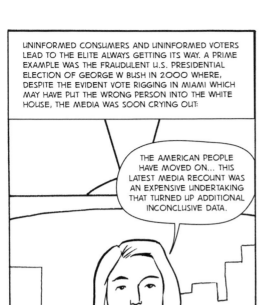

THE AMERICAN PEOPLE HAVE MOVED ON... THIS LATEST MEDIA RECOUNT WAS AN EXPENSIVE UNDERTAKING THAT TURNED UP ADDITIONAL INCONCLUSIVE DATA.

BUSH SPOKESWOMAN NICOLLE DEVENISH

KATIE BAUR, YOU ARE A SPOKESWOMAN FOR GOVERNOR JEB BUSH, WHO WAS CHAIRMAN OF HIS BROTHER'S FLORIDA CAMPAIGN. WHAT SAY YOU TO THIS?

TWO WORDS, JOHNNY: 'WHO CARES?'

THE AMERICAN PEOPLE ARE MORE CONCERNED ABOUT OUR NATION'S SECURITY AND ECONOMY THAN ANY UMPTEENTH RECOUNT OF AN ELECTION THAT WAS DECIDED OVER A YEAR AGO.

WHO CARES ABOUT VOTER FRAUD? WHO CARES ABOUT A CORRUPT DEMOCRACY? WHO CARES ABOUT ACCOUNTABLE GOVERNMENT? IF THE ELITE AND ITS MASS MEDIA GET THEIR WAY, THE ANSWER WILL BE: NOT ENOUGH OF US.

IN THE BUILD-UP TO THE 2003 INVASION OF IRAQ WE SAW SIMILAR TECHNIQUES OF DISTORTION AND DISTRACTION AND HOW THE U.S. AND UK ELITES OVERCAME THE CONSIDERABLE RELUCTANCE TO GO TO WAR ON THE PART OF MOST OF THE POPULATION OF THOSE COUNTRIES – THE SO-CALLED 'VIETNAM SYNDROME' (AS IF AN AVERSION TO KILLING FELLOW HUMANS WERE SOME KIND OF DISEASE).

WHAT'S WRONG WITH YOU, BOY? DON'T YOU WANT TO KILL INNOCENT PEOPLE THAT HAVE NEVER DONE YOU ANY HARM?

YET PROGRAMS LIKE CNN'S 'THE SITUATION ROOM' FOCUS ON TECHNO-LOGICAL SUPREMACY AND PRECISION BOMBING. THEY USE BUZZWORDS LIKE 'COLLATERAL DAMAGE' THAT DISTRACT US FROM THE FACT THAT MILITARY ACTIONS RESULT IN THE DEATHS OF REAL, FLESH-AND-BLOOD PEOPLE – ORDINARY FOLK MUCH LIKE US, WITH HOMES AND FAMILIES.

CONCERN FOR FELLOW HUMANS

PORTRAITS OF VIOLENCE

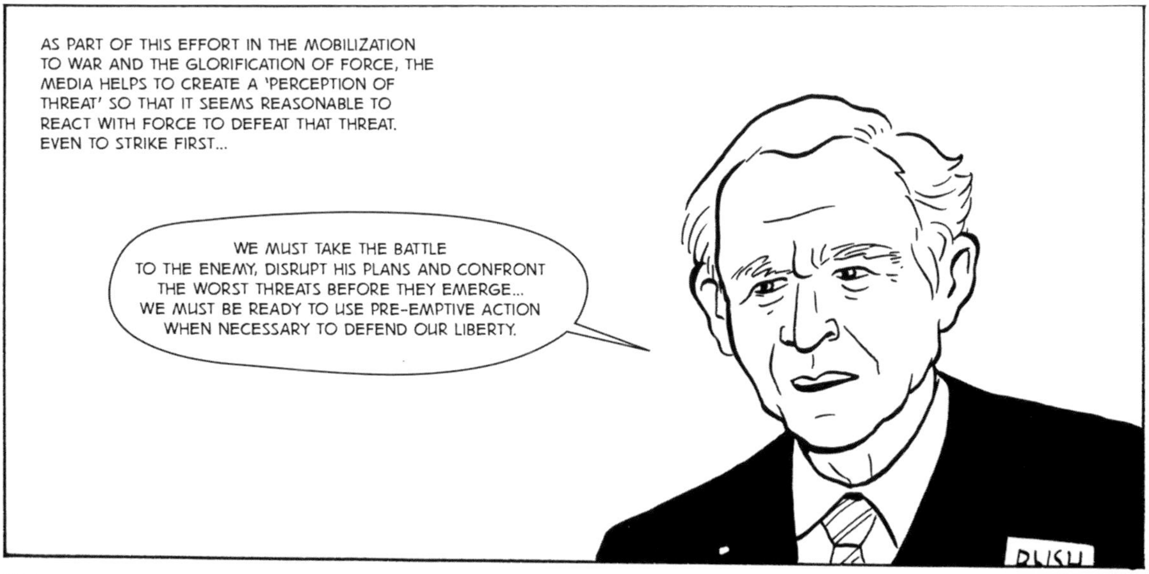
AS PART OF THIS EFFORT IN THE MOBILIZATION TO WAR AND THE GLORIFICATION OF FORCE, THE MEDIA HELPS TO CREATE A 'PERCEPTION OF THREAT' SO THAT IT SEEMS REASONABLE TO REACT WITH FORCE TO DEFEAT THAT THREAT. EVEN TO STRIKE FIRST...
WE MUST TAKE THE BATTLE TO THE ENEMY, DISRUPT HIS PLANS AND CONFRONT THE WORST THREATS BEFORE THEY EMERGE... WE MUST BE READY TO USE PRE-EMPTIVE ACTION WHEN NECESSARY TO DEFEND OUR LIBERTY.

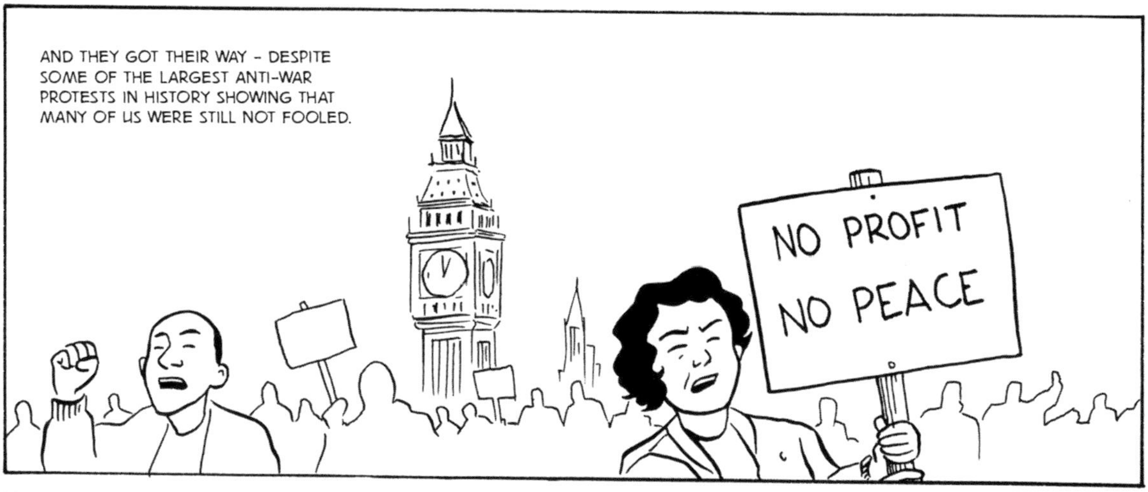
AND THEY GOT THEIR WAY - DESPITE SOME OF THE LARGEST ANTI-WAR PROTESTS IN HISTORY SHOWING THAT MANY OF US WERE STILL NOT FOOLED.
NO PROFIT NO PEACE

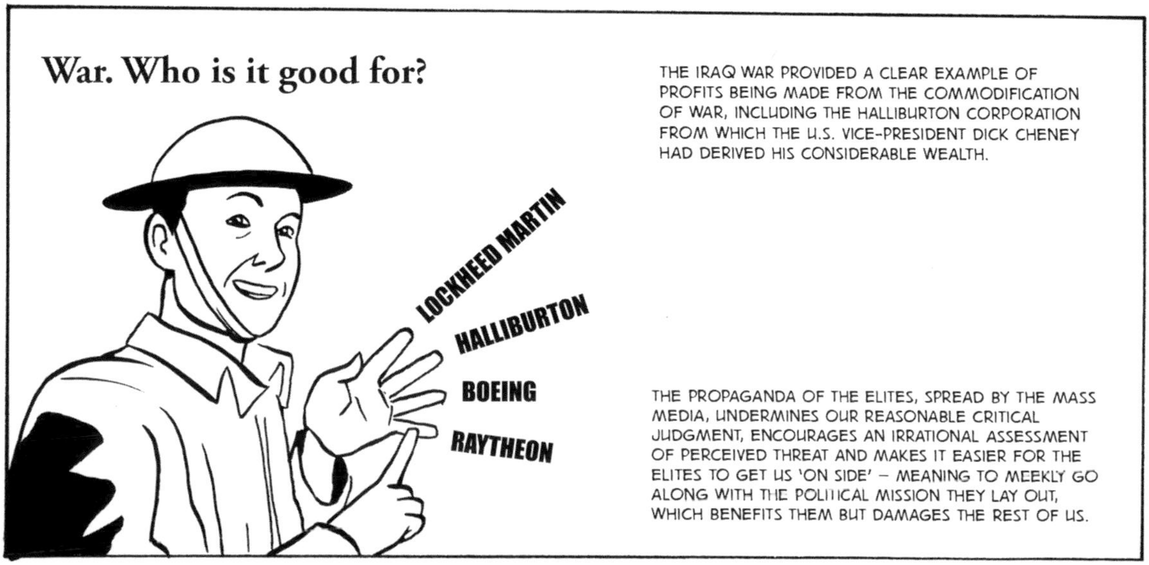
War. Who is it good for?
THE IRAQ WAR PROVIDED A CLEAR EXAMPLE OF PROFITS BEING MADE FROM THE COMMODIFICATION OF WAR, INCLUDING THE HALLIBURTON CORPORATION FROM WHICH THE U.S. VICE-PRESIDENT DICK CHENEY HAD DERIVED HIS CONSIDERABLE WEALTH.
LOCKHEED MARTIN
HALLIBURTON
BOEING
RAYTHEON
THE PROPAGANDA OF THE ELITES, SPREAD BY THE MASS MEDIA, UNDERMINES OUR REASONABLE CRITICAL JUDGMENT, ENCOURAGES AN IRRATIONAL ASSESSMENT OF PERCEIVED THREAT AND MAKES IT EASIER FOR THE ELITES TO GET US 'ON SIDE' – MEANING TO MEEKLY GO ALONG WITH THE POLITICAL MISSION THEY LAY OUT, WHICH BENEFITS THEM BUT DAMAGES THE REST OF US.

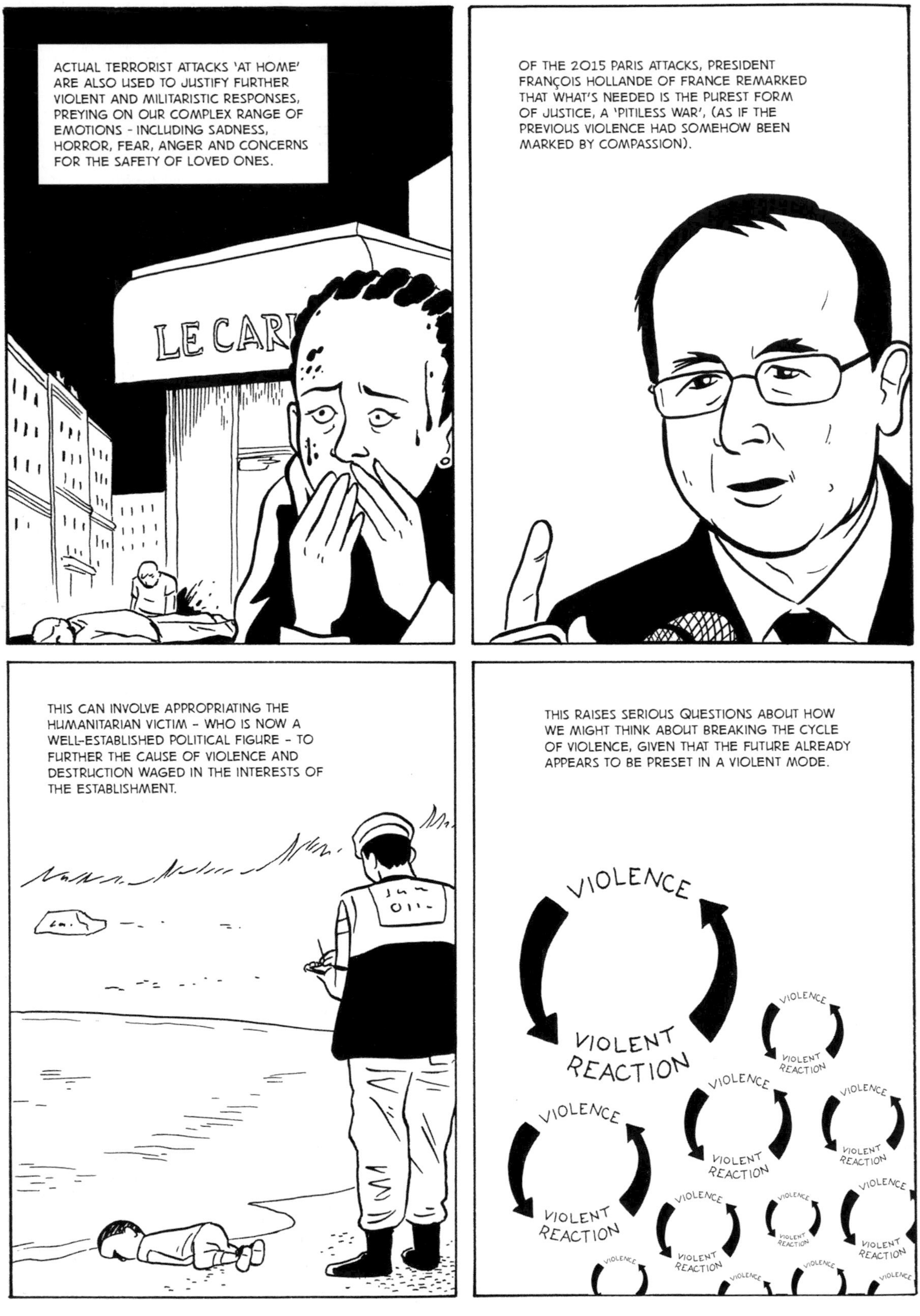
ACTUAL TERRORIST ATTACKS 'AT HOME' ARE ALSO USED TO JUSTIFY FURTHER VIOLENT AND MILITARISTIC RESPONSES, PREYING ON OUR COMPLEX RANGE OF EMOTIONS - INCLUDING SADNESS, HORROR, FEAR, ANGER AND CONCERNS FOR THE SAFETY OF LOVED ONES.
LE CAR
OF THE 2015 PARIS ATTACKS, PRESIDENT FRANÇOIS HOLLANDE OF FRANCE REMARKED THAT WHAT'S NEEDED IS THE PUREST FORM OF JUSTICE, A 'PITILESS WAR', (AS IF THE PREVIOUS VIOLENCE HAD SOMEHOW BEEN MARKED BY COMPASSION).
THIS CAN INVOLVE APPROPRIATING THE HUMANITARIAN VICTIM - WHO IS NOW A WELL-ESTABLISHED POLITICAL FIGURE - TO FURTHER THE CAUSE OF VIOLENCE AND DESTRUCTION WAGED IN THE INTERESTS OF THE ESTABLISHMENT.
THIS RAISES SERIOUS QUESTIONS ABOUT HOW WE MIGHT THINK ABOUT BREAKING THE CYCLE OF VIOLENCE, GIVEN THAT THE FUTURE ALREADY APPEARS TO BE PRESET IN A VIOLENT MODE.
VIOLENCE
VIOLENT REACTION
VIOLENCE
VIOLENT REACTION
VIOLENCE
VIOLENT REACTION
VIOLENCE
VIOLENT REACTION
VIOLENCE
VIOLENT REACTION
VIOLENCE
VIOLENT REACTION
VIOLENCE
VIOLENT REACTION
VIOLENCE
VIOLENT REACTION

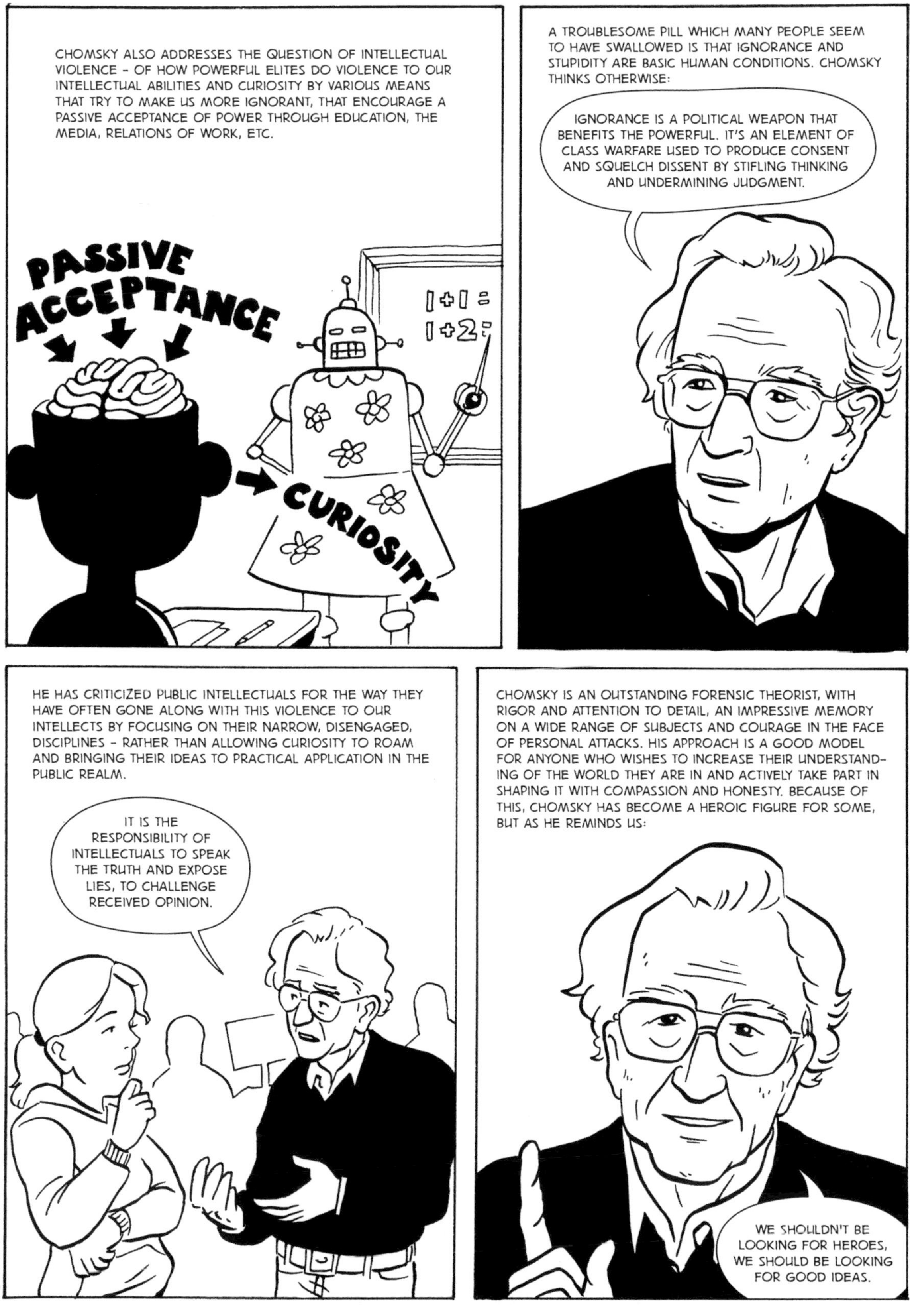
CHOMSKY ALSO ADDRESSES THE QUESTION OF INTELLECTUAL VIOLENCE – OF HOW POWERFUL ELITES DO VIOLENCE TO OUR INTELLECTUAL ABILITIES AND CURIOSITY BY VARIOUS MEANS THAT TRY TO MAKE US MORE IGNORANT, THAT ENCOURAGE A PASSIVE ACCEPTANCE OF POWER THROUGH EDUCATION, THE MEDIA, RELATIONS OF WORK, ETC.
PASSIVE ACCEPTANCE
1+1=
1+2=
CURIOSITY
A TROUBLESOME PILL WHICH MANY PEOPLE SEEM TO HAVE SWALLOWED IS THAT IGNORANCE AND STUPIDITY ARE BASIC HUMAN CONDITIONS. CHOMSKY THINKS OTHERWISE:
IGNORANCE IS A POLITICAL WEAPON THAT BENEFITS THE POWERFUL. IT'S AN ELEMENT OF CLASS WARFARE USED TO PRODUCE CONSENT AND SQUELCH DISSENT BY STIFLING THINKING AND UNDERMINING JUDGMENT.
HE HAS CRITICIZED PUBLIC INTELLECTUALS FOR THE WAY THEY HAVE OFTEN GONE ALONG WITH THIS VIOLENCE TO OUR INTELLECTS BY FOCUSING ON THEIR NARROW, DISENGAGED, DISCIPLINES – RATHER THAN ALLOWING CURIOSITY TO ROAM AND BRINGING THEIR IDEAS TO PRACTICAL APPLICATION IN THE PUBLIC REALM.
IT IS THE RESPONSIBILITY OF INTELLECTUALS TO SPEAK THE TRUTH AND EXPOSE LIES, TO CHALLENGE RECEIVED OPINION.
CHOMSKY IS AN OUTSTANDING FORENSIC THEORIST, WITH RIGOR AND ATTENTION TO DETAIL, AN IMPRESSIVE MEMORY ON A WIDE RANGE OF SUBJECTS AND COURAGE IN THE FACE OF PERSONAL ATTACKS. HIS APPROACH IS A GOOD MODEL FOR ANYONE WHO WISHES TO INCREASE THEIR UNDERSTANDING OF THE WORLD THEY ARE IN AND ACTIVELY TAKE PART IN SHAPING IT WITH COMPASSION AND HONESTY. BECAUSE OF THIS, CHOMSKY HAS BECOME A HEROIC FIGURE FOR SOME, BUT AS HE REMINDS US:
WE SHOULDN'T BE LOOKING FOR HEROES, WE SHOULD BE LOOKING FOR GOOD IDEAS.

Judith Butler

Precarious Lives

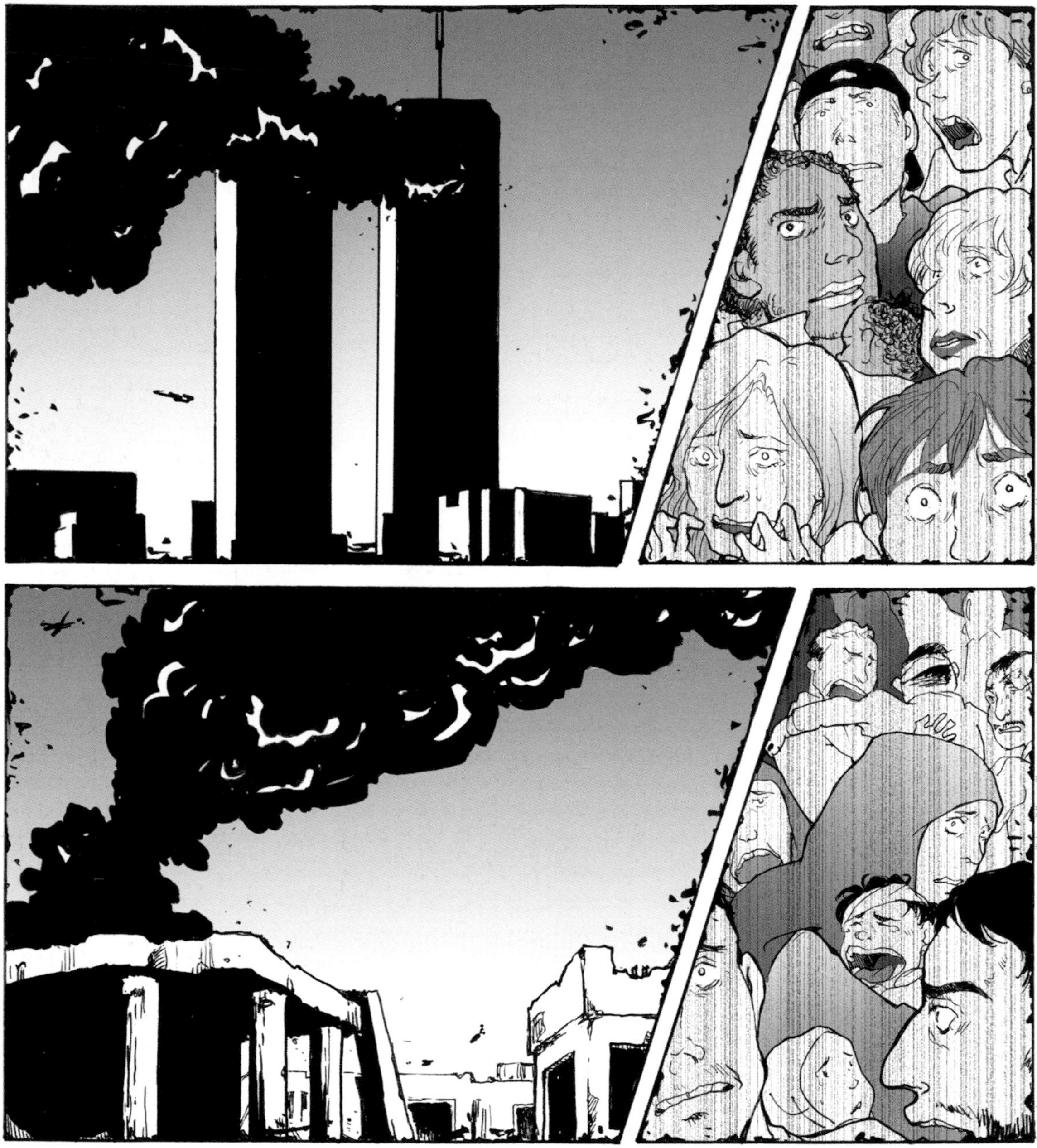

THE PROFESSOR AND WRITER JUDITH BUTLER STRIKES WITH THIS POWERFUL THOUGHT: IN THIS TIME OF MOURNING AND LOSS, THIS TIME WHEN BRUTE VIOLENCE KNOCKS OUR TOWERS OF ISOLATION DOWN, THERE IS A CHANCE TO UNDERSTAND THAT THE USA IS PART OF THE WIDER WORLD, IS IN RELATIONSHIP WITH IT.

IN HER BOOK *PRECARIOUS LIFE: THE POWERS OF MOURNING AND VIOLENCE* JUDITH BUTLER RESPONDS TO POST-9/11 AMERICA'S KNEE-JERK REACTION TO WAGE PERPETUAL WAR. SHE FOCUSES ON A DEEPER UNDERSTANDING OF MOURNING AND VIOLENCE AND HOW THESE COULD INSPIRE SOLIDARITY AND A STRONG EFFORT FOR GLOBAL JUSTICE.

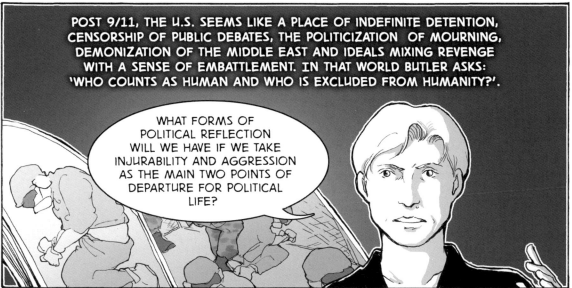

POST 9/11, THE U.S. SEEMS LIKE A PLACE OF INDEFINITE DETENTION, CENSORSHIP OF PUBLIC DEBATES, THE POLITICIZATION OF MOURNING, DEMONIZATION OF THE MIDDLE EAST AND IDEALS MIXING REVENGE WITH A SENSE OF EMBATTLEMENT. IN THAT WORLD BUTLER ASKS: 'WHO COUNTS AS HUMAN AND WHO IS EXCLUDED FROM HUMANITY?'.

WHAT FORMS OF POLITICAL REFLECTION WILL WE HAVE IF WE TAKE INJURABILITY AND AGGRESSION AS THE MAIN TWO POINTS OF DEPARTURE FOR POLITICAL LIFE?

SINCE THE UNSETTLING ATTACKS THE U.S. HAS BEEN TRYING TO RE-CENTER ITSELF VIA A FIRST-PERSON FOCUSED NARRATIVE ABOUT ITS SUPREMACY IN A WAY THAT ONCE AGAIN GIVES PRIMACY TO MILITARISM.

BUTLER BRINGS OUR ATTENTION TO THE NEED TO THINK OF OURSELVES AS GLOBAL ACTORS WITHIN AN INTERRELATED WORLD. THIS REQUIRES SEEING THE WORLD AS A SHARED SPACE, HISTORICALLY CONDITIONED, AND THUS REFLECT UPON THE IMPACT OUR LIVES HAVE ON THE LIVES OF OTHERS.

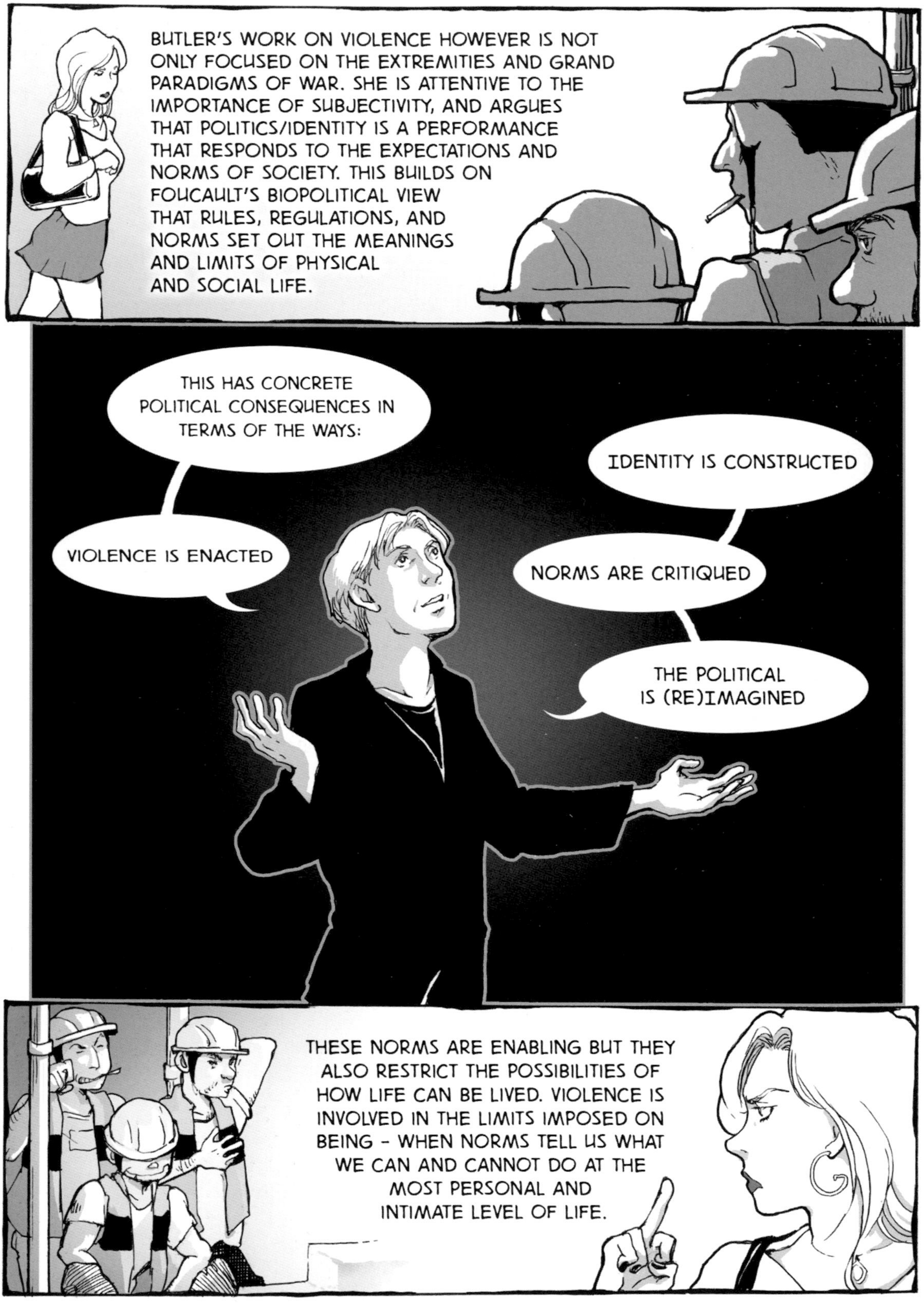
BUTLER'S WORK ON VIOLENCE HOWEVER IS NOT ONLY FOCUSED ON THE EXTREMITIES AND GRAND PARADIGMS OF WAR. SHE IS ATTENTIVE TO THE IMPORTANCE OF SUBJECTIVITY, AND ARGUES THAT POLITICS/IDENTITY IS A PERFORMANCE THAT RESPONDS TO THE EXPECTATIONS AND NORMS OF SOCIETY. THIS BUILDS ON FOUCAULT'S BIOPOLITICAL VIEW THAT RULES, REGULATIONS, AND NORMS SET OUT THE MEANINGS AND LIMITS OF PHYSICAL AND SOCIAL LIFE.
THIS HAS CONCRETE POLITICAL CONSEQUENCES IN TERMS OF THE WAYS:
VIOLENCE IS ENACTED
IDENTITY IS CONSTRUCTED
NORMS ARE CRITIQUED
THE POLITICAL IS (RE)IMAGINED
THESE NORMS ARE ENABLING BUT THEY ALSO RESTRICT THE POSSIBILITIES OF HOW LIFE CAN BE LIVED. VIOLENCE IS INVOLVED IN THE LIMITS IMPOSED ON BEING – WHEN NORMS TELL US WHAT WE CAN AND CANNOT DO AT THE MOST PERSONAL AND INTIMATE LEVEL OF LIFE.

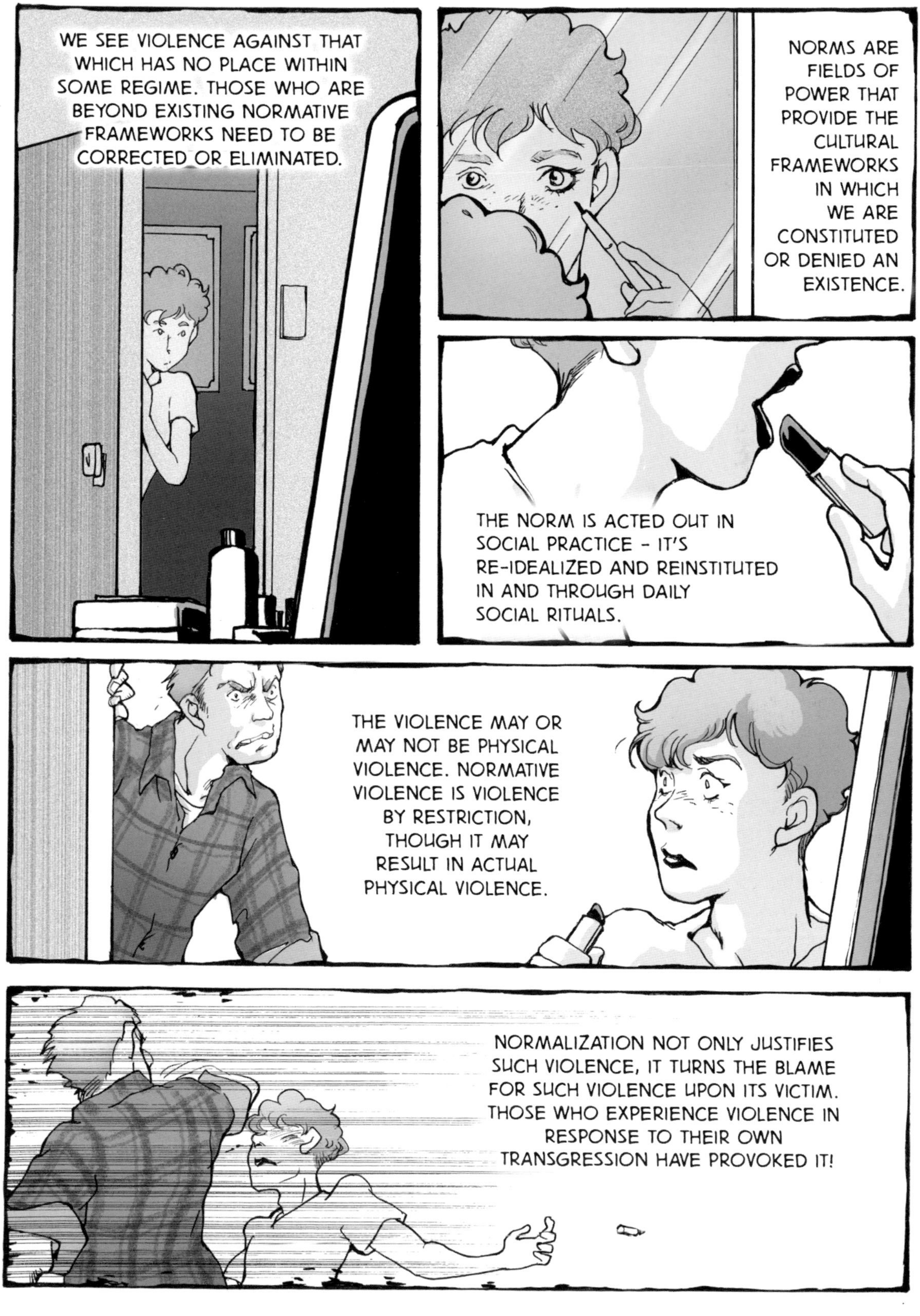
WE SEE VIOLENCE AGAINST THAT WHICH HAS NO PLACE WITHIN SOME REGIME. THOSE WHO ARE BEYOND EXISTING NORMATIVE FRAMEWORKS NEED TO BE CORRECTED OR ELIMINATED.
NORMS ARE FIELDS OF POWER THAT PROVIDE THE CULTURAL FRAMEWORKS IN WHICH WE ARE CONSTITUTED OR DENIED AN EXISTENCE.
THE NORM IS ACTED OUT IN SOCIAL PRACTICE - IT'S RE-IDEALIZED AND REINSTITUTED IN AND THROUGH DAILY SOCIAL RITUALS.
THE VIOLENCE MAY OR MAY NOT BE PHYSICAL VIOLENCE. NORMATIVE VIOLENCE IS VIOLENCE BY RESTRICTION, THOUGH IT MAY RESULT IN ACTUAL PHYSICAL VIOLENCE.
NORMALIZATION NOT ONLY JUSTIFIES SUCH VIOLENCE, IT TURNS THE BLAME FOR SUCH VIOLENCE UPON ITS VICTIM. THOSE WHO EXPERIENCE VIOLENCE IN RESPONSE TO THEIR OWN TRANSGRESSION HAVE PROVOKED IT!

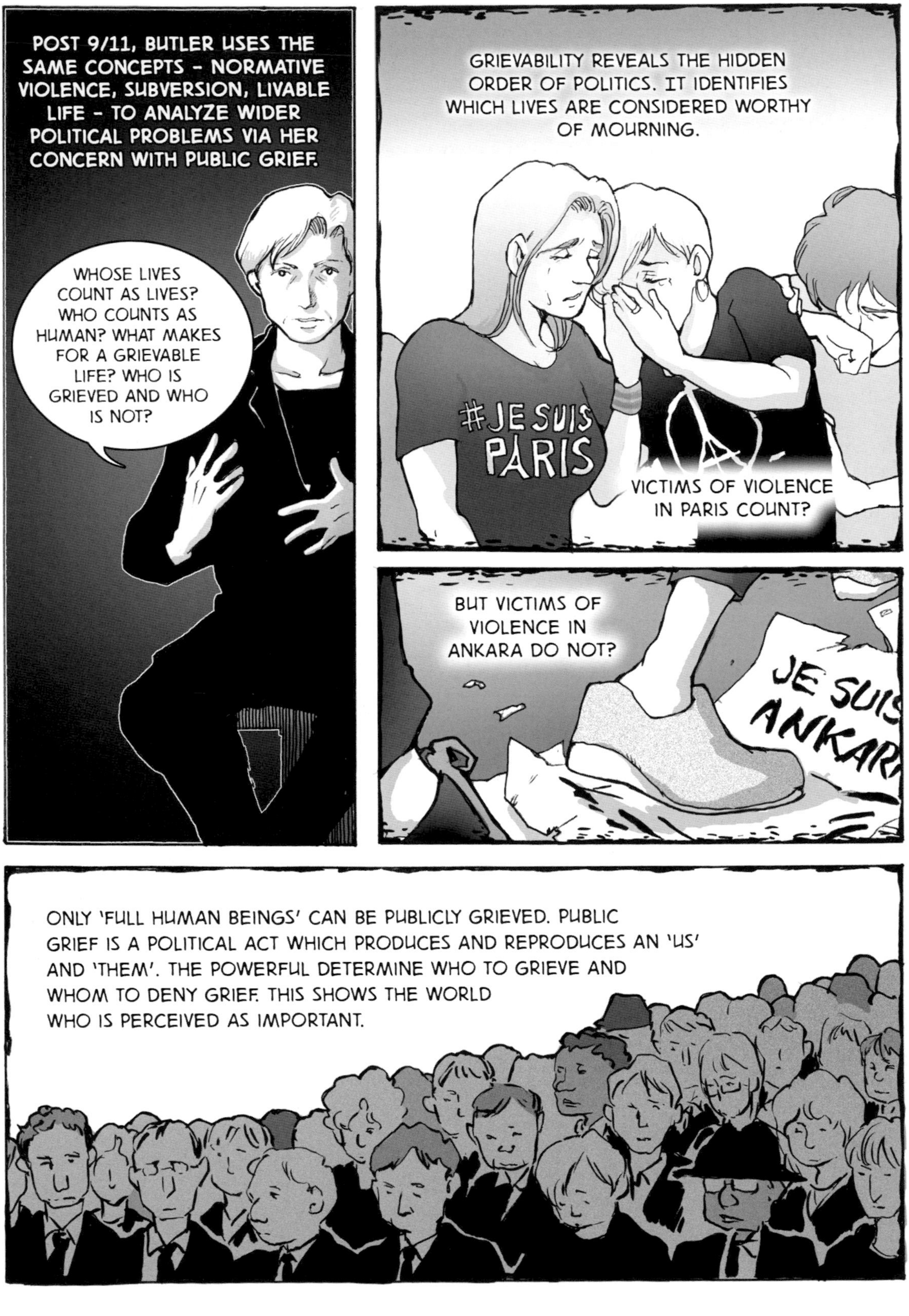
POST 9/11, BUTLER USES THE SAME CONCEPTS - NORMATIVE VIOLENCE, SUBVERSION, LIVABLE LIFE - TO ANALYZE WIDER POLITICAL PROBLEMS VIA HER CONCERN WITH PUBLIC GRIEF.
WHOSE LIVES COUNT AS LIVES? WHO COUNTS AS HUMAN? WHAT MAKES FOR A GRIEVABLE LIFE? WHO IS GRIEVED AND WHO IS NOT?
GRIEVABILITY REVEALS THE HIDDEN ORDER OF POLITICS. IT IDENTIFIES WHICH LIVES ARE CONSIDERED WORTHY OF MOURNING.
#JE SUIS PARIS
VICTIMS OF VIOLENCE IN PARIS COUNT?
BUT VICTIMS OF VIOLENCE IN ANKARA DO NOT?
JE SUIS ANKAR
ONLY 'FULL HUMAN BEINGS' CAN BE PUBLICLY GRIEVED. PUBLIC GRIEF IS A POLITICAL ACT WHICH PRODUCES AND REPRODUCES AN 'US' AND 'THEM'. THE POWERFUL DETERMINE WHO TO GRIEVE AND WHOM TO DENY GRIEF. THIS SHOWS THE WORLD WHO IS PERCEIVED AS IMPORTANT.

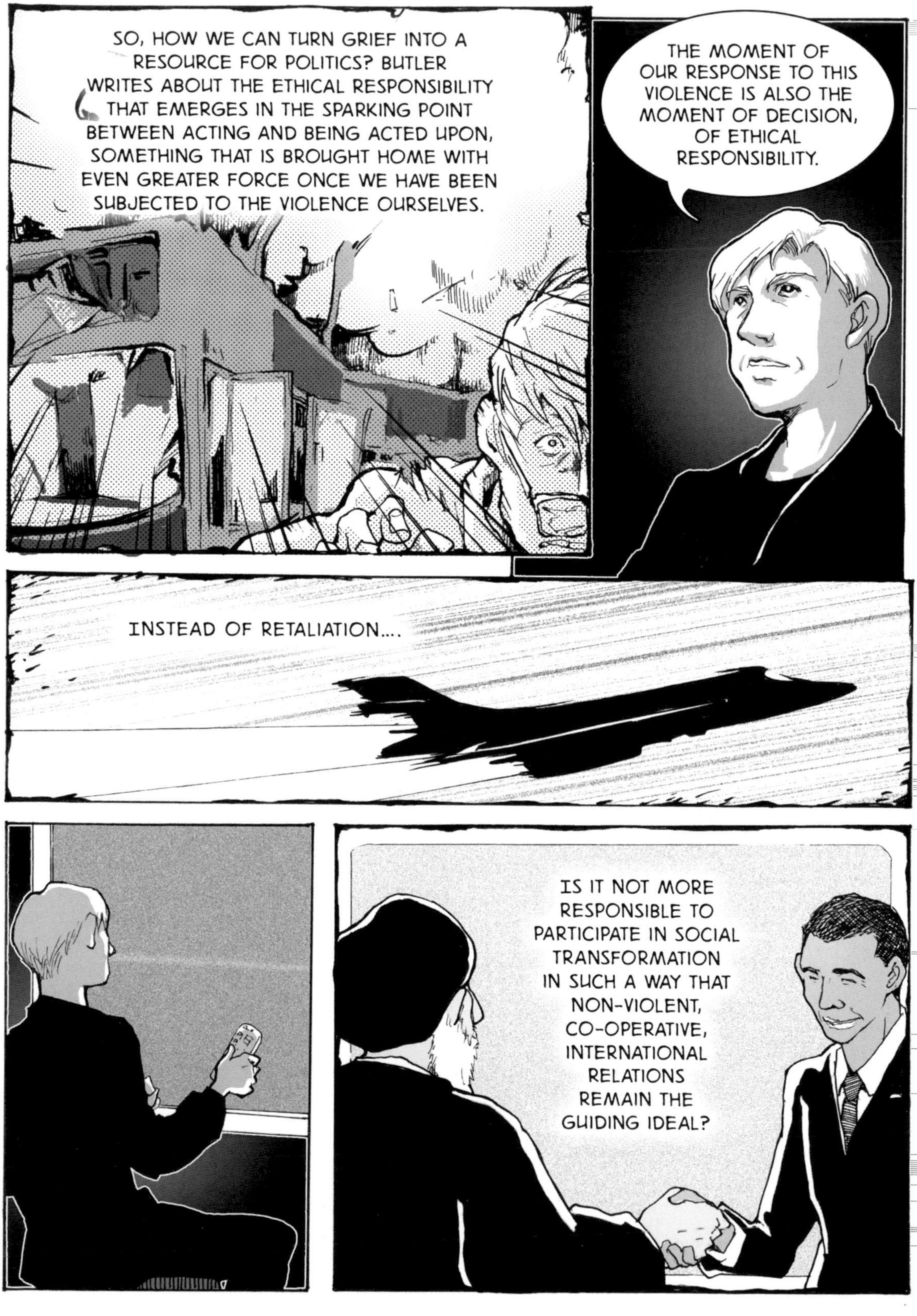
SO, HOW WE CAN TURN GRIEF INTO A RESOURCE FOR POLITICS? BUTLER WRITES ABOUT THE ETHICAL RESPONSIBILITY THAT EMERGES IN THE SPARKING POINT BETWEEN ACTING AND BEING ACTED UPON, SOMETHING THAT IS BROUGHT HOME WITH EVEN GREATER FORCE ONCE WE HAVE BEEN SUBJECTED TO THE VIOLENCE OURSELVES.
THE MOMENT OF OUR RESPONSE TO THIS VIOLENCE IS ALSO THE MOMENT OF DECISION, OF ETHICAL RESPONSIBILITY.
INSTEAD OF RETALIATION....
IS IT NOT MORE RESPONSIBLE TO PARTICIPATE IN SOCIAL TRANSFORMATION IN SUCH A WAY THAT NON-VIOLENT, CO-OPERATIVE, INTERNATIONAL RELATIONS REMAIN THE GUIDING IDEAL?

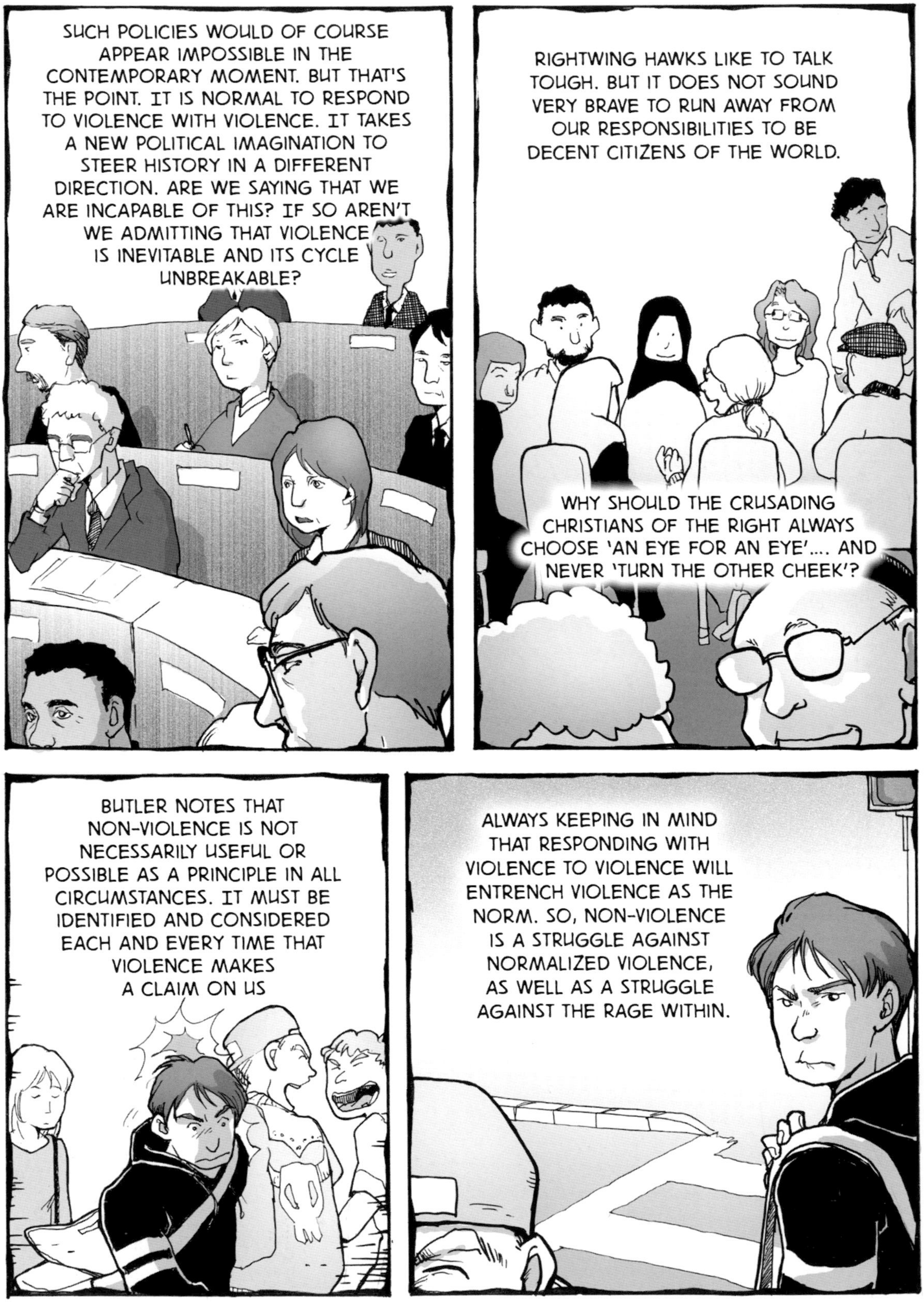
SUCH POLICIES WOULD OF COURSE APPEAR IMPOSSIBLE IN THE CONTEMPORARY MOMENT. BUT THAT'S THE POINT. IT IS NORMAL TO RESPOND TO VIOLENCE WITH VIOLENCE. IT TAKES A NEW POLITICAL IMAGINATION TO STEER HISTORY IN A DIFFERENT DIRECTION. ARE WE SAYING THAT WE ARE INCAPABLE OF THIS? IF SO AREN'T WE ADMITTING THAT VIOLENCE IS INEVITABLE AND ITS CYCLE UNBREAKABLE?
RIGHTWING HAWKS LIKE TO TALK TOUGH. BUT IT DOES NOT SOUND VERY BRAVE TO RUN AWAY FROM OUR RESPONSIBILITIES TO BE DECENT CITIZENS OF THE WORLD.
WHY SHOULD THE CRUSADING CHRISTIANS OF THE RIGHT ALWAYS CHOOSE 'AN EYE FOR AN EYE'.... AND NEVER 'TURN THE OTHER CHEEK'?
BUTLER NOTES THAT NON-VIOLENCE IS NOT NECESSARILY USEFUL OR POSSIBLE AS A PRINCIPLE IN ALL CIRCUMSTANCES. IT MUST BE IDENTIFIED AND CONSIDERED EACH AND EVERY TIME THAT VIOLENCE MAKES A CLAIM ON US
ALWAYS KEEPING IN MIND THAT RESPONDING WITH VIOLENCE TO VIOLENCE WILL ENTRENCH VIOLENCE AS THE NORM. SO, NON-VIOLENCE IS A STRUGGLE AGAINST NORMALIZED VIOLENCE, AS WELL AS A STRUGGLE AGAINST THE RAGE WITHIN.

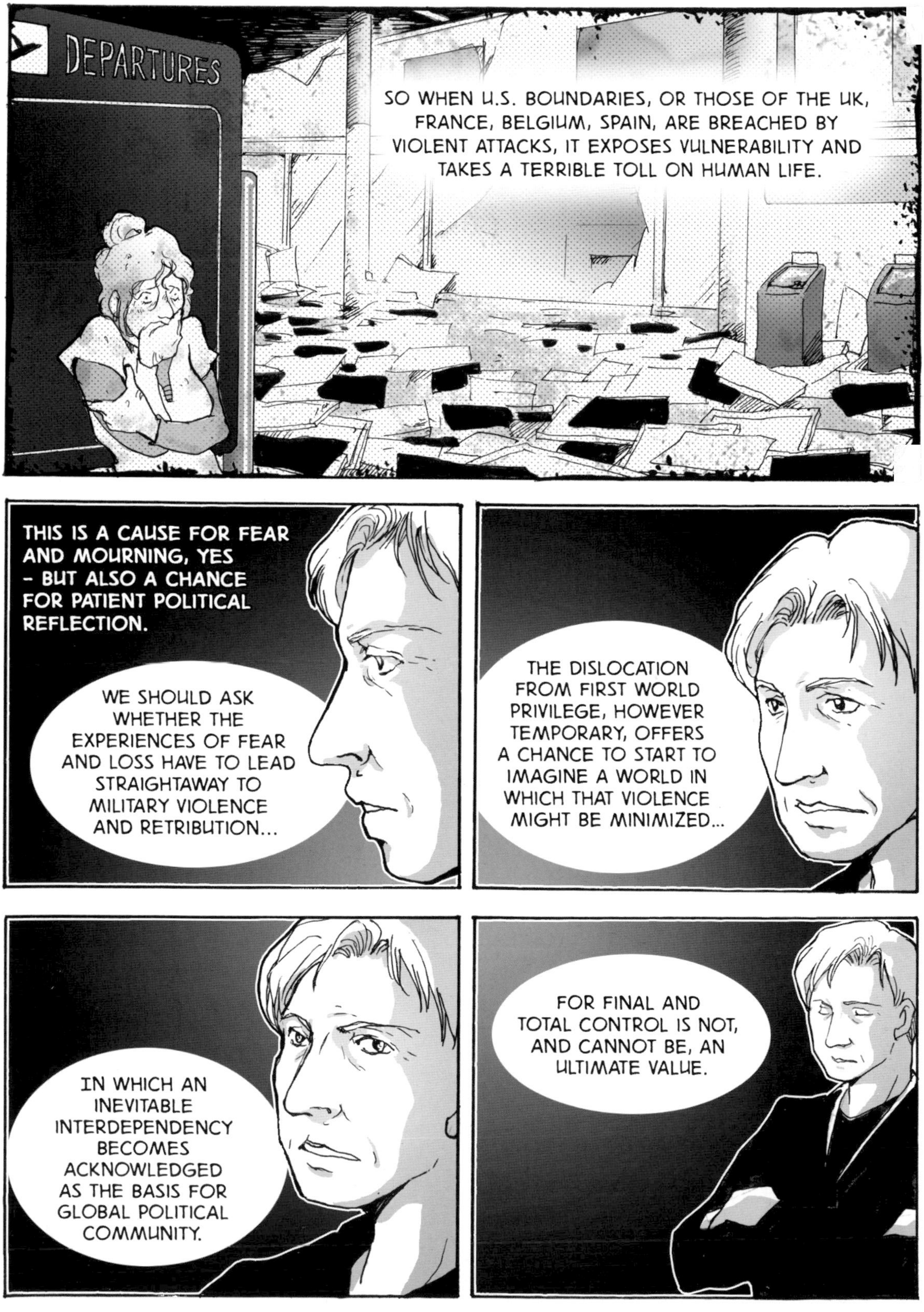
DEPARTURES
SO WHEN U.S. BOUNDARIES, OR THOSE OF THE UK, FRANCE, BELGIUM, SPAIN, ARE BREACHED BY VIOLENT ATTACKS, IT EXPOSES VULNERABILITY AND TAKES A TERRIBLE TOLL ON HUMAN LIFE.
THIS IS A CAUSE FOR FEAR AND MOURNING, YES - BUT ALSO A CHANCE FOR PATIENT POLITICAL REFLECTION.
WE SHOULD ASK WHETHER THE EXPERIENCES OF FEAR AND LOSS HAVE TO LEAD STRAIGHTAWAY TO MILITARY VIOLENCE AND RETRIBUTION...
THE DISLOCATION FROM FIRST WORLD PRIVILEGE, HOWEVER TEMPORARY, OFFERS A CHANCE TO START TO IMAGINE A WORLD IN WHICH THAT VIOLENCE MIGHT BE MINIMIZED...
IN WHICH AN INEVITABLE INTERDEPENDENCY BECOMES ACKNOWLEDGED AS THE BASIS FOR GLOBAL POLITICAL COMMUNITY.
FOR FINAL AND TOTAL CONTROL IS NOT, AND CANNOT BE, AN ULTIMATE VALUE.

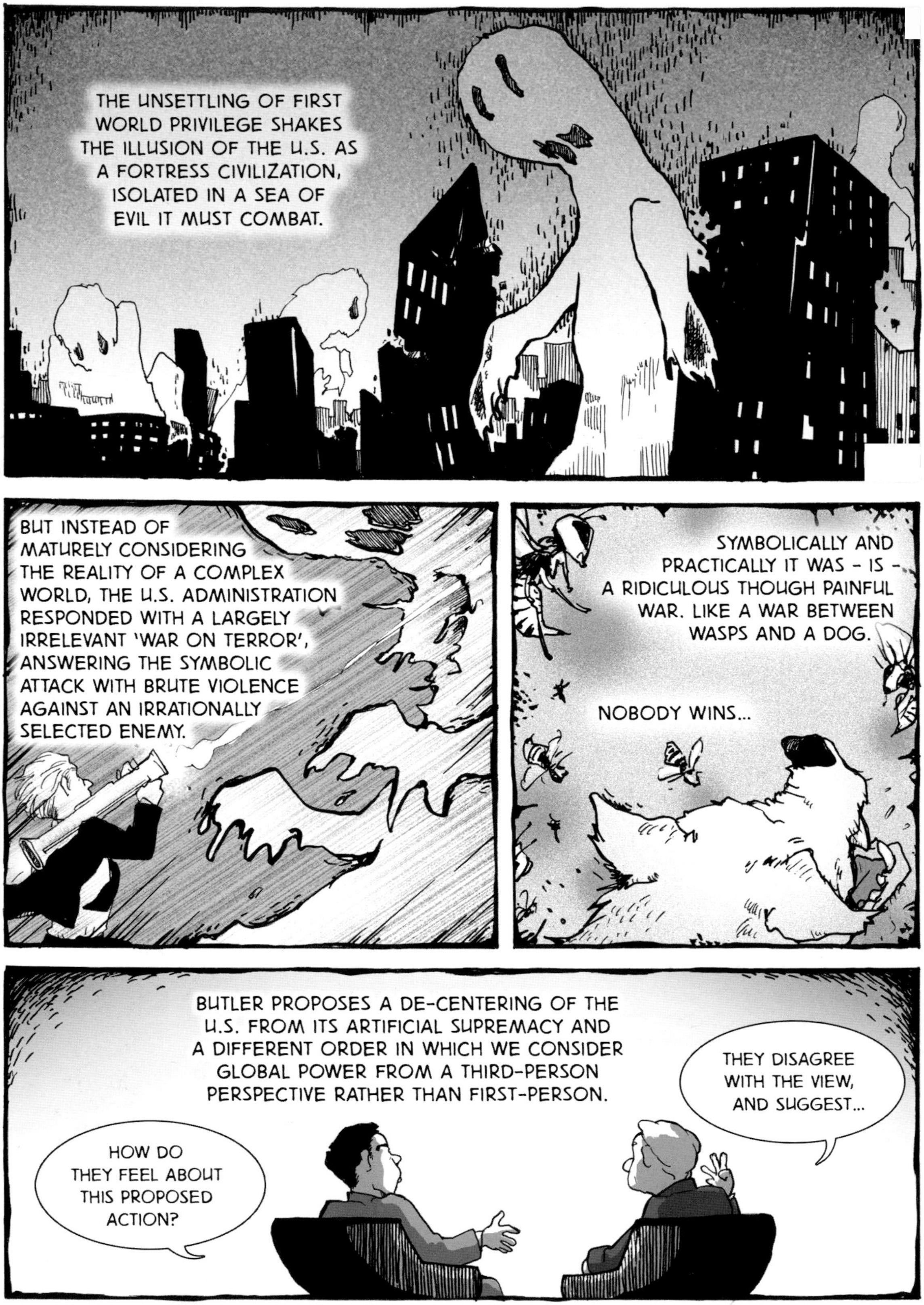
THE UNSETTLING OF FIRST WORLD PRIVILEGE SHAKES THE ILLUSION OF THE U.S. AS A FORTRESS CIVILIZATION, ISOLATED IN A SEA OF EVIL IT MUST COMBAT.
BUT INSTEAD OF MATURELY CONSIDERING THE REALITY OF A COMPLEX WORLD, THE U.S. ADMINISTRATION RESPONDED WITH A LARGELY IRRELEVANT 'WAR ON TERROR', ANSWERING THE SYMBOLIC ATTACK WITH BRUTE VIOLENCE AGAINST AN IRRATIONALLY SELECTED ENEMY.
SYMBOLICALLY AND PRACTICALLY IT WAS – IS – A RIDICULOUS THOUGH PAINFUL WAR. LIKE A WAR BETWEEN WASPS AND A DOG.
NOBODY WINS...
BUTLER PROPOSES A DE-CENTERING OF THE U.S. FROM ITS ARTIFICIAL SUPREMACY AND A DIFFERENT ORDER IN WHICH WE CONSIDER GLOBAL POWER FROM A THIRD-PERSON PERSPECTIVE RATHER THAN FIRST-PERSON.
HOW DO THEY FEEL ABOUT THIS PROPOSED ACTION?
THEY DISAGREE WITH THE VIEW, AND SUGGEST...

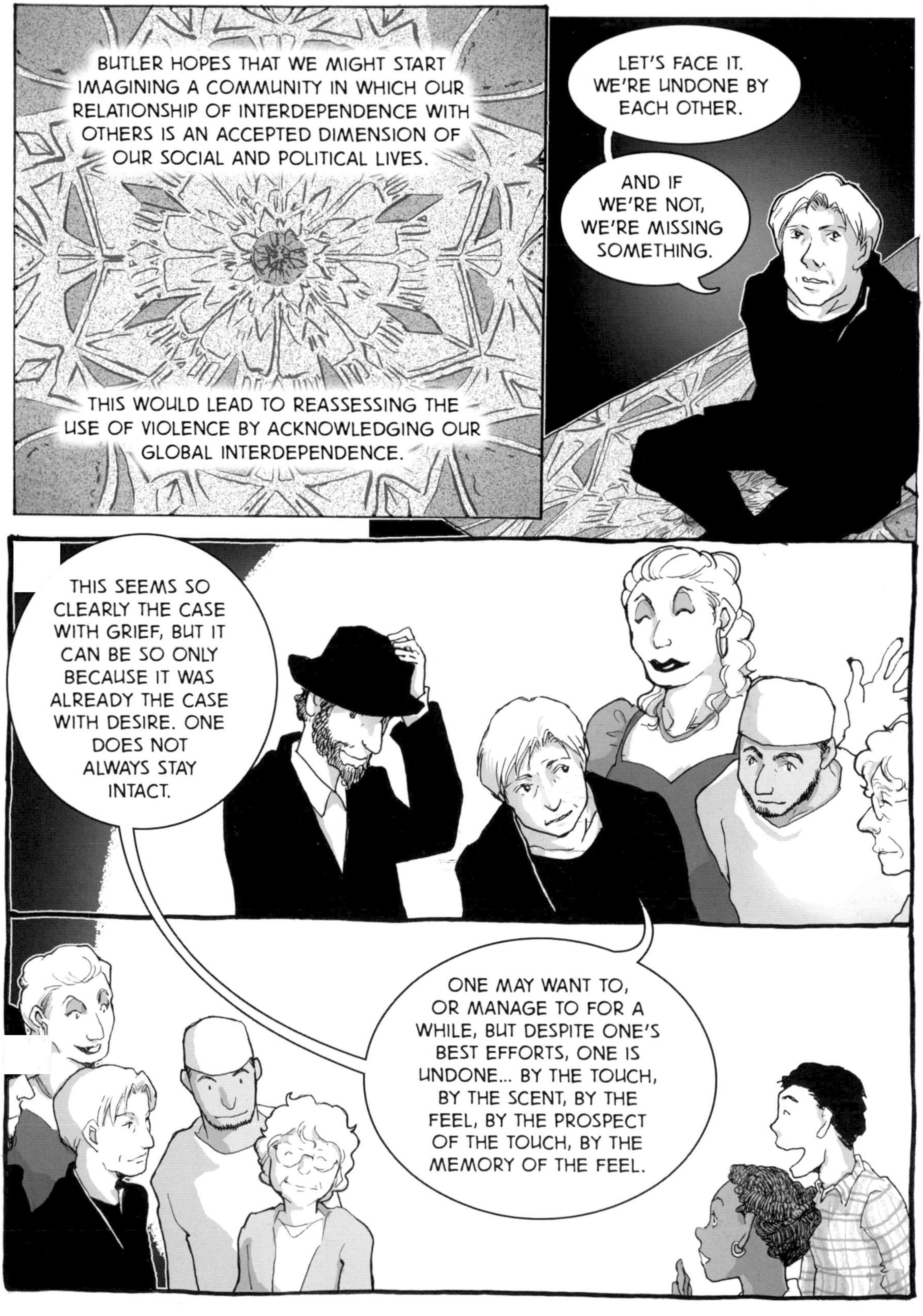
BUTLER HOPES THAT WE MIGHT START IMAGINING A COMMUNITY IN WHICH OUR RELATIONSHIP OF INTERDEPENDENCE WITH OTHERS IS AN ACCEPTED DIMENSION OF OUR SOCIAL AND POLITICAL LIVES.
THIS WOULD LEAD TO REASSESSING THE USE OF VIOLENCE BY ACKNOWLEDGING OUR GLOBAL INTERDEPENDENCE.
LET'S FACE IT. WE'RE UNDONE BY EACH OTHER.
AND IF WE'RE NOT, WE'RE MISSING SOMETHING.
THIS SEEMS SO CLEARLY THE CASE WITH GRIEF, BUT IT CAN BE SO ONLY BECAUSE IT WAS ALREADY THE CASE WITH DESIRE. ONE DOES NOT ALWAYS STAY INTACT.
ONE MAY WANT TO, OR MANAGE TO FOR A WHILE, BUT DESPITE ONE'S BEST EFFORTS, ONE IS UNDONE... BY THE TOUCH, BY THE SCENT, BY THE FEEL, BY THE PROSPECT OF THE TOUCH, BY THE MEMORY OF THE FEEL.

Giorgio Agamben

Sovereign Power/
Bare Life

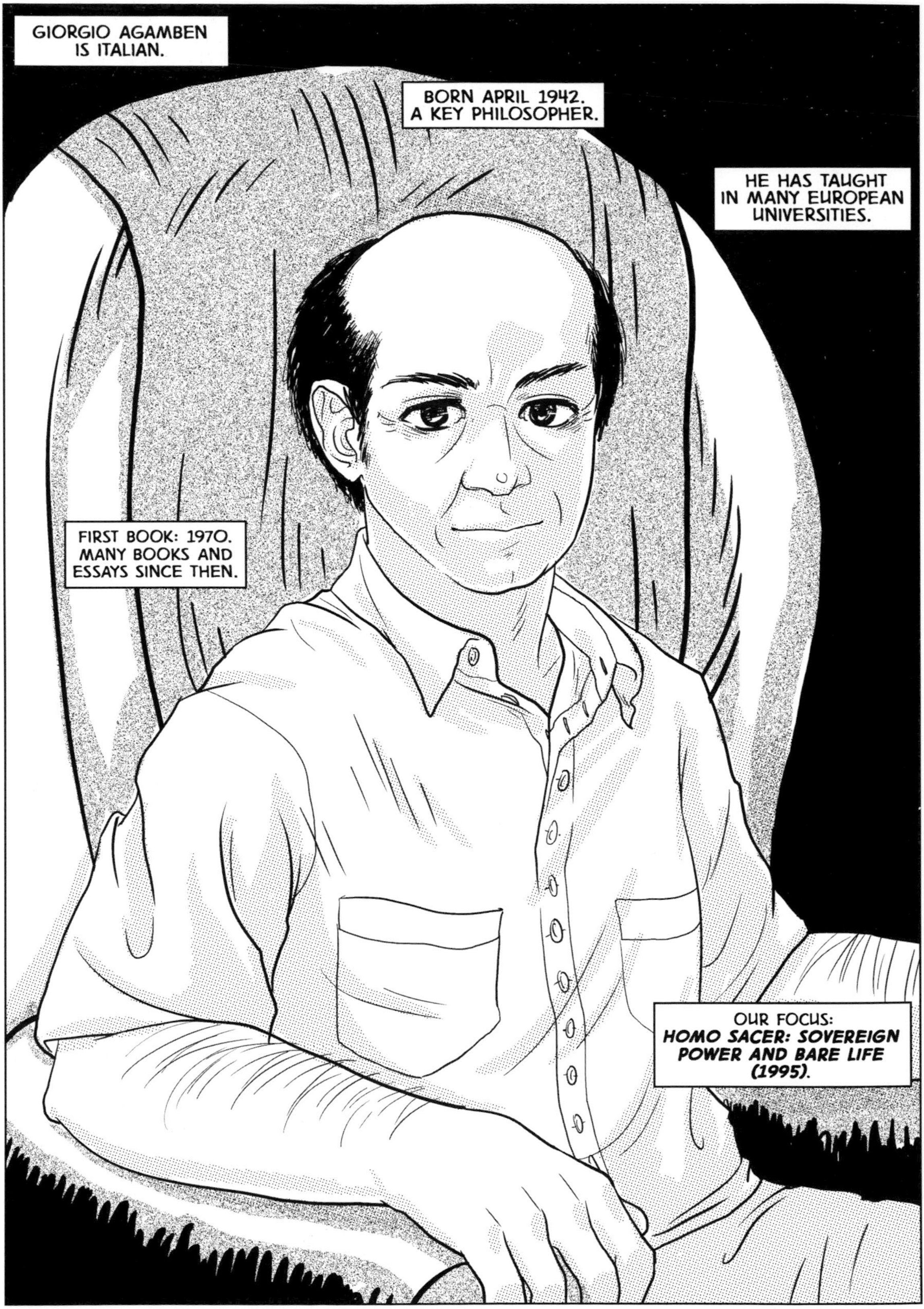
GIORGIO AGAMBEN IS ITALIAN.
BORN APRIL 1942. A KEY PHILOSOPHER.
HE HAS TAUGHT IN MANY EUROPEAN UNIVERSITIES.
FIRST BOOK: 1970. MANY BOOKS AND ESSAYS SINCE THEN.
OUR FOCUS: *HOMO SACER: SOVEREIGN POWER AND BARE LIFE (1995).*

AGAMBEN STUDIED AT THE UNIVERSITY OF ROME AND HIS IDEAS WERE FUNDAMENTALLY INFLUENCED BY ARISTOTLE'S *POLITICS*, *NICOMACHEAN ETHICS* AND *TREATISE ON THE SOUL*.

HIS MORE RECENT INFLUENCES INCLUDE WALTER BENJAMIN, MICHEL FOUCAULT, MARTIN HEIDEGGER, CARL SCHMITT AND HANNAH ARENDT.

HE EDITED BENJAMIN'S WORKS IN ITALIAN AND IN 1981 DISCOVERED SEVERAL LOST MANUSCRIPTS IN THE ARCHIVES OF THE BIBLIOTHEQUE NATIONALE DE FRANCE, INCLUDING FOR BENJAMIN'S THESIS *ON THE CONCEPT OF HISTORY*.

BENJAMIN'S THOUGHT WAS THE ANTIDOTE THAT ALLOWED ME TO SURVIVE HEIDEGGER.

IN 2004, HE CAUSED A CONTROVERSY WHEN HE REFUSED TO GO THROUGH WHAT HE CALLED THE 'BIOPOLITICAL TATTOOING' PROCESS — ELECTRONIC FINGERPRINTING BY THE UNITED STATES IMMIGRATION DEPARTMENT FOR ENTRY TO THE USA.

I HAVE NO INTENTION OF SUBMITTING MYSELF TO SUCH PROCEDURES.

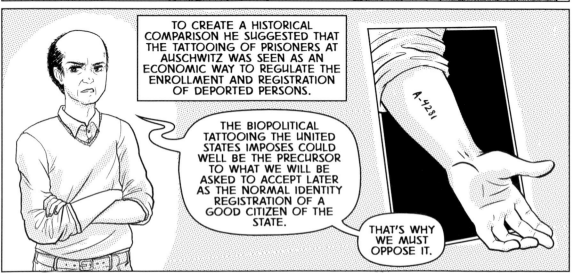

TO CREATE A HISTORICAL COMPARISON HE SUGGESTED THAT THE TATTOOING OF PRISONERS AT AUSCHWITZ WAS SEEN AS AN ECONOMIC WAY TO REGULATE THE ENROLLMENT AND REGISTRATION OF DEPORTED PERSONS.

THE BIOPOLITICAL TATTOOING THE UNITED STATES IMPOSES COULD WELL BE THE PRECURSOR TO WHAT WE WILL BE ASKED TO ACCEPT LATER AS THE NORMAL IDENTITY REGISTRATION OF A GOOD CITIZEN OF THE STATE.

THAT'S WHY WE MUST OPPOSE IT.

AGAMBEN FOCUSES ON THE IDEA OF SOVEREIGNTY IN AN INTERESTING WAY — HE SEES IT NOT AS A SECONDARY ASPECT BUT AS A PRIMARY ASPECT OF SOCIAL LIFE.

WHEREAS HOBBES NOTED THAT THE STATE OF NATURE CONDEMNED HUMANS TO A CONDITION THAT WAS 'SHORT, NASTY AND BRUTISH', FOR AGAMBEN, SOVEREIGNTY ITSELF APPEARS AS A FORM OF VIOLENCE.

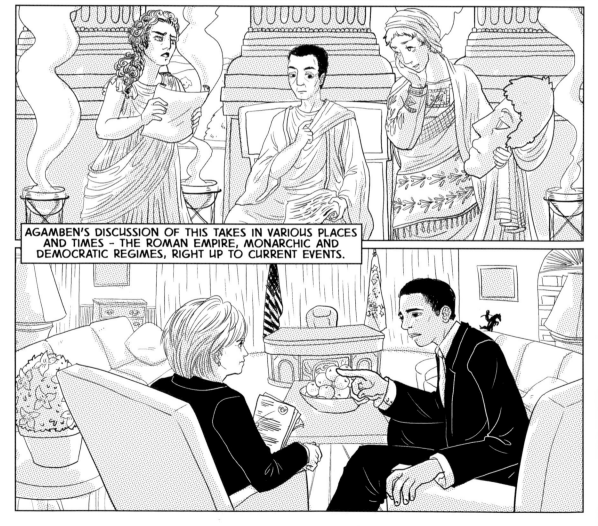

AGAMBEN'S DISCUSSION OF THIS TAKES IN VARIOUS PLACES AND TIMES — THE ROMAN EMPIRE, MONARCHIC AND DEMOCRATIC REGIMES, RIGHT UP TO CURRENT EVENTS.

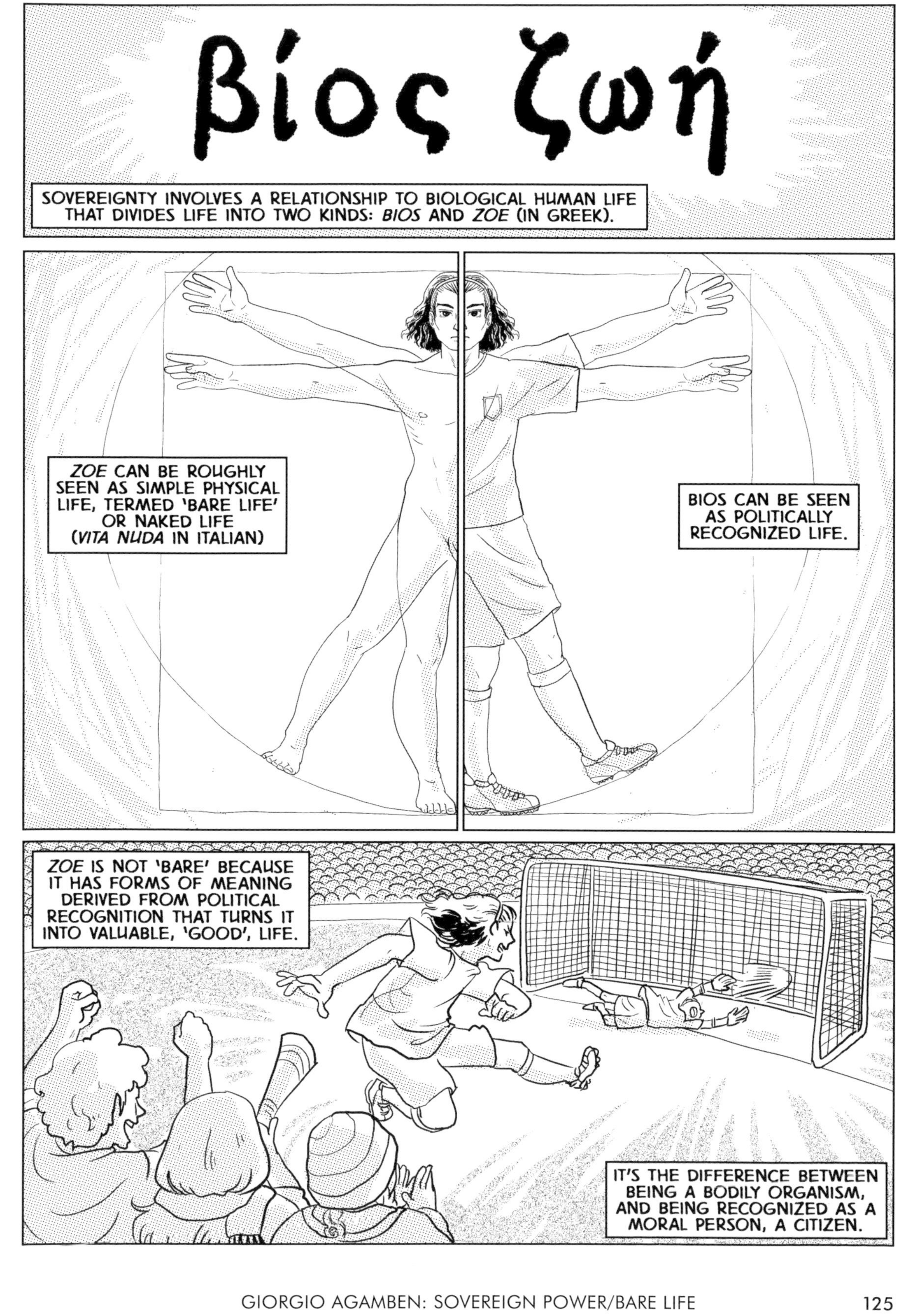
βίος ζωή
SOVEREIGNTY INVOLVES A RELATIONSHIP TO BIOLOGICAL HUMAN LIFE THAT DIVIDES LIFE INTO TWO KINDS: *BIOS* AND *ZOE* (IN GREEK).
ZOE CAN BE ROUGHLY SEEN AS SIMPLE PHYSICAL LIFE, TERMED 'BARE LIFE' OR NAKED LIFE (*VITA NUDA* IN ITALIAN)
BIOS CAN BE SEEN AS POLITICALLY RECOGNIZED LIFE.
ZOE IS NOT 'BARE' BECAUSE IT HAS FORMS OF MEANING DERIVED FROM POLITICAL RECOGNITION THAT TURNS IT INTO VALUABLE, 'GOOD', LIFE.
IT'S THE DIFFERENCE BETWEEN BEING A BODILY ORGANISM, AND BEING RECOGNIZED AS A MORAL PERSON, A CITIZEN.

A CONCENTRATION-CAMP INMATE AND A DETAINEE AT GUANTÁNAMO BAY: THESE ARE EXAMPLES OF PEOPLE WHO HAVE *ZOE*, BUT ARE NOT RECOGNIZED AS MORAL CITIZENS OF ETHICAL IMPORTANCE.

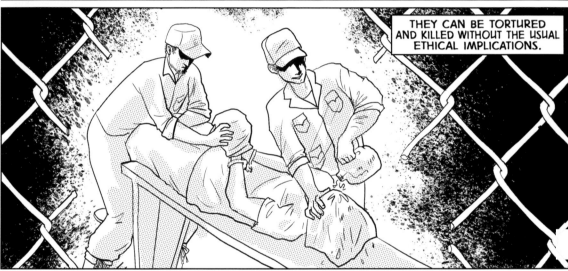

THEY CAN BE TORTURED AND KILLED WITHOUT THE USUAL ETHICAL IMPLICATIONS.

'BARE LIFE' CAN BE SEEN AS THE REMAINDER OF THE DESTROYED POLITICAL *BIOS*.

BARE LIFE IS NOT SIMPLY *ZOE* OR *BIOS*. IT'S A ZONE OF INDISTINCTION AND CONTINUOUS TRANSITION BETWEEN HUMAN AND BEAST.

IT IS LIFE EXPOSED TO DEATH, ESPECIALLY IN THE FORM OF SOVEREIGN VIOLENCE.

PORTRAITS OF VIOLENCE

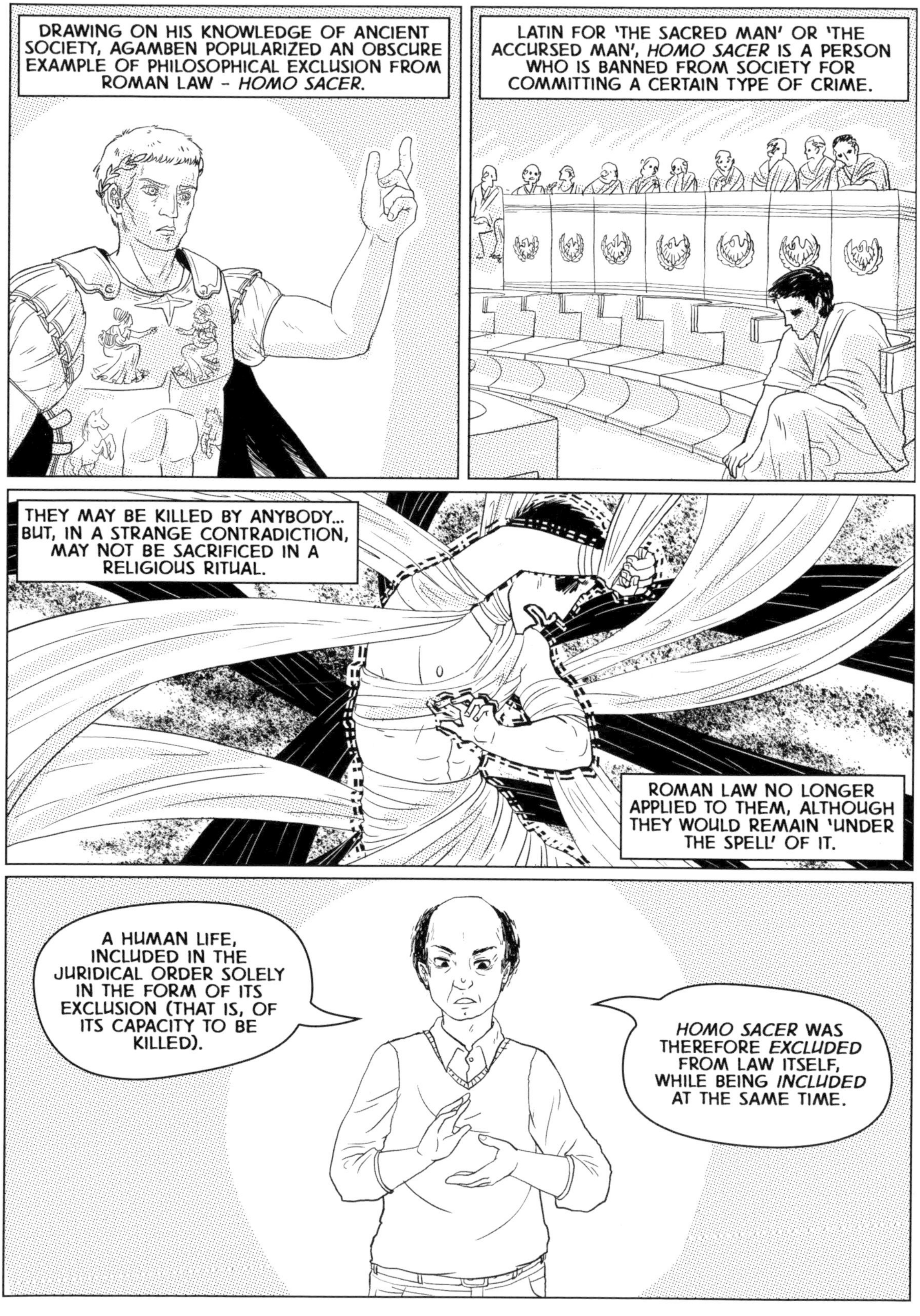
DRAWING ON HIS KNOWLEDGE OF ANCIENT SOCIETY, AGAMBEN POPULARIZED AN OBSCURE EXAMPLE OF PHILOSOPHICAL EXCLUSION FROM ROMAN LAW - *HOMO SACER*.
LATIN FOR 'THE SACRED MAN' OR 'THE ACCURSED MAN', *HOMO SACER* IS A PERSON WHO IS BANNED FROM SOCIETY FOR COMMITTING A CERTAIN TYPE OF CRIME.
THEY MAY BE KILLED BY ANYBODY... BUT, IN A STRANGE CONTRADICTION, MAY NOT BE SACRIFICED IN A RELIGIOUS RITUAL.
ROMAN LAW NO LONGER APPLIED TO THEM, ALTHOUGH THEY WOULD REMAIN 'UNDER THE SPELL' OF IT.
A HUMAN LIFE, INCLUDED IN THE JURIDICAL ORDER SOLELY IN THE FORM OF ITS EXCLUSION (THAT IS, OF ITS CAPACITY TO BE KILLED).
HOMO SACER WAS THEREFORE *EXCLUDED* FROM LAW ITSELF, WHILE BEING *INCLUDED* AT THE SAME TIME.

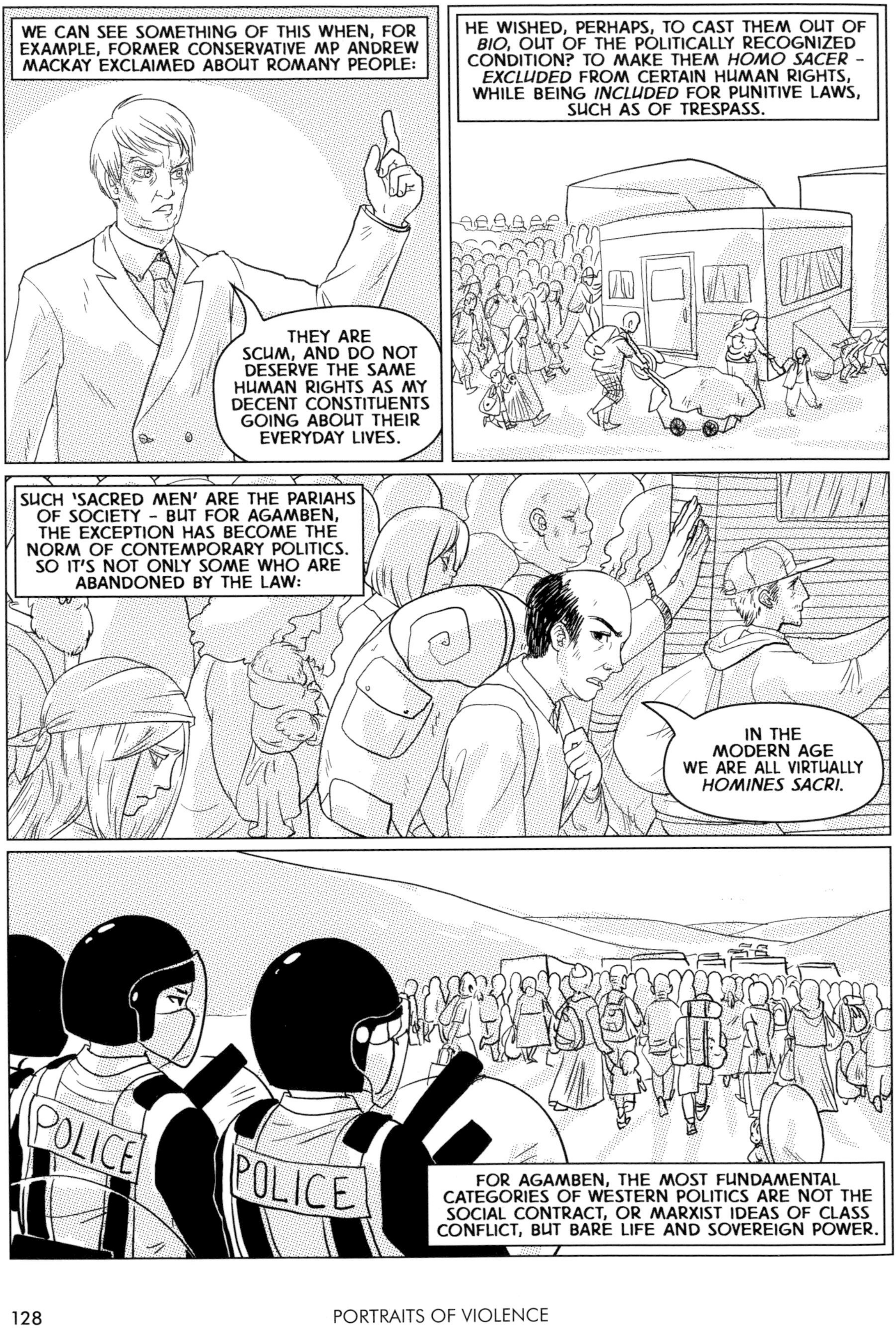
WE CAN SEE SOMETHING OF THIS WHEN, FOR EXAMPLE, FORMER CONSERVATIVE MP ANDREW MACKAY EXCLAIMED ABOUT ROMANY PEOPLE:
THEY ARE SCUM, AND DO NOT DESERVE THE SAME HUMAN RIGHTS AS MY DECENT CONSTITUENTS GOING ABOUT THEIR EVERYDAY LIVES.
HE WISHED, PERHAPS, TO CAST THEM OUT OF *BIO*, OUT OF THE POLITICALLY RECOGNIZED CONDITION? TO MAKE THEM *HOMO SACER* – *EXCLUDED* FROM CERTAIN HUMAN RIGHTS, WHILE BEING *INCLUDED* FOR PUNITIVE LAWS, SUCH AS OF TRESPASS.
SUCH 'SACRED MEN' ARE THE PARIAHS OF SOCIETY – BUT FOR AGAMBEN, THE EXCEPTION HAS BECOME THE NORM OF CONTEMPORARY POLITICS. SO IT'S NOT ONLY SOME WHO ARE ABANDONED BY THE LAW:
IN THE MODERN AGE WE ARE ALL VIRTUALLY *HOMINES SACRI*.
POLICE
POLICE
FOR AGAMBEN, THE MOST FUNDAMENTAL CATEGORIES OF WESTERN POLITICS ARE NOT THE SOCIAL CONTRACT, OR MARXIST IDEAS OF CLASS CONFLICT, BUT BARE LIFE AND SOVEREIGN POWER.

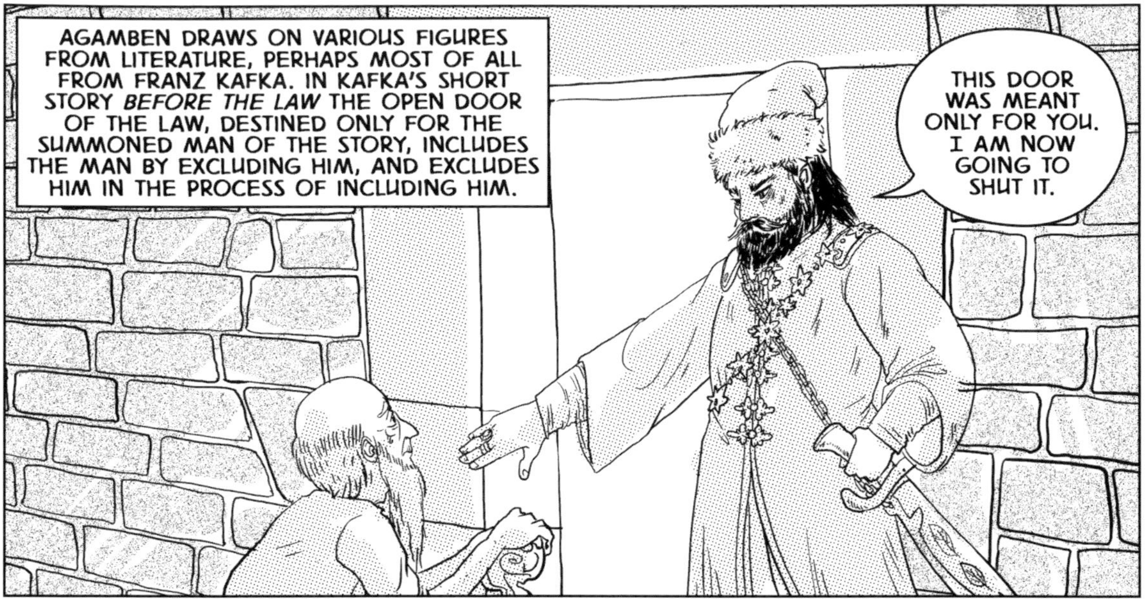
AGAMBEN DRAWS ON VARIOUS FIGURES FROM LITERATURE, PERHAPS MOST OF ALL FROM FRANZ KAFKA. IN KAFKA'S SHORT STORY *BEFORE THE LAW* THE OPEN DOOR OF THE LAW, DESTINED ONLY FOR THE SUMMONED MAN OF THE STORY, INCLUDES THE MAN BY EXCLUDING HIM, AND EXCLUDES HIM IN THE PROCESS OF INCLUDING HIM.
THIS DOOR WAS MEANT ONLY FOR YOU. I AM NOW GOING TO SHUT IT.

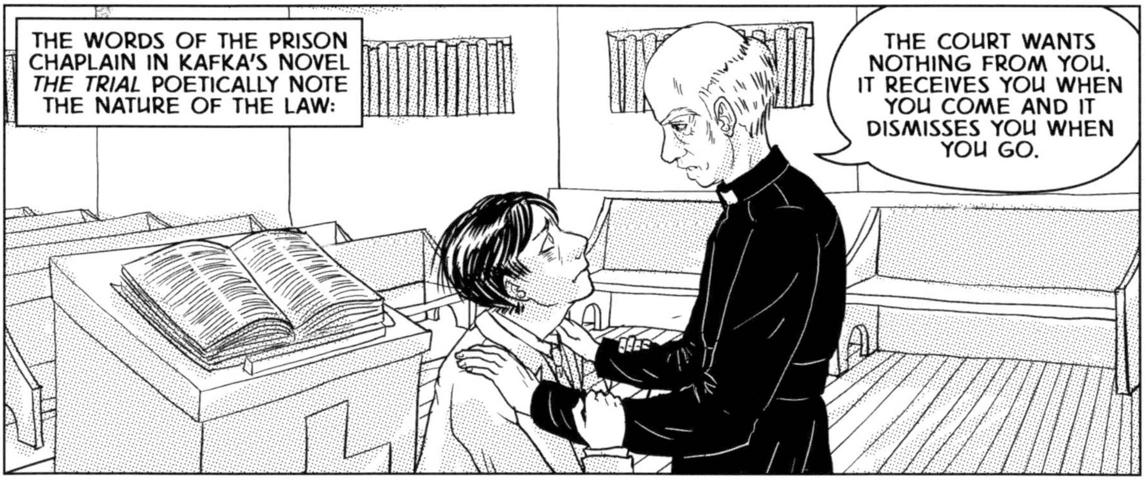
THE WORDS OF THE PRISON CHAPLAIN IN KAFKA'S NOVEL *THE TRIAL* POETICALLY NOTE THE NATURE OF THE LAW:
THE COURT WANTS NOTHING FROM YOU. IT RECEIVES YOU WHEN YOU COME AND IT DISMISSES YOU WHEN YOU GO.

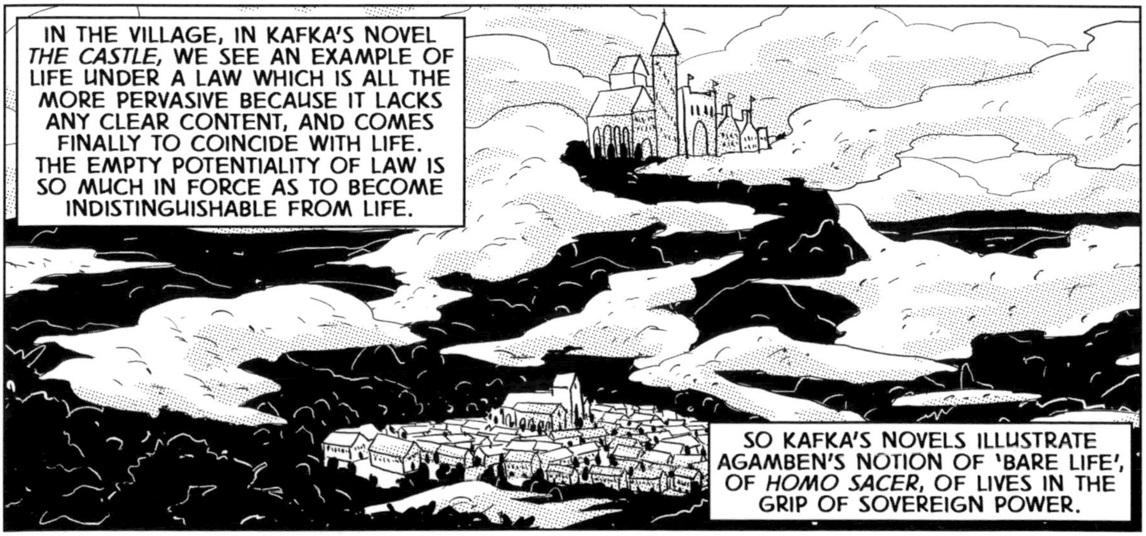
IN THE VILLAGE, IN KAFKA'S NOVEL *THE CASTLE*, WE SEE AN EXAMPLE OF LIFE UNDER A LAW WHICH IS ALL THE MORE PERVASIVE BECAUSE IT LACKS ANY CLEAR CONTENT, AND COMES FINALLY TO COINCIDE WITH LIFE. THE EMPTY POTENTIALITY OF LAW IS SO MUCH IN FORCE AS TO BECOME INDISTINGUISHABLE FROM LIFE.
SO KAFKA'S NOVELS ILLUSTRATE AGAMBEN'S NOTION OF 'BARE LIFE', OF *HOMO SACER*, OF LIVES IN THE GRIP OF SOVEREIGN POWER.

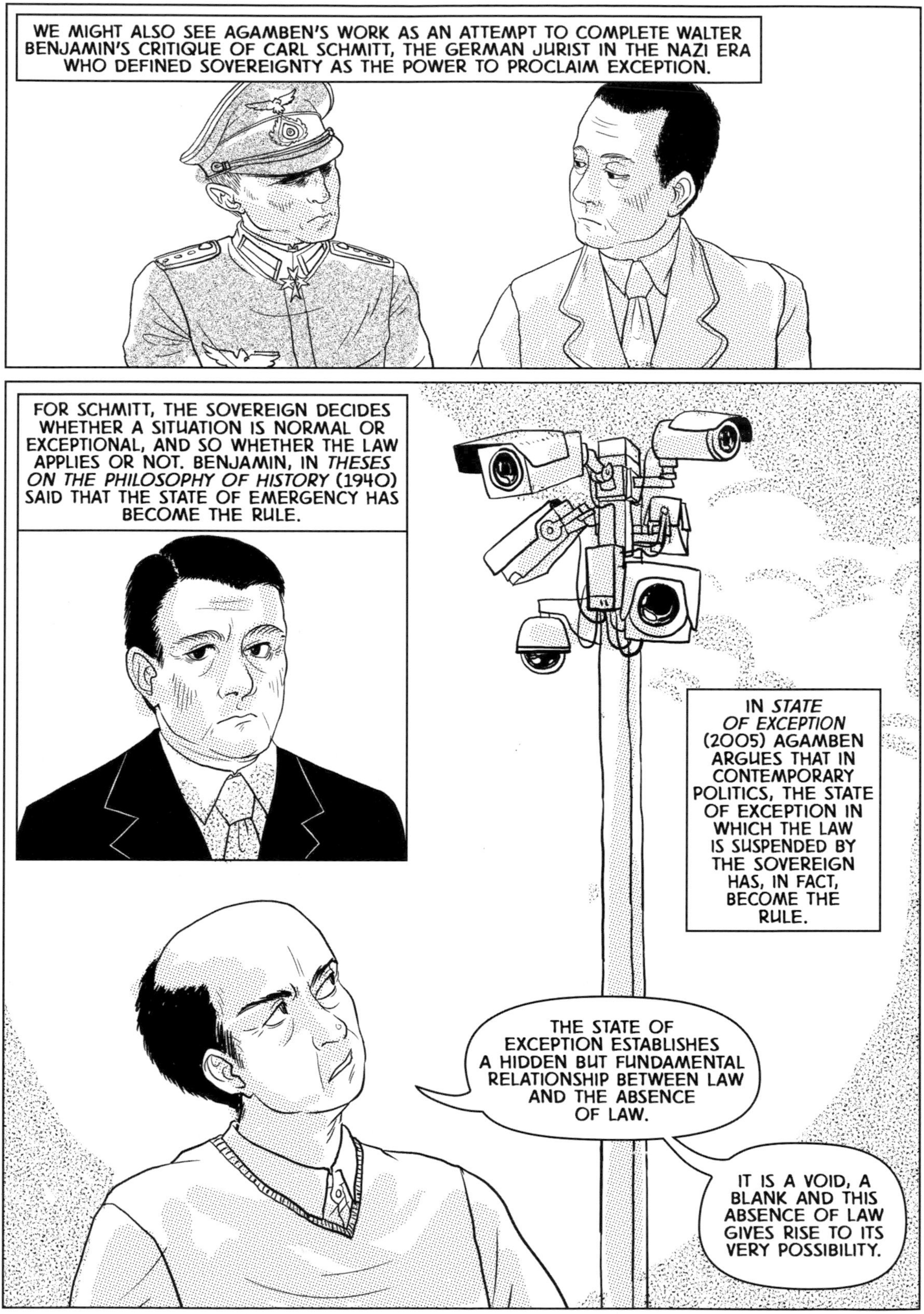
WE MIGHT ALSO SEE AGAMBEN'S WORK AS AN ATTEMPT TO COMPLETE WALTER BENJAMIN'S CRITIQUE OF CARL SCHMITT, THE GERMAN JURIST IN THE NAZI ERA WHO DEFINED SOVEREIGNTY AS THE POWER TO PROCLAIM EXCEPTION.
FOR SCHMITT, THE SOVEREIGN DECIDES WHETHER A SITUATION IS NORMAL OR EXCEPTIONAL, AND SO WHETHER THE LAW APPLIES OR NOT. BENJAMIN, IN *THESES ON THE PHILOSOPHY OF HISTORY* (1940) SAID THAT THE STATE OF EMERGENCY HAS BECOME THE RULE.
IN *STATE OF EXCEPTION* (2005) AGAMBEN ARGUES THAT IN CONTEMPORARY POLITICS, THE STATE OF EXCEPTION IN WHICH THE LAW IS SUSPENDED BY THE SOVEREIGN HAS, IN FACT, BECOME THE RULE.
THE STATE OF EXCEPTION ESTABLISHES A HIDDEN BUT FUNDAMENTAL RELATIONSHIP BETWEEN LAW AND THE ABSENCE OF LAW.
IT IS A VOID, A BLANK AND THIS ABSENCE OF LAW GIVES RISE TO ITS VERY POSSIBILITY.

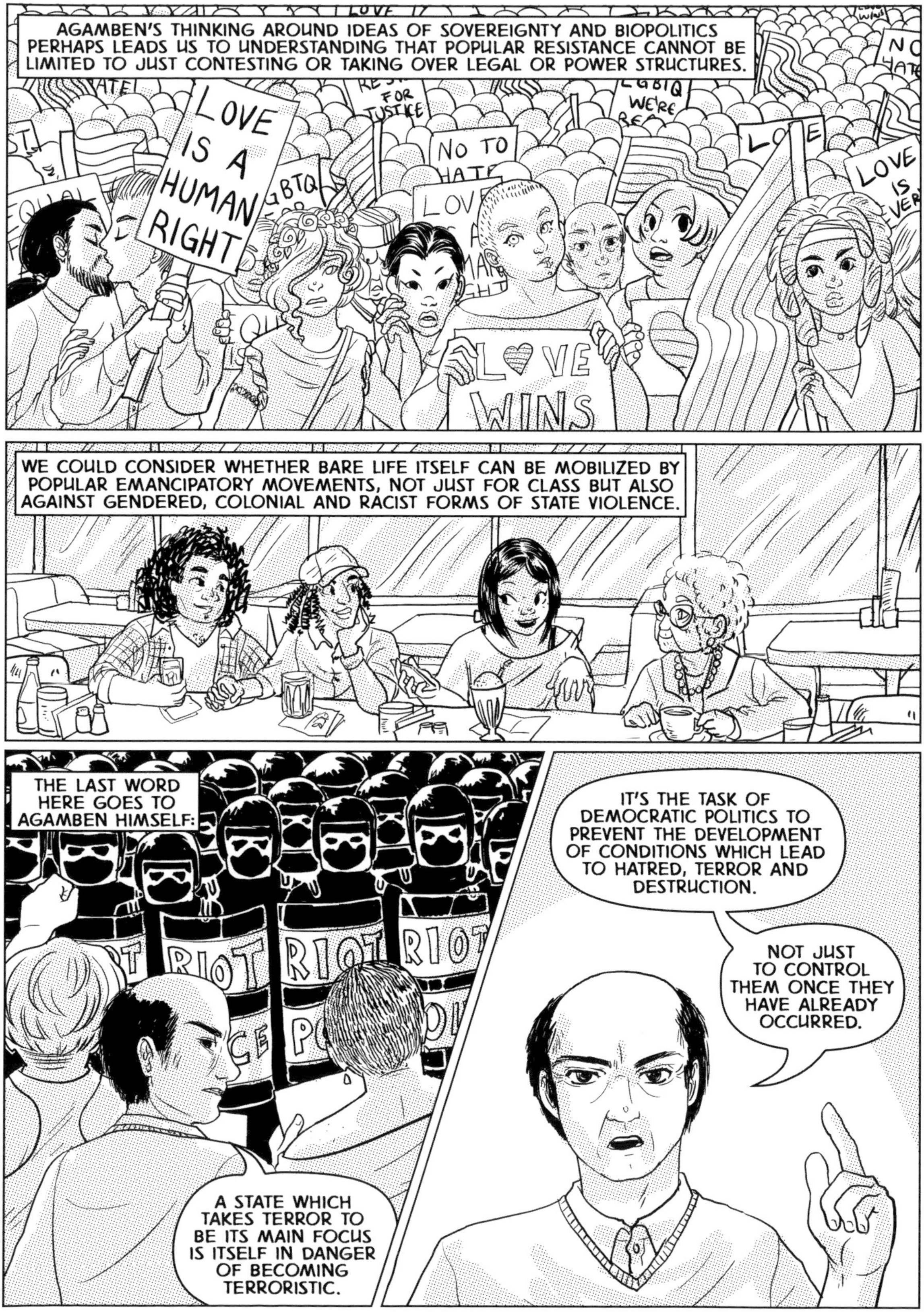
AGAMBEN'S THINKING AROUND IDEAS OF SOVEREIGNTY AND BIOPOLITICS PERHAPS LEADS US TO UNDERSTANDING THAT POPULAR RESISTANCE CANNOT BE LIMITED TO JUST CONTESTING OR TAKING OVER LEGAL OR POWER STRUCTURES.
LOVE IS A HUMAN RIGHT
LOVE WINS
WE COULD CONSIDER WHETHER BARE LIFE ITSELF CAN BE MOBILIZED BY POPULAR EMANCIPATORY MOVEMENTS, NOT JUST FOR CLASS BUT ALSO AGAINST GENDERED, COLONIAL AND RACIST FORMS OF STATE VIOLENCE.
THE LAST WORD HERE GOES TO AGAMBEN HIMSELF:
A STATE WHICH TAKES TERROR TO BE ITS MAIN FOCUS IS ITSELF IN DANGER OF BECOMING TERRORISTIC.
IT'S THE TASK OF DEMOCRATIC POLITICS TO PREVENT THE DEVELOPMENT OF CONDITIONS WHICH LEAD TO HATRED, TERROR AND DESTRUCTION.
NOT JUST TO CONTROL THEM ONCE THEY HAVE ALREADY OCCURRED.

The writers

Brad Evans is a political philosopher, critical theorist and writer, whose work specializes on the problem of violence. He is currently leading a series of articles and dialogues dedicated to the problem of violence for the opinions section of *The New York Times* (The Stone), and also edits the Violence Section of the *Los Angeles Review of Books*. Brad serves as a Reader in Political Violence at the School of Sociology, Politics & International Studies (SPAIS), University of Bristol, UK. He is also the founder and director of the histories of violence project.
brad-evans.co.uk

Sean Michael Wilson is a comic-book writer from Scotland, living in Japan. He has had many books published with a variety of US, UK and Japanese publishers, such as *A Christmas Carol* (Sunday Times 'Best of 2008'), *Fight the Power!* (New Internationalist), *The Book of Five Rings* (Shambhala Publications) and edited the critically acclaimed *AX:alternative manga* (Publishers Weekly's 'Best ten books of 2010'). In 2016 his book *The Faceless Ghost* was nominated for the prestigious Eisner Book Awards, and received a medal in the 2016 'Independent Publisher Book Awards'.
seanmichaelwilson.weebly.com

The artists

Robert Brown is a cartoonist based in Manchester, UK. He studied at the University of Gloucestershire, where he helped inaugurate the BA Illustration annual *Olio*. He has contributed strip cartoons to anthologies such as *Solipsistic Pop, Paper Tiger Comix* and *Sea Mouse*. He began publishing his current comic book series, *Killjoy*, in 2011.
robertbrowncomi.cz

Inko is a Japanese manga artist based in the UK. Her works often imply crossovers between traditional Eastern and Western cultures. She graduated from Kyoto Zokei University of Art & Design in Japan, and Central Saint Martins College of Art & Design in the UK. She frequently attends conventions, art projects such as Art on the Underground, gives talks at museums, and delivers manga workshops in and outside Britain. Among

her works currently available are: the webcomic *Go! Go! Metro!* (co-written with Chie Kutsuwada); the action manga story *Ketsueki* (written by Richmond Clements); and the art book *Uniform Girls I.*
dokoteiinko.wix.com/inkoredible

Chris Mackenzie is an artist from Glasgow, Scotland who has done illustration work for newspapers and magazines, including *The Japan Times.*

Michiru Morikawa is a Japanese illustrator and manga artist. She won the prestigious International Manga and Anime Award in Britain, and received a prize for Best New Manga Artist from Kodansha. As a graphic artist, Morikawa has illustrated concert and theater posters in Japan and public-service posters in Birmingham, UK. With Sean Michael Wilson she has created several graphic novels so far: *Yakuza Moon* (Kodansha), *Demon's Sermon*, *Musashi* and *The Faceless Ghost* (Shambhala Publications).

Carl Thompson graduated from the Minneapolis College of Art and Design in 2011 but currently lives and works in Dallas, Texas. He has worked with writer Sean Michael Wilson on the political comic strip 'Green Benches', which was published monthly in the British magazine *Blue and Green Tomorrow* and the ground-breaking strip 'A history of Mr X', published in a collection by the University of Dundee. They also collaborated on the graphic novel *Parecomic: The Story of Michael Albert and Participatory Economics.*
cargocollective.com/carlthompsonart

Yen Quach is a Vietnamese artist and regular contributor to/maker of self-published zines and comics. She began the #draweveryday challenge in 2013 and has not missed a day yet. In 2015, Yen graduated from Coventry University (UK) in Illustration & Animation. She works in both digital and traditional media equally well, with a preference for character design and narrative-based art. When not drawing, Yen moonlights as the Astral Assistant and records her forays into the real world through urban sketching.
yendraws.com